Southeast Asia

A Political Introduction

RICHARD BUTWELL

PRAEGER PUBLISHERS
New York

Published in the United States of America in 1975
by Praeger Publishers, Inc.
111 Fourth Avenue, New York, N.Y. 10003

© 1975 by Praeger Publishers, Inc.

Library of Congress Cataloging in Publication Data

Butwell, Richard A.
    Southeast Asia.

    Bibliography: p.
    1. Asia, Southeastern—Politics. I. Title.
JQ96.A2B87   320.9′59   73–8177
ISBN 0–275–19700–X
ISBN 0–275–84710–1 (pbk.)

Printed in the United States of America

Southeast Asia

A Political Introduction

Contents

I

The Setting

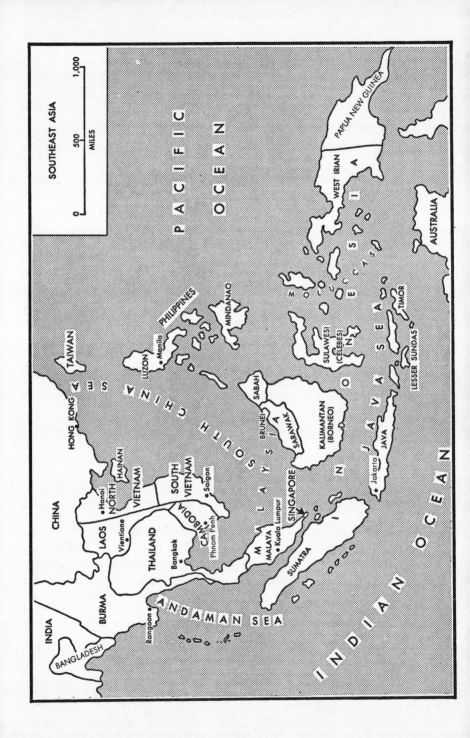

SOUTHEAST ASIA

0   500   1,000
      MILES

1

Introduction

There is a widespread belief about Southeast Asia—that this vast and sprawling region would "settle down" and resolve many of its problems if "outside powers" would only halt their interference in its affairs. The governments of the region would then be able to manage their own activities without the distractions (and, often, destruction) that seemed so much a part of the impact of major power rivalries upon their area. But is it really the case that "outsiders"—Americans, Chinese, Russians, Japanese, or others—were mainly responsible for the principal problems that plagued the "new states" of Southeast Asia in the period after the end of World War II and their liberation from European colonial control?

The United States clearly gave the war in Vietnam a particular character as a result of its major intervention in the conflict. Some opponents of U.S. involvement in Vietnam in the years after 1954 appeared almost to believe that the Americans created the problem of Vietnam, through their support of the French against the Communists and later of the anti-Communist Ngo Dinh Diem against the Communist Ho Chi Minh. But was the problem that was (and still is) Vietnam of American making? The answer is no. The real problems of Vietnam were there before the American intervention, and they are there today after the United States has disengaged itself from direct combat participation in the persisting military conflict in that divided land.

One of the most outspoken critics of great-power interference in the area, Malaysia, sought in the 1970's to establish Southeast Asia as a "zone of peace and neutrality" free from such intervention. Neutralization, if possible, could be the best of all means for the immunization of the area from unwanted and extraneous influences. And yet Malaysia's own major difficulties in the third quarter of the twentieth century had their roots within the country itself: the long Communist insurgency that partly derived from the nonassimilation of a sizable Chinese minority; the rioting and resulting deaths of May, 1969, in the capital city of Kuala Lumpur that reflected the racial antagonisms of an inadequately integrated land; and the undeclared war with Indonesia in the mid–1960's that was occasioned by the former Malaya's territorial expansion to become the new Malaysia (and the opposition to this move of the neighboring Indonesians, who could hardly be called "outsiders"). Similarly, the Philippine Communist insurgency of the late 1940's and early 1950's was an indigenous, not foreign-prompted, phenomenon—just as the southern Muslim uprising in the same country in the 1970's was provoked primarily by the neglect and exploitation of an increasingly resentful Islamic minority by elements of the Christian majority on the islands.

This is not to say that there has not been extraregional foreign intervention in both Malaysia and the Philippines as well as Vietnam. But such intervention has been, on the whole, secondary in importance to the indigenous causes of conflict and related difficulties in establishing functioning political institutions and solving problems of great urgency to whole populations. Moreover, much of the foreign intervention that has taken place—and let there be no doubt that there has been such intervention on a large scale!—has been by one Southeast Asian state at the expense of a neighboring Southeast Asian state. Almost every Southeast Asian country has, at one time or another, intervened in a major way to create or worsen political problems for the government of a nearby state. The list of such interventions reads like a chronology of Southeast Asian crisis situations: Communist Vietnamese military activity in Laos and Cambodia (which should not be confused with the war in Vietnam itself); long-term South Vietnamese efforts to subvert the former regime of Prince Norodom Sihanouk in neighboring Cambodia; Thailand's support until 1973 of ex-Burmese Premier U Nu in his campaign to overthrow the government of General Ne Win in adjacent Burma; Indonesia's unsuccessful military campaign to force Malaysia to relinquish the newly absorbed Bornean states of Sarawak and Sabah in the mid-1960's; and the support given Filipino Muslim rebels in the 1970's by the leadership of the nearby Malaysian constituent state of Sabah (as contrasted with the federal government in Kuala Lumpur). And these are by no means all of the instances of such troublesome intervention!

The fact is that Southeast Asia is one of the most politically unstable areas in all the world today in terms of unresolved conflicts both within almost all its countries and between many of the states that adjoin one another in the region. Southeast Asia's most important problems in the 1950's and 1960's were largely internal and political; in the two decades preceding the 1970's, however, after the region was catapulted into the world's headlines, its political problems, though internally rooted, became internationalized. Governments of countries outside Southeast Asia may continue to exacerbate some of these problems, or even to alleviate others, as they have done in the past. They may also create a few new problems themselves. But the major problems are—and will continue to be—overwhelmingly indigenous in origin, importance, and necessary solution.

THE TWO SOUTHEAST ASIAS

Geographically, Southeast Asia is divided almost in half, forming two physically quite distinct subregions. One is the southeastern periphery of the Asian mainland immediately to the south of China and east of India; the other is the heavily populated island world to its south and east. Although these two Southeast Asias differ from one another in various ways, yet in many of their circumstances, problems, and patterns of development they are sufficiently similar to justify their being treated together by both policy-makers and scholars.

The mainland countries, from west to east, are Burma, Thailand, Laos, Cambodia, and Vietnam (whether regarded as a single country with a still raging internal war or as the separate states of North and South Vietnam). Three of these lands—Burma,

Laos, and Vietnam—share frontiers with China; the Chinese occupation of a large portion of adjacent northern Laos makes Thailand, too, a *de facto* neighbor of the Chinese People's Republic. It
is these countries, principally Vietnam, Laos, and Cambodia and,
to a lesser extent, Thailand, that have dominated the world's
headlines about Southeast Asia in the years since the 1950's.
Most of their basic problems, however, are similar to those of the
sea-surrounded countries to the south—which have commanded
so much less of the rest of the world's attention.

This other, "insular Southeast Asia" has experienced far fewer
internal wars and other upheavals, although it has by no means
escaped such experiences altogether. It contains about two-thirds
of the population of the region as a whole, and almost half of the
people in all Southeast Asia are to be found in the largest of the
insular lands, Indonesia, which had an estimated population of
132 million in 1974. Although far more sparsely inhabited than
neighboring Indonesia, the Philippines, the second largest island
country, still had more people in 1974 than any of the mainland
states (approximately 42 million). The region's smallest country,
the 224-square-mile island-state of Singapore, is important because of its strategic location in the commercial and transportation heart of the region, its predominantly Chinese population,
and its economy and standard of living, which are the most advanced in the area. Neighboring Malaysia is generally considered
to be part of insular Southeast Asia, too, its easternmost (and
largest) two states, Sarawak and Sabah, occupying the northern
portion of the big island of Borneo, the rest of which is ruled by
Indonesia. Western Malaysia, smaller in territory than Sarawak
and Sabah, from which it is divided by sea, serves as a link between insular and mainland Southeast Asia.

In addition to geographical differences, there are also various
social and historical factors peculiar to the mainland and insular
countries that give each of these subregions a character of its
own. The predominant religion in all the mainland countries is
Buddhism, which is not a major spiritual force in any of the insular lands (although it once was). The Buddhist faith made its
way to Burma, Thailand, Laos, and Cambodia from India, where
it originated, but it entered Vietnam via China, where it had been

altered in important ways. The Chinese cultural impact in general is greater on the mainland than among the insular countries to the south (Singapore notably excepted), although only in Vietnam has the influence of China been historically more important than that of India. Unlike the inhabitants of insular Southeast Asia, the mainland peoples are variously differentiated from one another—on the basis of ethnic factors, language, and historical rivalries (not to mention geography, which contributed to the development of distinct "valley civilizations" separated by forested mountain ranges). The major peoples of mainland Southeast Asia —the Burmans, the Thai, the Khmers (or Cambodians), and the Vietnamese—are not closely related ethnically, speak different languages (which are not related to each other, as are, for example, French, Spanish, and Italian), and historically fought (and often subjugated) one another.

Because of their more distant location from the historical sea routes, the mainland countries were also colonized later than Indonesia, Malaysia, and the Philippines (while the Thai managed to escape becoming a Western colony altogether). Today, however, being physically nearer a resurgent and interventionist China, they have been drawn more intimately into international rivalries involving China, both its would-be containment by other governments and Peking's own interference in the affairs of adjacent states. There is no parallel in insular Southeast Asian experience to major Chinese aid of insurgents in Burma and Thailand, to China's *de facto* occupation of a large portion of northern Laos, or to Peking's important support of North Vietnam in the latter's long war with South Vietnam or of Prince Norodom Sihanouk in his attempt in the 1970's to return to a leadership role in Cambodia.

The people of insular Southeast Asia, unlike their neighbors to the north, are relatively homogeneous ethnically as well as linguistically and culturally. Islam is the dominant religion in Indonesia and among the Malays of Malaysia, and in the Philippines it is the faith of 5 per cent of the population (the majority of which is Christian). The preponderance of the population in both Indonesia and the Philippines is Malay, while a slight majority of all the inhabitants of Malaysia are also Malays ethnically. About

36 per cent of Malaysia's population, however, is Chinese (as are three-quarters of the people of adjacent Singapore), the result of a major migratory movement that took place during British colonial rule. The seas that superficially seem to divide insular Southeast Asia, moreover, have had quite the opposite effect through the centuries. The Malays, a skilled seafaring people, spread throughout the Indonesian and Philippine archipelagos by boat. At different times in the period before Western colonial rule, Indonesian kingdoms established a commercial and partial political presence as far away as the southern shores of mainland Southeast Asia as well as the Philippines. The waters of insular Southeast Asia thus served historically much the same purpose as the Mediterranean Sea in linking to one another the peoples living along their shores.

Although the precolonial kingdoms of insular Southeast Asia warred among themselves, these conflicts were for the most part over by the early 1700's, so that they have only a very limited continuing impact today. By contrast, mid-nineteenth-century clashes among the Vietnamese, Khmers, Thai, and Lao were interrupted by colonization; the end of the colonial era in mainland Southeast Asia, especially in Indochina (Vietnam, Laos, and Cambodia) and Thailand, seems to have politically thawed historical rivalries that had apparently been only suspended during French occupation. The fact, moreover, that the majority peoples of Indonesia, the Philippines, and Malaysia are so closely related ethnically—and are otherwise culturally linked—has minimized, if not altogether eliminated, the only too human tendency to think in terms of "us" and "them."

Distance and intervening water have also lessened the sense of urgency with which the leaders of the four insular nation-states have viewed the "Chinese threat" (which all of them, however, perceive). This is not to say that Indonesians and Filipinos have not feared China as much as the Thai or Burmese have. Certainly no government in Southeast Asia at any time has had quite the fear of China that President (and General) Suharto of Indonesia has evinced in the late 1960's and early 1970's. But even Indonesia's soldier-rulers of these years acknowledged that the "Chinese threat" was not as immediate for them as it was for the countries of the mainland. And Malaysia's recognition of Peking in 1974 was designed to check China—still very much feared by Kuala Lumpur's largely Malay political rulers.

The differences found in Southeast Asia today, of course, are not only regional ones between mainland and insular Southeast Asia. Almost everywhere, except in diminutive Singapore, there is a cultural and economic gap between city and countryside—between, for example, Indonesian or Thai modern life-styles, on the one hand, and the much more traditional ways of the rural peasantry of these lands, on the other. Almost everywhere, too, though in varying degrees, there are political differences between those who espouse strong-arm ruling methods and those who favor consensual politics, not to mention differences between right and left, which may or may not coincide with the clash between authoritarians and democrats. Furthermore, the values and expectations of the generation that has come of age since independence often differ dramatically from those of the men and women who struggled for, and won, liberation from colonial rule. And, by no means least important, there are the differences between the majorities and various minorities to be found in almost every country of both mainland and insular Southeast Asia. Many of Burma's minorities, for example, have had as much difficulty in relating to the majority Burmans of their own land as some of the majority peoples of the mainland have had in living peacefully with neighboring countries.

THE ENVIRONMENT OF POLITICS

The political environment in Southeast Asia is complex and changing, shaped by history, geography, economic resources and development, colonialism and postindependence problems, and the changing Asian international setting. Understanding this environment can increase our comprehension of why Southeast Asian leaders and followers behave as they do, why people possess particular attitudes and pursue certain goals, and why institutional governing arrangements have undergone various alterations in the last quarter of a century. The similar, though by no means identical, responses of various of the Southeast Asian

countries to different aspects of this environment justify their being treated together in political analysis, because these responses
reflect a region-wide attempt to come to grips with many of the
same political realities. For example, the setting for, and the
problems of, the Communist government of Hanoi after American combat disengagement from Vietnam are not all that different from the political circumstances and challenges confronting
the anti-Communist Jakarta soldier-regime of Indonesia. Both
must deal with questions of national unity, leadership, consensus,
opposition, development, and great-power interests and reliabil-
ity, among other problems.

Colonial Legacy. Every one of the Southeast Asian countries,
except Thailand, was a colony of a Western nation when the
twentieth century began. Some of these lands (or parts of them)
had been colonies for several centuries. And, although Thailand
escaped the fate of formal political colonization, its effective independence was limited by a sizable foreign economic presence
on its soil, the loss of some previously ruled territory, the humiliation of extraterritoriality (that is, not being able to try foreigners
for violations of its own laws), its agrarian economy, and the
need to relate to its immediate neighbors through the foreign offices of their colonial rulers in distant London or Paris.

The main political legacy of the colonial era for the various
countries of Southeast Asia was the limited experience of their
peoples in governing themselves, whether through authoritarian
or democratic political institutions. Understandably, although
they resented foreign rule and worked for its abolition, they
also doubted their ability to rule themselves, a self-doubt manifested in various ways in the first years of independence, such as
Burma's fear that Western foreign aid could lead to a return to
colonialism. In the Philippines even today, more than a quarter
of a century after independence, large numbers of Filipinos—
young as well as old—believe that the country was better ruled by
the Americans than it has been at any time since.

Because so much has happened in Southeast Asia since the formal ending of the colonial era, it is easy to overlook the fact that
today's Southeast Asians are only a generation removed from the
reality of foreign political rule in their countries. Continuing pre-

occupation with Vietnam, even after the termination of American participation in the war there, and the consequences for all Southeast Asians of the emerging post-Vietnam, multipolar Asian setting have drawn attention to problems essentially of the future, to the neglect of an appreciation of the continuing impact of the legacy of the past. The political outlook of nearly all the rulers of today's Southeast Asian governments, the character of the economic systems they variously seek to change, and many other factors were set in the colonial period. The Vietnam war itself, which still continues among the Vietnamese combatants, was fought to determine which group of Vietnamese should succeed the French as rulers of the formerly colonized country. The Western powers that ruled Southeast Asia ran their respective colonies differently, and these different methods of governing continue to influence the indigenous regimes that succeeded them. Some of these recent colonies, moreover, had to fight to throw off foreign rule, while others gained their freedom through peaceful negotiations. How colonial rule ended had an extraordinary impact on some lands—particularly Vietnam, Laos, and Cambodia.

Historical Identity. The various Southeast Asian peoples also had a history and related identity that preceded the period of Western colonial conquest and rule. Americans and the first postcolonial generation of Filipino leaders emphasized the legacy of representative government bequeathed to the Philippines by the United States, but President Ferdinand E. Marcos in the early 1970's seemed to draw greater inspiration from the indigenous institution of the *barangay,* or local council, which existed before the coming of the Spanish to his archipelago land four centuries ago. It is not just institutionally, however, that the precolonial past has seemed to exercise an increasing influence over the "new states" of Southeast Asia in recent years. The attempt by the Vietnamese Communists to extend their influence over the weaker adjacent lands of Laos and Cambodia, begun while the French still ruled Indochina and long before the "Americanization" of the Vietnam war, was a revival of an expansionist thrust that had clearly expressed itself in the precolonial era.

History did not begin for the peoples and governments of Southeast Asia with the end of colonial rule—any more than it ended for them with the loss of their independence when the Europeans established their colonies. Great though the Western impact was (and still is) upon Southeast Asia, it penetrated society far less than politics—and influenced hardly at all the minds of many of the peoples of the area. Not surprisingly, with some very conspicuous exceptions, the several Southeast Asian societies —or, perhaps more accurately, cultures—have influenced politics more since independence than they have themselves been changed by politics or political action. Both the regal and mystical dimensions of traditional Cambodian culture, for example, shaped the politics of Norodom Sihanouk and Lon Nol far more than either of these quite different rulers altered the way most of their countrymen perceived basic questions of law and authority.

"Plural Societies." Most of the countries of Southeast Asia emerged from the colonial era very much "plural societies," that is, with two or more different societies, or cultures, existing within the structure of a single state. The most frequently cited example of such a plural society is Malaysia, where an economically powerful Chinese minority is almost as large as the Malay majority. These two population groups were more or less separated from one another in colonial times in occupation, residential location, language, religion, and even food and style of dress. When independence came in 1957 to Malaya, which later became Malaysia, there may have been a single state (or government), but there was far from a united nation within that state. State and society were not, in fact, one: Most Malays viewed themselves as Malays, and most Chinese regarded themselves as Chinese; only a minority of people really thought in Malayan or, later, Malaysian terms.

In the first half of the 1970's, rebellion flared in the southern Philippines as some Muslims rose in arms against the Christian majority, whose leaders generally looked down upon this religious minority and had not protected it against "land-grabbing" and various other types of exploitation. The Muslims had probably never been part *in fact* of the Filipino nation, and their civil war was a reflection of this state of nonintegration. The same can be said of some members of the many minorities, such as the Karens, Shans, Kachins, and Chins of Burma or of the Malay, Lao, or Meo minorities of Thailand, and, to a less dramatic extent, of other minorities in most of the other lands of Southeast Asia. Are the countries of Southeast Asia really nations? The next few years may tell whether these lands have become sufficiently integrated to withstand the tests of internal—and possible international—conflict.

"Conditions" of Independence. The Western colonial powers that used to govern nearly all Southeast Asia were, by. the twentieth century at least, political democracies, even if they did not rule their colonies in a democratic fashion. The postcolonial "new states" of Southeast Asia, accordingly, were explicitly expected to adopt democratic political institutions as part of the "conditions" of independence and to follow democratic "political rules" in the way in which they selected their leaders and otherwise governed themselves. Moreover, most of the first generation of postcolonial Southeast Asian political leaders wanted their countries to be ruled democratically; their own "identity" and "self-confidence" crises required them to prove to the Europeans that they were not their inferiors and could govern themselves as democratically as the peoples of the West.

Democracy's "Failure." Democratic political institutions proved to be too foreign to the traditions, experiences, and possibly needs of most of the Southeast Asian peoples—or, where they were not irrelevant, they turned out not to be sufficiently entrenched to withstand the assault of autocrats. As a result, representative democracy "failed" in Indonesia, Burma, Vietnam, Cambodia, Laos, Thailand (which "tried" democratic political institutions, following World War II, to demonstrate its change of heart after half a decade of only partly forced collaboration with Japan), and even the Philippines (which for so long regarded itself as a "bastion of democracy" in Southeast Asia). In Malaysia and particularly Singapore, moreover, formally democratic institutions were variously limited in practice in the first half of the 1970's, raising the question of how really democratic these former British colonies were. Could the ruling elites of either country, for example, be displaced by means of the ballot? Many inside, and outside, both lands thought not.

Democracy, of course, did not truly "fail" anywhere in Southeast Asia (except possibly in the Philippines). In some countries, it was not seriously tried; in others, leaders failed democracy. Whatever the reasons for this lack of success, which will be examined later, experimentation with democratic governing institutions—and the results thereof—has left a strong imprint on the political environment of most Southeast Asian countries and of Southeast Asia as a whole in the 1970's.

Economic Influences. There were, and still are, several aspects of the economic environment of major importance to the nature and functioning of the various national political systems in Southeast Asia. Probably foremost among these is the limited economic development of the countries of the area. The preponderance of Southeast Asians (except the largely urban and affluent population of Singapore) are peasants of very modest means; the economies within which they function, moreover, are mainly agricultural and extractive. Politically, these circumstances have meant two things in particular: that there is an enormous, and growing, gap between the wealthy ruling class and most of the people, and that most of the ruling elites have had as one of their leading policy goals the modernization of their countries' economies. Leaders have sought modernization both for its own sake and to lessen the continuing "neocolonial" dependence of their economies on the more developed nations.

Is democratic government possible when a country's people are very poor and largely lacking in education? Can a wealthy ruling class—often of corrupt entrepreneurs, as in the Philippines, or luxury-loving soldiers, as in Indonesia or Thailand up to late 1973 —really be expected to seek to improve the economic condition of the "lower classes"? Can economic modernization be most expeditiously accomplished through competitive, privately owned or largely state-operated enterprises? The political development of the Southeast Asian countries will be determined, as it has been to a very large degree, by how these questions can be answered.

Types of Leaders. The men who rose to political importance in Southeast Asia after World War II could not help influencing what kinds of political systems were favored and established as well as the way in which the political systems operated. Leaders like Indonesia's Sukarno and Burma's U Nu, though otherwise quite different, both gained their political reputations and experience in an era of anticolonial nationalist agitation. The task of governing highly complex countries in the process of unparallelled social change was a circumstance for which history had not adequately prepared them or others of Southeast Asia's leaders, including Cambodia's Prince Norodom Sihanouk.

Other leaders similarly reflected the political circumstances in which they had been socialized or out of which they had emerged. Indonesia's General Suharto, Thailand's Field Marshals Sarit and Thanom (in the years 1957–73), Marshal Thieu of South Vietnam, and General Ne Win of Burma were all soldiers who gained office by force and whose concepts of politics reflected their military origins. Politics under all of these leaders was authoritarian and hierarchical, in the manner of a military organization, whatever the system was called.

Political systems themselves, of course, also influence the men who mature under them. But the independent political systems of the Southeast Asian countries began largely with the termination of colonial rule, although considerable continuity in personnel and practices of the late colonial era existed in such countries as the Philippines and Malaysia, as contrasted with the sharp break with the political past that occurred in Indonesia. There were, accordingly, no functioning political systems to make the men, only men of uneven ability to set up such systems. The men, and women, who launched the Southeast Asian lands on independent courses uniquely contributed to shaping their politics, as those who succeeded them, the political leaders of the 1970's, still continue to do in an extraordinarily unstable, flexible, and malleable political setting.

Need for Institutionalization. Governments in Southeast Asia have generally been ones of men, not of institutions, as evidenced under Sukarno in Indonesia, U Nu in Burma, and, more recently, Marcos in the Philippines and Thieu in South Vietnam. Men have often substituted for institutions, as Prince Norodom Sihanouk did for so long during the 1950's and 1960's in Cambodia. Whether it was always necessary for them to do so, however, is an open question.

The need in most Southeast Asian countries, therefore, is for the institutionalization of politics. In most of these lands, there are not even designated or accepted procedures for succession of leadership. Even where "legislatures" or "elections" exist, these are largely window-dressing, not effective elements in highly personalized real political systems. Laws, moreover, are often arbitrarily proclaimed at dictatorial whim or, even worse, in angry response to some challenge from another would-be leader or perhaps only a critic of the regime. Unfortunately, some Southeast Asian lands are a long way from effectively institutionalizing their political behavior—by democratic or nondemocratic means.

Problems of Representation. Institutionalization of politics is only one of the unfulfilled needs of Southeast Asian ruler-ruled relations. There is also the problem of representation; that is, how (if at all) to reflect the general will and the several particular wills that constitute the countries in question. The government of the late President Ngo Dinh Diem of South Vietnam in 1954–63 was increasingly unrepresentative of the will of his country's Buddhist majority or its leadership, and this is one reason why it fell.

Many Chinese in Malaysia contend that their central government is a pro-Malay one that takes insufficient account of the Chinese point of view and of the interests of the large Chinese community. Members of nearly all of Burma's indigenous minorities have felt similarly ignored by the Burman majority in the years since independence in 1948 and have expressed their feelings in continual revolts against the central political authority of the country. And in Cambodia it was the lack of popular backing that threatened the political survival of the increasingly unrepresentative Lon Nol government in the first half of the 1970's.

Representation is not identical with popularity, but a regime that is representative will probably be popular, at least with key sectors of the population. It is an important fact of the political environment in most Southeast Asian countries today that governments are not representative of major groups in their populations and, in some cases, even of the general will. They are, as a result, usually not very popular, often holding power only by force, and highly unstable.

International Setting. Throughout modern history, Southeast

Asia has been a subordinate area in international politics, the object (indeed, often the victim) of the foreign policies of more formidable powers external to the area. Its neighbor to the immediate north today is a revolution-minded and interventionist China; its chief trading (and investment) partner is developed but resource-lacking Japan; and the most important external ally of many of its governments is the United States. The relations among these three powers are changing, however, and this will have an impact on some of the policies—if not politics, more generally defined—of the Southeast Asian lands. The Soviet Union and its *de facto* ally India are also increasing their activities, and influence, in the area. The immediate international setting in which Southeast Asia finds itself, that of heavily populated and adjacent East and South Asia, is undergoing considerable change, as is, indeed, the larger global environment. The era of bipolarity between the democratic and Communist superpowers, America and Russia, which encouraged revolution, counterrevolution, and probably the emergence of military regimes, is receding into history. It is being replaced by a new and uncertain age of untested multipolarity. This international setting will influence, though probably not as decisively as a variety of internal factors, the fate of Southeast Asian governments in the years ahead.

How to Evaluate?

The task of evaluating the progress—or perhaps, more accurately, the accomplishments and failures—of the Southeast Asian governments since independence is not easy. Many analysts try to do so in terms of the success or failure of democratic political institutions. Others emphasize effectiveness of the administrative management of the countries in question. Still others base their evaluation on achievements in program development and implementation, that is, public policy or problem solution.

It is important, of course, to evaluate the key areas of political activity, but each of these three factors seems significant, none really more or less so than the others. No less important, however, is the approach to evaluation. What is expected? What can be reasonably and fairly expected? Too many observers have measured the Southeast Asian nations against abstract, often irrelevant, and resultingly unfair standards. Quite frankly, the outlook for successful self-government was bleak with independence coming in the wake of war, without preparation, and sometimes through revolution. Yet, the record of the first twenty-five years of national independence is a surprisingly impressive and inspiring one—if it is evaluated in terms of what might have reasonably been expected instead of what partisans of particular ideologies, within and without the various countries of the area, unrealistically hoped for. It is in terms of the realities of Southeast Asia rather than such political dreams and biases that the politics of the lands of this part of the world will be described and analyzed in the pages that follow.

II

The Countries

2

The Mainland Lands

The mainland lands of Southeast Asia—particularly Vietnam, Laos, and Cambodia—have come to symbolize Southeast Asia in the eyes of most of the rest of the world. Together with Thailand, the three formerly French-ruled Indochinese countries have often been perceived as being ruled by right-wing leaders who enrich themselves at the expense of their countrymen and remain in power as a result of American support. Only Burma of the mainland countries has not generally been viewed in such terms, largely because it is the least known of all the Southeast Asian lands (yet the Burmese, too, were ruled at the start of the 1970's by a strong-armed military government). The adversaries of these regimes, on the other hand, have frequently been depicted as representing the will of the people, social justice, and the prospect of a better life and way of government.

Are such images realistic reflections of the governments, political processes, and contending forces of mainland Southeast Asia? Could the politics of these lands be adequately understood in the 1960's and first half of the 1970's in terms of American-backed authoritarian regimes increasingly challenged by popular forces of revolt (led by Communist reformist elements)? The answer to such questions is a qualified no. It is no because the political processes and problems of these lands are more complex (and even contradictory) than these simplified images suggest. The answer is qualified, on the other hand, because, like many popular political explanations (whether largely right or wrong), there is some truth to them. That is, the military did dominate the politics of most of the mainland Southeast Asian countries in the 1960's and early 1970's, many soldier-rulers did line their own pockets, and the United States did give support to such governments in their internal wars with Communist insurgents. It is open to serious question, however, whether such Communist elements were as generally popular as they depicted themselves to be. Moreover, although they emphasized social justice as one of their objectives, the restrictions they placed on political, religious, intellectual, and other freedoms were far greater than those of most of the regimes they opposed. And, like the governments they fought, they also enjoyed very considerable foreign support.

No less important, however, is the fact that the political life of the several mainland Southeast Asian nations is more complicated than such images suggest. The political story of Vietnam can by no means be wholly told in terms of Communists versus anti-Communists. The military did not rule by itself—very far from it!—in Thailand in the years from 1947 through 1973. Burma's government, though military-controlled, was left-, not right-, wing in the early 1970's (and it was nonetheless opposed by Peking-supported rebels). Cambodian Prince Sihanouk, far from a Communist himself and the central figure in a highly corrupt regime at the time of his 1970 overthrow, enjoyed the widespread respect of most of his rural countrymen as a result of his royal status—not as politician or reformer, let alone left-wing revolutionary!

Simplified explanations just will not suffice to indicate why the several mainland Southeast Asian lands are so conflict-ridden, why their political institutions have become increasingly authoritarian through the years, why they have the particular political (and related) problems they have, and why even their very existence as nation-states is in doubt a quarter of a century after the end of Western colonial rule. To understand better the complexities and causes underlying these conditions, one must look at the individual lands.

VIETNAM

The Vietnam war that dominated the world's political headlines in the 1960's and early 1970's was very much an outgrowth of France's efforts to hold on to its prized Asian colony in the first decade after World War II. To be sure, Soviet and Chinese recognition of Ho Chi Minh's revolutionary movement as a government as early as 1950 and later massive American direct participation in the war between Ho and the elite that ruled the southern part of the divided country made Vietnam a major point of contention in the world-wide clash between the Communist countries and the United States. But there were two Vietnams, to begin with—and, thus, to fight over—as a result of the French colonial strategy of "divide and continue to rule." In this sense, the French imperial legacy persists in Vietnam, tormenting those who have sought to succeed France in the governance of the country.

In the period between World Wars I and II, Ho Chi Minh emerged as a leading figure in developing Vietnamese nationalist resistance to continued French rule in the country. Ho had turned to Communism as a means of ousting the French partly because he was disillusioned by other approaches (including his attempt to win support for a free Vietnam from the United States and the other powers that convened at Versailles after World War I). The 1920's were the formative years in the shaping of Ho as a Communist; in addition to the nationalist that he already was, he became, in 1929, one of the founders of the Indochinese Communist Party (the name of which indicates that, even then, Ho and his Vietnamese comrades conceived their political stage to be all of the French-ruled territory of Indochina, not just their native Vietnam).

There were both Communist and non-Communist wings of Vietnamese nationalism in the 1930's, and it was not until the Pacific phase of World War II that Ho Chi Minh emerged as the pre-eminent leader of the nationalist movement, not just the Communists, that was ultimately to catapult the French out of their prized Indochinese colonial territory. In 1941, Ho founded the Viet Minh, a multigroup nationalist coalition to oppose the French as well as the Japanese, whom the Vichy regime had allowed to move into the country militarily (partly because it had no real choice about it). During the war, Ho and the Viet Minh monopolized the resistance against the French and the Japanese with the help of many sympathetic Frenchmen and some Americans. With the war's end in sight and defeat imminent for themselves, the

Japanese turned on the cooperative Vichy French and gave inde-
pendence to Vietnam, as well as to adjacent Laos and Cambodia.
Responding to *de facto* Viet Minh monopolization of indigenous
political power in the country, Emperor Bao Dai—of the line of
Vietnamese rulers who had governed the country before the
French established their colony (and who had continued in a
titular role subsequently)—abdicated his position. On September
2, 1945, ironically the day on which U.S. General Douglas Mac-
Arthur was receiving the official Japanese surrender, Ho Chi
Minh proclaimed the establishment of the "Democratic Repub-
lic of Vietnam"—for all Vietnam!

The French, however, were able subsequently to re-establish
themselves in Vietnam (and Indochina as a whole) and were of
no mind to quit the colony, let alone turn over power to the Communist Ho Chi Minh. Although the French Government variously
negotiated with Ho, sometimes seriously and sincerely, key French
officials in Vietnam itself were opposed even to sharing power
with any Vietnamese. The result was the Franco–Viet Minh war,
which raged from late 1946 to July 21, 1954. The "Geneva Accords" seemed to end the war in Indochina, after the fighting had
spread to Laos and even, in a much more limited fashion, to
hitherto tranquil Cambodia.

A political war was probably unavoidable among the elites contending for the mantle of vanquished French political authority
over all Vietnam and, apparently, the whole of Indochina, too.
But that war need not have been internationalized, and might not
have been, under different American political leadership than
that of President Lyndon Johnson, who oversaw the U.S. military
escalation of the conflict in the middle and late 1960's. The intent
of the Geneva Accords was to head off renewed resort to force and
to determine which Vietnamese should rule Vietnam by means of
elections scheduled for 1956. The plan, though sincere, was a mis-
guided one, premised, as it was, on the hope that one or the other
contending elite would give up power without a real fight; that
is, that either faction would agree to elections it would not be
able to win.

Such a fight was made almost inevitable as a consequence of
previous French efforts to oppose Vietnamese nationalism and to

hold on to the profitable colony as long as possible. The Americans in the Philippines, the British in Burma, and the Dutch in Indonesia relinquished power, albeit in very different ways, to a single successor elite. Rivals to such elites were to develop later, but, when colonial rule ended, there was no doubt who would succeed the departing imperial powers in those three countries. In Vietnam, however, there were four definable elites—three of them, to make the matter more complex, overlapping in various ways. Best known among these was Ho Chi Minh's overwhelmingly Communist elite, the leadership of the successfully insurgent Viet Minh. They controlled most of the countryside (but none of the cities, including Hanoi and Haiphong) at the time of Geneva and were given *temporary* occupation of all the Vietnamese territory north of the 17th parallel in 1954. Foreign critics of France argued in the late years of the war with the Viet Minh that French policies forced many non-Communist Vietnamese nationalists into the Viet Minh, which was partly true. France, it was said, gave non-Communist Vietnamese no alternative to alliance with Ho Chi Minh except acquiesence in continued French dominance of the country, an alternative that, by 1954, had become unacceptable to most Vietnamese politicians. In fact, however, some Vietnamese continued to oppose the French without siding with the Viet Minh. Of these, one of the best known was the expatriate Ngo Dinh Diem, who became Premier of all Vietnam shortly before the Geneva settlement and was later to become President of South Vietnam (and, subsequently, to be assassinated by soldier rivals for his power).

Ngo Dinh Diem was himself a member of two of the three other elites opposed to Communist rule of all of Vietnam; he was a member of the large and well-educated Catholic minority, and he was a nationalist who would not follow the Communist leadership of Ho Chi Minh. The largely anti-Communist Catholic minority in South Vietnam was to be swelled dramatically after 1954 by the influx of refugees from the north; this would make it even less likely that the differences between the two Vietnams could be peacefully resolved. The Catholics ultimately came to represent approximately 10 per cent of South Vietnam's population, and they were, on the whole, prosperous and *much*

better educated than the population in general. They also dominated both the civil and military bureaucracies as well as political
life in general, exercising an influence out of proportion to their
numbers.

The fourth elite was the indigenous military who had fought
on the French side against the Viet Minh in the years 1946–54.
This elite was, on the whole, not unhappy to see the French leave,
but it was of no mind at all to surrender the country to Ho and
his comrades, against whom it had so recently and fiercely warred.
Like Diem, such soldiers represented a non-Communist Vietnamese alternative to rule by Ho Chi Minh and the Communists. A
disproportionate number of them, too, were Catholics. Although
he was not the key figure in the overthrow of Diem in 1963, later
President Nguyen Van Thieu was to emerge as the strongest personality among the anti-Communist soldier-nationalists, and it
was he who was to lead the South Vietnamese side against the
Communists after 1967.

The point is that, when the French quit Vietnam in 1954, there
was not a single elite in a position to succeed to the ruling role
they relinquished. Diem, and his various allies among non-
Communist nationalists, Catholics, and the military, made Communist rule of the entire country impossible without a war, while
the Communists, the largest and best-organized political force in
all the country, prevented the non-Communists from governing
the whole of Vietnam, too. This is really why Vietnam was divided, however temporarily in the eyes of the Geneva diplomats
in 1954. It is also why war was probably inevitable if either the
Communists or the non-Communists were not content to rule only
half a Vietnam. Moreover, the division of the larger South Vietnamese political elite into at least three groups—non-Communist
civilian nationalists, Catholics (in a predominantly Buddhist
country), and soldiers—is also the reason that the Americans
were tempted to intervene militarily so dramatically in the mid–
1960's. Divisions among the South Vietnamese elite were seriously
weakening the anti-Communist cause, and a Communist victory
appeared likely as the different South Vietnamese elites endlessly
jockeyed for political power among themselves.

This does not explain why the United States felt that Vietnam was all that important in the first place, but it does suggest why the Johnson Administration despaired of the South Vietnamese pulling themselves together in time to avert a Communist victory in the country's deteriorating internal war. Ultimately, behind the U.S. military shield, the soldiers so strengthened their hand politically within South Vietnam that by 1973, when the United States and the Communist Vietnamese reached agreement to end direct American participation in the war, greater political unity, unquestionably partly forced, prevailed within the South Vietnamese political elite. The struggle to succeed the French, however, was by no means over.

South Vietnam. The path of political development followed by Premier (and subsequently President) Ngo Dinh Diem after 1954 was a classic one of "new states" the world over seeking to attract, or retain, the favor of the United States. Diem declared South Vietnam a republic and held elections to demonstrate its democratic character, but he controlled the outcome of the voting. Popular selection or control of national leaders was wholly foreign to Vietnamese historical experience under indigenous emperors, while French colonial rule fell far short of the British, let alone American, policy of preparing colonial subjects for eventual self-government. Diem, in addition, was very much of an autocratic disposition personally, not given to easy or effective contact or consultation with the people or even groups within the country. And he was to fall under the excessive influence of his brother and sister-in-law, who possessed highly developed skills in conspiratorial politics.

Following Diem's refusal to acquiesce in the scheduled 1956 elections, war with the Communists began in earnest, hardly enhancing the climate for development of a democratic political process in a setting already wholly unprepared for it. It was this same war and setting that facilitated the military takeover of the government in 1963. By that time, the armed forces had become so large that only fear of American disapproval held the soldiers back. Professional soldier Nguyen Van Thieu, who ultimately emerged as Vietnam's new strong-man, did retain a façade of democratic institutions, including a Presidential election without an opponent in 1971, to play up to the Americans, whose multisided military and economic support was regarded as essential to the survival of the non-Communist elite.

North Vietnam. "The Democratic Republic of Vietnam," the formal name of North Vietnam (as it is commonly known outside the Communist countries), has often been described as having a typical Communist government, ruling party, and political process. This, however, is probably not the case—a result of the pressures of war and the still incomplete struggle to unify the country, partly through appeal to non-Communist groups and individuals. The Vietnamese Communists proclaimed the Democratic Republic of Vietnam in 1945 for *all* Vietnam, and they have far from abandoned their claim to the whole country. Their political process is, accordingly, a very complicated one that operates on at least two levels. There is, first of all, the government—and political support institutions such as party, functional groups, and media—of North Vietnam itself, which must be regarded as highly effective in light of its survival and only slightly restricted operation during a period of unprecedented American bombing. In addition, there is the "Provisional Revolutionary Government" in South Vietnam, the Communists' political counterpart to the Saigon government of the anti-Communist soldiers and successor to the previous Communist National Liberation Front. The Provisional Revolutionary Government has its own political system but interacts with the Hanoi government within the larger all-Vietnam Communist political process.

North Vietnam's government includes both a Prime Minister, the real head of government, and, since Ho Chi Minh's death in 1969, an ornamental or ceremonial President. Pham Van Dong was Premier in the early 1970's but, because of recurrent illness, willingly shared power in collegial fashion with comrades of nearly half a century. The *Lao Dong* (or Workers') Party monopolized institutional political power and established policy priorities for the government. Government and party consultative bodies could be convened to endorse important decisions, but this was not frequently done in the 1960's and early 1970's because of the war. The National Assembly, however, did convene in early 1974, a year after the "cease-fire agreement," to ratify the new party line of priority of economic rehabilitation policies over expanded war activity against the south.

LAOS

Laos was the least prepared of the French or any other Southeast Asian colonies for independence. The French did almost nothing to prepare its people for directing their own destiny, and, to compound the problem, Laos did not really exist as a country even when the 1954 Geneva Accords confirmed its "freedom." No area in the whole region resumed its independence after World War II with so little political or administrative experience, with less national integration, or with an economy as underdeveloped. Much experience was gained in political leadership and problem-solving in the quarter-century after World War II, but it was acquired at a most extraordinary cost in terms of loss of life, physical destruction, and political subordination to the neighboring Communist Vietnamese.

The Lao people, who largely inhabit the lowland portion of the country that lies across the Mekong River from Thailand, are of the same ethnic stock as the Thai. Like the Shan minority of northeastern Burma, they represent a wave of Thai migration out of southern China several centuries ago that moved in a different direction from the main Thai group. The language and general culture of the three peoples—Thai, Lao, and Shan—are very much alike, and the three "Thai" groups form an ethnocultural population bridge across the central portion of mainland Southeast Asia between Vietnam and Burma.

Before the coming of the French in the nineteenth century, the peoples of present-day Laos composed three feudal kingdoms, the political legacy of which persists to this day in the form of the main contending families in the country's non-Communist politics. Although Laos was ruled largely by the French as a single unit within the supercolony of Indochina, it was not until the immediate post–World War II period that France formally created the single-state structure of the kingdom of Laos. By this time (1945), Laos had already been declared independent by the Japanese as they prepared to retreat from Indochina. There had been no nationalist movement seeking to replace French with Laotian rule before the war, nor did even the elite of the land think in Laos-wide terms (but rather in terms of the three traditional feudal kingdoms). The Japanese occupation, however, stimulated nationalism, as it did elsewhere in Southeast Asia, and Laos was never again to be the same politically.

The French imperial experience did more than merely unite the people into a single new political community called Laos. Colonial rule also linked the Laotian people—the minorities of the northern and eastern hill country as well as the majority Lao of the western lowlands—with the dynamic neighboring Vietnamese and with the once historically great Khmers or Cambodians to the south in an artificial governmental structure called "French Indo-china." Before the coming of the French, the Vietnamese had been expanding at the expense of their neighbors, primarily the Khmers. France arrested this expansionist drive by conquering the Vietnamese and temporarily depriving them of their inde-pendence altogether. But the French may also have facilitated Vietnamese subjugation of both the Lao and the Khmers in the long run by placing all three peoples together in a single political structure. It is of considerable significance, in light of the later interaction of the three peoples, that Ho Chi Minh's new Commu-nist party in 1929 was called the Indochinese Communist Party and that left-wing dissident nationalist movements in Laos and Cambodia in the early 1950's were part of a coalition led by Ho's Viet Minh. The Viet Minh, indeed, treated all Indochina as the battleground in its war with the French and fought in Laos against France before the termination of the Franco–Viet Minh war in 1954.

In the wake of World War II, the young and extremely inex-perienced Laotian nationalist leadership split into two main fac-tions, which continue to persist in the politics of the country. One of these sought to negotiate independence from French rule and, after independence was obtained, tried to steer a middle ground in terms of political tactics and, no less important, foreign policy. This faction was represented from the late 1950's to the 1970's by the highly astute Prince (and, more often than not, Premier) Souvanna Phouma. The other chief faction chose to fight for free-dom from the French, joined in alliance with the Viet Minh in adjacent Vietnam, and became the insurgent Pathet Lao, which was not wholly Communist in the beginning but became very much so by 1954. The Pathet Lao, which has been strongly aided by the Vietnamese Communists through the years, controlled an estimated three-quarters of the total territory of Laos (in which, however, lives a minority of the population) at the time of the February, 1973, Laotian political agreement that ended most of the fighting in the country.

Although Laos was a battlefield in the eight-year Viet Minh war to oust the French from all Indochina, it did not assume any real importance in the struggle until toward the end. It was the moderates, moreover, who controlled the government of the country in the wake of the 1954 Geneva settlement, although the two northeasternmost provinces of the land were held by the Pathet Lao (who were never to give them up, even when they entered into coalition governments with the non-Communists in 1957 and 1962). In a very real sense, its independence was won for Laos by the Ho Chi Minh–led Viet Minh in neighboring Vietnam, a fact that has not been lost on any of the major parties involved in Laotian politics since 1954–the moderate nationalists, the Pathet Lao, and the Communist Vietnamese.

The political history of Laos since the 1954 Geneva Accords illustrates the difficulty for the great powers in seeking to legislate the framework within which the political development or growth of a country like Laos should proceed. The Geneva settlement clearly provided for the international neutralization of Laos and for the establishment of a coalition government in which the Pathet Lao should participate together with the moderate nationalists (who in the immediate post-1954 years were dominated by their right- rather than left-wing). The non-Communist nationalists sought the integration of the Pathet Lao into the government, but the Communists, suspicious of the moderates or pursuing an intentionally delaying tactic, resisted such incorporation into the legitimate Laotian political process. Elections were held, accordingly, in 1956 without the Communists.

In 1957, Prince Souvanna Phouma, as Premier, was able to negotiate a political agreement with the Pathet Lao, supplementary elections were held in which the Communists made a very impressive showing, and a coalition government was formed. Right-wingers within the government, however, then moved against the

Communists, possibly with American CIA encouragement, and
the Pathet Lao military forces, in the process of being incorporated into the government's ranks, were fortunate to escape
liquidation. The political die, accordingly, was cast for the Laotian internal struggle for years to come: The Communists, denied
a legitimate role in the country's political process, seemed to be
justified in their renewed resort to force and even, possibly, their
alliance with the North Vietnamese.

Things went rapidly from bad to worse, as the CIA did play a
role in the emergence of the right-wing as the dominant force in
the national government and may have aided the military takeover of that government in 1960. In August of the same year, however, the limits of great-power direction of Laotian politics were
most dramatically demonstrated when a hitherto obscure Laotian
Air Force captain, Kong Le, led a *coup d'état* that unseated the
pro-American regime and returned the popular and politically
skillful Prince Souvanna Phouma to the premiership. The United
States, acting largely through the CIA and with the aid of allied
Thailand, sought to establish Prince Boun Oum, of one of the
three onetime independent Laotian kingdoms, and General
Phoumi Nosavan as the political leaders of the country. This bold
and unconcealed power play of the Americans provoked a strong
counterresponse from the North Vietnamese, who intervened even
more dramatically than they had hitherto been doing. The result
was a veritable rout of the pro-Americans, a second Geneva conference that produced the 1962 Laotian Accords, and U.S. acqui-
escence in the return of Souvanna Phouma as the country's Prime
Minister. This sequence of events was to seem particularly ironic
in the middle and late 1960's and early 1970's, when the United
States accorded strong diplomatic, economic, and military support to the same Souvanna Phouma as Premier against the Communists. Yet, on two occasions in the late 1950's and early 1960's,
the Americans endeavored to engineer Souvanna's replacement as
leader of the Laotian Government for his allegedly excessive willingness to negotiate with the Pathet Lao.

The 1962 Geneva Accords, like those for all Indochina eight
years earlier, sought the neutralization of Laos and a nationalist-
Communist coalition to rule the country. Such a coalition was, in

fact, set up but was quickly abandoned by the Pathet Lao, who resumed their military struggle against the moderate nationalists, including Souvanna Phouma. In all likelihood, the Laotian Communists developed second thoughts about the wisdom of a political coalition with the able and adroit Souvanna Phouma, but events, such as the murder of the anti-American "neutralist" Foreign Minister of the country, probably also renewed their fears of a new right-wing move against themselves.

In the decade that followed the break-up of the 1962 coalition government, the Communist Pathet Lao was to increase dramatically the amount of national territory under its control. It was able to do this despite all-out U.S. military, economics, and other aid to the Souvanna Phouma government; American bombing activity in support of the non-Communist regime; U.S. training, support, and leadership of the fiercely fighting Meo tribesmen of the country against the Communists; participation of more than 20,000 Washington-paid Thai "mercenaries" in the war (largely in Laotian uniform); and the steady and general improvement of the Laotian armed forces (though not to the level of the fighting ability of the Pathet Lao). The reasons for the Pathet Lao military successes are not easy to determine. Although variously aided by the more militarily capable North Vietnamese, who often fought the Laotian Government forces directly, the Pathet Lao was outnumbered by Souvanna Phouma's army, was far less equipped, and had no air power at its disposal whatsoever. The Communist Vietnamese on whom the Pathet Lao depended, moreover, were themselves foreigners—whose visible participation in the war ought to have provoked some kind of nationalist reaction. The North Vietnamese, in addition, were interested primarily in the battle for control of Vietnam itself and clearly gave the Laotian struggle secondary priority—except, of course, for the purpose of keeping open the so-called Ho Chi Minh Trail for the movement of supplies through eastern Laos into South Vietnam.

In February, 1973, a month after the U.S.–Communist Vietnamese agreement to end American direct participation in the Vietnam war, the two Laotian factions—the nationalists and the Communists—agreed to end their fighting, too. Actually, they reached much greater political agreement than was to be achieved between the two Vietnamese sides in the political war in that adjacent country. This was probably because there were fewer—and less deep—divisions between the Communists and the Souvanna Phouma–led nationalists (except for the extreme right-wing military and feudal elements among the latter). The Pathet Lao, for its part, seemed tacitly to realize that it had partly forced Souvanna Phouma into his dependence on the Americans. The United States had probably helped to save the non-Communist Souvanna Phouma nationalist faction from political extinction—but for how long?

More than half a year after the fighting had largely stopped in the war for Laos, Souvanna Phouma's anti-Communist side and the Pathet Lao reached an agreement in principal on the sharing of portfolios in a new coalition government, the third to be attempted in the country since the end of French colonial rule. The superior military position of the Communists, who controlled about three-quarters of the country, was not reflected in the proposed composition of the cabinet. Souvanna Phouma would again be Premier; probably everybody, including the Pathet Lao, recognized that the popular Prince, at 72, was nearing the end of his political career. Deputy premierships were to be shared by the nationalists and the Communists, each having one, with the portfolios otherwise to be equally divided between the two sides, the Souvanna group holding most of the key ministries. Another half-year passed, however, without the establishment of such a government, but in February, 1974, on the eve of the first anniversary of the 1973 cease-fire, agreement was reached on the composition of police and military forces guarding the country's twin capitals, royal and administrative, and in April, for the third time since 1957, a coalition government finally took office.

The September, 1973, coalition pact could possibly succeed—unlike the previous unity agreements of 1957 and 1962—because of the disengagement of the Americans from Laos under the Nixon Doctrine* and the preoccupation of the Vietnamese Com-

---

* The Nixon Doctrine, proclaimed in July, 1969, while the American President was en route to Southeast Asia, emphasized local responsibility for peace-keeping in the region and signaled an apparent U.S. intention to reduce its military role in the area.

munists with the struggle for power in South Vietnam. Although the war had been temporarily ended without a Communist triumph, nonetheless most political and military factors seemed to favor an ultimate Communist victory in Laos, though not necessarily in subordination to Hanoi or any other foreigners.

CAMBODIA

Of all the lands of formerly French Indochina, Cambodia, under the leadership of Prince Norodom Sihanouk, was the most successful for the longest period of time in avoiding civil war. This was so not because Sihanouk was more earnest or able in his pursuit of peace than Prince Souvanna Phouma of neighboring Laos, but because, for many years, the objective circumstances of Cambodia favored Sihanouk and his strategy—until the colorful Prince's forced removal, possibly with American assistance, in 1970.

The sorry and bloody situation in which Cambodia found itself in the first years of the 1970's, with Cambodians fighting each other and U.S. bombers relentlessly seeking to break up "enemy" concentrations, was a far cry from the glory of a bygone era. No state in the whole history of this part of Southeast Asia ever ruled as large a territory as Sihanouk's royal ancestors did in the early centuries of the present millennium, but the kingdom declined, largely for reasons of internal weakness, leaving for posterity the great royal-religious complex known as Angkor Wat (temple). By the nineteenth century, when Angkor was nearly completely overgrown by jungle, the Khmers (Cambodians) were struggling for their very survival as a separate people against expansion by the Vietnamese in the east and the Thai in the west. Most of what is today known as South Vietnam was still part of the Khmer Kingdom a couple of centuries ago, which is why there are so many ethnic Cambodians to be found in that country. (Some of these were used by both the Diem and Thieu governments against Prince Norodom Sihanouk in a local illustration of the internationalization of the Cambodian power struggle.)

Khmer rulers of the mid-nineteenth century acquiesced in the establishment of a French colonial protectorate over their kingdom because they saw it as a way of ensuring their national survival against local foreign foes. Yet, while in the short run Cambodia may have been "saved" (although this was hardly the purpose of France's imperial intervention), in the long run it probably lost more than it gained from French colonial rule. If anyone profited, it was the Vietnamese. Already more advanced than any of the other Indochinese peoples, they acquired the administrative, technological, and commercial skills of Western civilization; significant numbers of them moved freely within the Indochinese political and territorial framework from Vietnam into Cambodia, performing the merchandising and money-lending functions associated with the "overseas Chinese" in most of the Southeast Asian colonial societies (although there were also such Chinese in Phnom Penh and other Khmer cities, too).

The French colonial presence served only to suspend the ancient rivalries among the Khmers and the neighboring Vietnamese and Thai; thus, when the French departed in 1954, these old animosities reasserted themselves. During the 1946–54 Franco–Viet Minh war, however, Cambodia was largely spared the death and destruction of that very bloody conflict. A pro-Communist satellite movement of the Viet Minh was established in the country, but, unlike the Pathet Lao to the north in Laos, it did not immediately become a significant force in the political life of the land. Indeed, at the time of the 1954 Geneva conference on all Indochina, Prince Sihanouk held up that important international meeting until he got the concessions he wanted to ensure his country's independence. Cambodia was then not deemed important enough by the Vietnamese Communists, France, or anyone else to risk the loss of an otherwise acceptable agreement to end the larger war in Indochina as a whole.

The policies pursued by Sihanouk after 1954 were designed to serve two ends: Cambodia's continued independence, largely through a "neutralist" foreign policy, and the prince's own survival as the country's political leader. Sihanouk had been King when independence returned to his country, but he stepped down from the throne in 1955, abdicating in favor of his father; he realized that his was not the age of monarchs, but he probably also appreciated that the country's traditionally oriented peasant population would still view him with royal awe whatever office he held. During the first years of Cambodia's independence, Sihanouk, besides being King, was also Prime Minister from time to time, resigning and resuming the premiership in the in-and-out fashion of a jack-in-the-box. After 1960, he served in the newly (and specially) created position of "Chief of State," which was generally indistinguishable from his former role as King, since there was no procedure whatsoever for picking another, or successor, chief of state.

Sihanouk seemed to favor a democratic political system for his land, but four consecutive parliamentary elections between 1955 and 1966 produced 100 per cent majorities for his "Popular Socialist Community" (or *Sangkum*) party. The *Sangkum* was a would-be mass political party created by Sihanouk to represent various points of view, promote consensus, mobilize the population, and guarantee his own political supremacy. In 1966, for the first time, the Prince refused to endorse the candidacies of any of the *Sangkum* nominees for Cambodia's single-chamber legislature, the National Assembly. Sihanouk's position, however, "set up" the defeat of *Sangkum's* increasingly assertive "left-wing," since "right-wing" candidates from the Prince's movement were clearly favored by the generally conservative Khmer population over "leftist" members of the same political organization. Thus, the election strategy was actually intended to promote his personal political standing—not to increase the competitiveness of elite-dominated Khmer politics.

No matter who was Prime Minister or King at any given time, Sihanouk clearly ruled as Cambodia's only modestly opposed leader during the years 1954–70. Indeed, even during those periods when he was out of office (or out of the country), his substitute either was a caretaker or surrogate or, as happened in early 1970, was given temporary leadership responsibilities in order to demonstrate Sihanouk's own indispensability. The Prince's concern, in short, seemed to be almost always the preservation of his own political position rather than permanent institution-building. The sixteen years 1954–70 were a much longer period than most national leaders have in office, but, when Sihanouk was ousted from power in March, 1970, there was very little to show by way of institution-development for his decade and a half as Cambodia's political leader.

The manner in which Sihanouk was overthrown and subsequent political developments in the country demonstrated the precarious fragility of Khmer political institutions as well as the inexperience and incompetence of most members of the ruling elite, who had shared little in the exercise of power in Sihanouk's heyday. Seemingly friendly rivals Marshal Lon Nol and Prince Sirik Matak were given responsibility for governing the country during Sihanouk's absence on a health-vacation in France in the first months of 1970. Cambodia was facing difficult economic problems, and Sihanouk expected Lon Nol and Sirik Matak to be embarrassed by their failure to deal effectively with these problems and to urge him to return to resume leadership of the country. Instead, they managed to cope with the problems and called Sihanouk home to cut him down to more manageable political size. When he refused to return and went instead on a peace-seeking trip to Moscow and Peking, they ousted him altogether as Cambodia's leader.

There is little doubt that the Prince's popularity was at its low point at the time of his overthrow. In his relations with other Khmer politicians, he was not always the charming human being that he inevitably seemed to be at international conferences or when meeting with world dignitaries, and the other members of the small Cambodian political elite had had their fill of his arrogance, insults, corruption, and nepotism. The Khmer economy, moreover, was seriously afflicted by inflation due in part to Sihanouk's unsophisticated leadership. Young educated Cambodians without jobs, and the army, commanded by Lon Nol, without weapons, equipment, or even decent uniforms, had lost faith in the political Prince. When he was overthrown by Lon Nol and Sirik Matak in March, 1970, Sihanouk had lost the confidence of nearly everyone in the capital city of Phnom Penh, the ordinary working people as well as the elite. But to the vast majority of rural Khmers he was probably very much still the latter-day manifestation of the country's historic "god-king."

There was no initial evidence to indicate foreign intervention in Sihanouk's overthrow, and there is still none. But the evidence revealed at the 1973 hearings of the Senate Armed Services Committee of secret U.S. bombing of Cambodia during this period, and of other clandestine political and military activity in the whole of Indochina during the Johnson and Nixon administrations, raises the question of possible still-secret CIA or other U.S. encouragement of Lon Nol and Sirik Matak in their ouster of the once popular Sihanouk. Be this as it may, the Americans quickly embraced the new Khmer regime, repeating the mistakes of their involvement in the Vietnam war by taking over and fighting the new and enlarged Cambodian conflict for the Cambodians, only this time in the air rather than on the ground. Lon Nol, who declared Cambodia a republic and became its first President, subsequently suffered a stroke and partial paralysis and turned out to be a far less competent and effective leader than Sihanouk in almost all respects. The politically unsophisticated President was even less prepared than the Prince to govern democratically; corruption, which had been extensive under Sihanouk, grew to almost astronomical proportions; and the war was waged unbelievably badly, despite massive American financial aid and U.S. training and tactical help. When American bombing in support of Lon Nol ended on August 15, 1973, as required by Congress, the survival of the pro-U.S. (and anti-Sihanouk) regime was very much in question. Although the Lon Nol regime survived a subsequent serious military assault on the capital of Phnom Penh, its general battlefield position remained precarious in mid-1974, as the Communist insurgents registered significant new gains.

Lon Nol's greatest mistake, however, was perhaps not in the way he governed Cambodia, although this probably would have brought his downfall in time, but in his abandonment of Prince Sihanouk's skillfully directed foreign policy of apparent neutrality. Sihanouk, in fact, had been far from neutral in his years of political leadership, clearly realizing, and fearing, Communist Vietnamese designs on his country. In 1954, he sought Khmer membership in the largely U.S.-created Southeast Asian Treaty Organization but was rebuffed by the Eisenhower Administration because Cambodian participation in SEATO would have obviously violated the Geneva Accords, and such open flaunting of these agreements did not then seem in the American interest. In

1969, President Nixon revealed in 1973, Sihanouk invited him to visit Cambodia, despite "secret" American bombing of Communist forces on Khmer soil and the Prince's knowledge thereof. At the time of his ouster in 1970, indeed, Sihanouk was on a trip to Moscow and Peking to urge the Soviets and the Chinese to persuade the Communist Vietnamese to quit Khmer soil, or at least dramatically reduce their violation of Cambodian sovereignty, lest Cambodia be drawn more directly into the larger Indochina military conflict.

In the years after 1970, this was, indeed, Cambodia's fate. As happened in both Vietnam and Laos, the Communist Vietnamese were the first to violate the terms of the 1954 Geneva Accords, but the United States proved subsequently capable of using its full military might to expand and internationalize the conflict—aiding, in the case of Cambodia, the "enemy" cause inestimably. As in Vietnam, American bombing of Cambodia gave the indigenous Communist "Khmer Rouge" a visible enemy, and the assisting North Vietnamese, who initially carried the main combat burden, justification for their quite open operations in the country. As for Sihanouk, a political exile in Peking, he maneuvered awkwardly as an avowed ally of the Khmer Rouge, once his enemy within Cambodia, and of the feared Communist Vietnamese (while seeking China's support as a counterweight to North Vietnam). China, reluctant to see Vietnamese hegemony over all of Indochina because of Peking's fear of future strong Soviet influence in Hanoi, delicately sought to aid the Prince.

THAILAND

The only country in all Southeast Asia—and one of very few in Asia as a whole—to escape the experience of being ruled by a Western imperial power was Thailand (or Siam, as it used to be called). This was the result largely of two factors: the extraordinarily enlightened Thai leadership of the second half of the nineteenth century and first years of the twentieth, and the fact that rival British and French imperial presences in Burma to the west and Indochina to the east balanced off one another. France wanted to exercise dominant influence over Thailand at the very least, but the extension of India-based British power to Burma, incorporated as a province of India in 1885, blocked the French. Skillful Thai diplomacy played a part, too, but even more important to continued Thai independence were the accomplishments of the great Kings Mongkut and Chulalongkorn in modernizing the nation. The leaders of Thailand's Burmese and Indochinese neighbors were almost helpless in the face of the accelerating European impact—economic, technical, and cultural no less than political, administrative, and military. Mongkut and Chulalongkorn directly faced up to the problem of national weakness and changed their nation's institutions and various aspects of their countrymen's behavior more than any other Southeast Asian rulers. And, partly as a result of their leadership, Thailand survived as an independent nation.

In many respects, Thailand was the first modern Southeast Asian nation, the first, that is, to confront various problems of a posttraditional society and to try to do something about them. Many things happened in independent Thailand in the 1930's that were to begin in the 1950's elsewhere in the region. Thailand was, in fact, already a nation (as contrasted with a country or kingdom) by the turn of the century, but it was not a *modern* nation, nor was it part of an international political system of interacting nation-states. Thailand, accordingly, was attempting to get started as a truly modern state and participant in international politics in the 1920's and 1930's; Indonesia, Burma, and Cambodia, among other lands, were to try to do this in the late 1940's and 1950's. The first military government in modern Southeast Asia was established in Thailand in the 1930's. And the Thai, seeking to protect their comparatively weak country against the clashing interests of the great powers in their part of the world, probably pursued, in the 1930's, Southeast Asia's first "neutralist" foreign policy.

As part of the process of modernization, Thailand developed an army, many of whose officers were trained abroad. Although Mongkut, Chulalongkorn, and their successors were enlightened rulers, government during their reigns was still highly autocratic, despite the fact that steadily larger numbers of Thai were acquiring various modern skills and the interest and desire to participate

in the political life of their country. In 1932, some such modernized soldiers and a handful of lawyers and bureaucrats joined to
bring about a bloodless coup that ended absolute monarchy in
Thailand. By 1938, the military, led by Phibun Songkhram, had
taken over the government in its own right, as soldiers were later
to do in neighboring Burma and Cambodia as well as Indonesia
and South Vietnam.

The larger world in which Phibun found himself as Thailand's
leader was hardly an attractive one politically or militarily. In the
late years of the previous century and the first decade of the twentieth century, the Thai had played off the British and French
against one another. In the 1930's, they similarly tried to balance
a militarily expansionist Japan against the European colonial
powers with territorial holdings in Southeast Asia—and, later,
Japan and the United States—but to no lasting avail. The result
was that Phibun ultimately sided with Japan to spare his country
the cost of a military invasion and occupation. Phibun permitted
Japan to use Thailand as a base against neighboring European
colonial territories in Southeast Asia, and this "pro-Japanese" policy permitted Thailand to come out of World War II with less
damage than any of the other countries of Southeast Asia. The
Thai still cite this today as yet another example of their historic
skill in diplomacy.

At the end of World War II, Phibun was initially treated as a
war criminal by the Allies, briefly jailed in Japan, and ultimately
allowed to return to his homeland. The Thai, inexperienced in the
ways of consensual politics after centuries of monarchical abso-
lutism and nearly a decade of military dictatorship, experimented
with elections and a pseudoparliamentary government in the
years 1945–47. Naturally, they had problems trying to reorder
their political institutions so drastically in such a short period of
time. The astute Phibun, seeing the difficulties that "democracy"
was encountering and anticipating an American desire for a
strong ally in mainland Southeast Asia in the event of a Communist victory in the Chinese Civil War, turned to the favored Thai
instrument for changing governments—the *coup d'état*—to return
to power in two stages, as the leading member of a new military
junta, in 1947–48. Within two years, the United States was pro-

viding economic and military assistance to the second government headed by Phibun Songkhram—its World War II enemy!

The junta headed by Phibun after 1948 was a fairly tightly run military dictatorship, but not an especially efficient government. Increasingly challenged by a new military strongman, army leader Sarit Thanarat, in the mid-1950's, Phibun turned to popular elections and a parliament in a belated and unsuccessful attempt to rally his countrymen to his support (his rigged balloting, however, hurt rather than helped his cause). Sarit succeeded Phibun, accordingly, by the traditional coup in 1957 and went on to head a much more vigorous and development-minded administration that was often compared at the time, much too flatteringly, with the great reigns of Mongkut and Chulalongkorn.

Sarit died in 1963, and he was succeeded by his hand-picked deputy, Marshal Thanom Kittikachorn, who ruled for six years before holding elections, in 1969, to a legislature created by a new constitution. This body was dismissed by Thanom in 1971, however, when he also abrogated the two-year-old constitution, because he felt that the parliamentarians were becoming too independent-minded, increasingly criticizing the government, and trying to exercise initiative in various ways on their own. Admittedly, the legislators, who were largely unqualified, hampered government operations through their bid for greater budgetary power and even dabbled directly in the sensitive area of national security. But the ruling military autocrats could also be criticized for their own inexperience, their unwillingness to share power, and their ineptness in dealing with the various insurgents challenging the government, as well as their excessive dependence on the United States as ally and protector and their related inability seriously to consider alternative foreign policies.

The Thai developed the political system they did in the twentieth century as an outgrowth of their own historical experiences, reflecting the ways their society had changed as a result of the modernization started by Mongkut and Chulalongkorn. At the beginning of the 1970's, with or without a partly elected legislature, but with the unifying symbol of the persisting and highly popular monarchy, Thailand's political system could best be described as a coalition between military and civilian bureaucrats;

the soldiers made the significant policy decisions but actually governed the country through a collaborating civilian bureaucracy.
The system, though largely internally derived, was nonetheless
highly vulnerable to external influences. This was demonstrated
dramatically in 1971, when the ruling soldier elite was visibly
stunned by the announcement of President Nixon's planned trip
to Peking. The Thai had actively solicited the anti-Communist defense partnership with the Americans, designed originally to protect themselves against the feared Chinese and, later, to keep the
once very much underestimated Communist Vietnamese as distant from their borders as possible. As a result of this major
change in U.S. policy toward China, badly frightened Premier
Thanom dissolved Parliament, abrogated the constitution, and
formed a very narrowly based National Executive Council to govern the country.

This overreaction to changing American foreign policy was to
prove politically fatal to Marshal Thanom and to his even less
democratic sidekick in the governance of Thailand, Deputy Premier Prapas Charusathien, who were overthrown by student demonstrators in October, 1973, and forced to flee from the country.
Thanom's main mistakes were the rigidity of his foreign policy in
an era of evolving multipolarity in Asia, for which student nationalists in particular criticized him, and his inability to appreciate
the altered Thai perception of the people's role in politics. Not
only was the postconstitution government of the two-year period
from late 1971 to October, 1973, ineffective and inefficient, it also
almost totally lacked any contact with relevant political groups
except ranking military officers, senior civil servants, and conservative business leaders.

For nearly forty years, the military had dominated Thai politics, forty years in which Thai society underwent great changes,
particularly in the 1960's and early 1970's. But the ruling military-
political elite took limited—and, indeed, decreasing—cognizance
of such changes and the political pressures building up as a result
of them. Thailand's popular monarch, on the other hand, Bhumibul Adulyadej, was aware of the changes in process in his increasingly stirring country and gave obvious indirect encouragement
to the student demonstrators (who originally did not set out to

topple the Thanom government). The overthrow of soldier rule in Thailand was followed by the election, by convention, of an interim National Assembly, the drafting of a democratic constitution, the legalization of previously banned political parties, and the promise of new parliamentary elections in 1974 or early 1975. Although student discontent with inflexible Thai foreign policy was a factor in setting up the overthrow of military dictatorship, the changes of 1973 and after were rooted in internal changes—and long overdue.

The war in neighboring Indochina, meanwhile, has yet really to "spill over" into Thailand, as had long been feared by Thanom, Prapas, and their American allies. Quite the opposite, in fact, has been the case: The Thai themselves have through the years willingly assumed an active role on the American and local anti-Communist side in the wars in Vietnam and Laos, dispatching combat personnel in surprisingly large numbers in view of the insurgency problem at home. Their objective was to keep the "enemy" as far away as possible from Thailand itself. Nonetheless, local Communists, aided by the North Vietnamese, made impressive military gains in both Laos and Cambodia, Thailand's immediate neighbors to the east. Furthermore, not only did the Communist Vietnamese (and Pathet Lao) retaliate by aiding Thai insurgents in the poverty-ridden northeastern area of the country, but also China provided aid to anti-Thai Mao tribesmen in the hilly northern reaches of the country. In the late 1960's, Thailand's own insurgency problems seemed to have been contained, but in the first years of the 1970's they assumed new and enlarged dimensions in the sensitive and strategic northern and northeast regions as well as in the peninsular south, adjacent to northern Malaysia, among the much-neglected Malay ethnic minority. Traditionally rice-surplus Thailand, moreover, experienced sizable declines in its harvests during these same years, while in 1973–74 trade unions and other long-suppressed groups openly and successfully defied the government for the first time ever, even after the students had toppled the hated Thanom regime. Would Thai leadership, institutions, modernization, and foreign policy be sufficient to the problem—as they had been in the past? Could democrats, new leaders, students, workers, and King rise to the challenge of a veritably revolutionary era? Or was it only a matter of time before the soldiers would be back in the political saddle again? These were the questions painfully confronting the Thai nation as the mid-1970's approached.

Burma

It has often been said that Burma alone of the mainland Southeast Asian countries has escaped the costly destruction of involvement in the international rivalries of the great powers in its part of the world. Since the beginning almost of its resumed independence in 1948, Burma has scrupulously pursued a policy of noninvolvement—an even more restrained foreign policy than nonalignment—in international affairs. It is this stance, it is said further, that explains why Burma has escaped the fate of Vietnam, Laos, Cambodia, and even, for that matter, Thailand.

This, however, is not entirely correct. It is true that the Burmese have been the most noninvolved of all the Southeast Asian states in international politics during the last twenty-five years, but they have not escaped interference in their affairs, first by the Americans and later by the Chinese. The U.S. intervention, which ended years ago, was seemingly the least harmful, although it could have caused considerable trouble at the time. For several years after the Communist victory in the Chinese Civil War, the American CIA supplied by air and otherwise supported remnant Chinese Nationalist forces across a section of the 1,200-mile-long Sino-Burmese border in the northeastern corner of the country. Former Premier U Nu terminated American aid to his land in protest of U.S. policy in 1953, and the CIA intervention was subsequently, but not immediately, stopped. Fortunately, it did not provide a pretext for Chinese Communist moves against the Burmese—which was what Nu feared.

China, apparently, did not need such a pretext. Beginning in the mid-1950's, it has intervened actively and continuously in support of various of Burma's "multicolored" rebels, as they are called in the country—ethnic minorities as well as indigenous ideological Communists in revolt against the Rangoon government. As early as 1956, Chinese soldiers appeared on Burmese soil, and, even after a border pact negotiated by General Ne Win with Peking in 1960, uniformed and other Chinese crossed over the frontier and enaged directly in clashes with Burmese troops (although the Rangoon government has always tried to keep such encounters as secret as possible). The irony is that active Chinese support of insurrectionary activity against the government in Burma preceded by almost a decade Peking's aid to insurrectionists in neighboring Thailand—despite the fact that the Thai, as early as 1950, began to ally themselves with the United States against Peking, while Burma remained scrupulously neutral through the years.

There are probably several reasons for this ironic circumstance, and these throw much light not only on Burma's political problems but also on those of the mainland Southeast Asian states in general. Direct Chinese intervention in Burma's internal affairs took place as early as it did, and has continued through the years without significant let-up (indeed, with some increase in aid in recent times), partly because the two countries are direct neighbors with the longest common border China has with any Southeast Asian country. The peoples on both sides of this frontier, moreover, are related more closely to one another than to the majority peoples of either land. Of no less importance is the fact that Burma's indigenous Communist organization was far more developed a quarter of a century ago than any other such movement in mainland Southeast Asia, except Vietnam. When there were almost no Communist partisans at all in Laos, Cambodia, or Thailand, Burma's Communists were almost strong enough to gain control of the country's independence-winning nationalist coalition, the Anti-Fascist People's Freedom League, on the eve of the end of British colonial rule. There were, then, indigenous Communists to support in Burma, but, unlike in Vietnam, Laos, and Cambodia, these local Communists were largely defeated in their onetime stronghold in the central region of the country by the late 1960's, despite Chinese support. They were subsequently to relocate in the northeastern part of the land—adjacent to China—where they more easily received Chinese aid.

The new Communist rebellion of the late 1960's and first half of the 1970's in the northeastern corner of the country includes some Shan, Kachin, and other ethnic minority opponents of the central government as well as more orthodox Communist insurgents. By no means a wholly domestic insurgent effort, it represents China's attempt to exploit Burma's badly fractured national unity to its own political advantage. The majority Burmans, who constitute three-quarters of the population, are to be found largely in the lower and central heartland of the country, which consists of about one-half of the national territory. The other half of the country, the jungled and hilly peripheral parts of the land, is inhabited by the remaining quarter of the people of Burma; they are not Burmans but members of different minorities, primarily Shans, Karens, Kachins, and Chins. Some leaders of all these and other, less important minorities have feared that they would lose their identities as distinct peoples in a Burman-dominated Burma. Portions (but considerably less than a majority) of various of these minorities have been in more or less continuous revolt against the central Burman-dominated government since the first years of independence. And it is elements of such alienated minorities that the Communists, aided by China, are trying to attract to their leadership against the Rangoon government today.

Burma, as such ethnopolitical disunity indicates, is not really a nation. Possibly more than half the people, in territorially half the country, do not identify with Burma as their "nation," although not all of them are in revolt against the regime. They are Shans, Karens, Kachins, or Chins but not Burmese (many members of such minorities do not distinguish between "Burmese" nationality and the "Burman" majority ethnic group). Both the country's first civilian Premier, U Nu, and General Ne Win, who unseated him, have feared, more than anything else, that Burma's national disunity would be exploited by outsiders—primarily the Chinese—with the result that the country would be divided like Vietnam, Laos, Cambodia, Korea, or China itself.

Nothing has concerned Burma's civilian and soldier-leaders through the years as much as the need for national unity. The democratic constitution with which the country began its independence in 1948 was parliamentary in form, after the model of Burma's departed British colonial ruler. It provided for a two-house national legislature, consisting of a Chamber of Nationalities, in which the minorities were represented as such, and a conventional and ordinarily elected Chamber of Deputies. The indigenous Communists had risen in revolt against the country's first democratic leaders largely because they wanted to rule in their place. But the minorities became increasingly alienated from the government after some had made at least a modest effort at coexistence with the majority Burmans; they feared Burmanization of their cultures and veritable "internal imperialism."

While U Nu, the country's first Premier, was in office, the emphasis was on reconciliation, although Nu did not hesitate to use force against either the Communists or the ethnic insurgents during the years of his initial leadership (1948–58). Both the Communists and the minorities were fairly well contained by the mid-1950's, but then the government party, the Anti-Fascist People's Freedom League, split in 1958. The rebels, particularly the Communists, took advantage of the break in the ranks of the democrats and posed a renewed danger to the country almost overnight. It was in this circumstance that General Ne Win first ousted U Nu from the premiership, largely restored law and order in the land, and then acquiesced, albeit with some reluctance, in Nu's return to power in 1960.

Minority disaffection, stimulated in part by the insensitivity of the Burman-dominated military during the first Ne Win regime, continued to grow after U Nu's return to power, and Nu discussed concessions with leaders of the non-Burman peoples to gain (or renew) their allegiance to the country. Ne Win reportedly feared that Nu's approach would only encourage a move toward separatism on the part of some of the minorities, and he overthrew Nu's government in March, 1962, for the second time in four years —jailing the widely respected Premier for half a decade (for no other apparent reason than his popularity), abolishing the constitution, and dismissing the elected Parliament. Burma's new and inexperienced soldier-leader, who at one time held hundreds of former civilian politicians in jail, also sought to revolutionize the national economy with almost unimaginable zeal, and an equally unbelievable ignorance of how an economy functions! Indian and Chinese traders were expropriated, almost everything in sight was nationalized, and even food in a once rice-rich country was rationed. Rice exports from the world's onetime leading exporter of that grain dropped dramatically, and the officially labeled "Burmese Way to Socialism" was almost universally judged an unmitigated failure—except by Ne Win. In the early 1970's, however, the Burmese leader did begin to make some modifications in the Burmese Way to Socialism, providing for limited private business activity and showing real interest in private foreign oil companies, including American, that might help him to find and exploit offshore petroleum deposits.

By then, Ne Win was also ready to attempt to construct a new political order for Burma. In 1972, he revealed the first draft of a new constitution that provided for a "socialist republic"—a one-party political system, with a single-house noncommunal national legislature. The Burma Socialist Program Party, created by Ne Win in 1962 and modeled essentially after the Communist parties of the U.S.S.R. and Eastern Europe, was to be the only political party allowed in the country. A plebiscite in which 90 per cent of the voters endorsed the new basic law was followed by elections in early 1974 and the convocation of the new People's Assembly—twelve years after Ne Win overthrew elected Premier U Nu. The new governing institutions, a far cry from the multiple political parties and contested elections of U Nu's day, were seemingly designed to check the historic divisiveness among Burma's chronically feuding politicians and minorities. The objective was a firm constitutional structure that could hold the state together, both in light of its own intrinsic weaknesses and against the efforts of China, and perhaps others, too, to exploit these weaknesses. But could the new political institutions accomplish this, and was unity more likely to be attained through controlled rather than consensual politics?

The "Mainland Problem"

The pre-eminent political problem of most of the mainland Southeast Asian lands appears to be their intrinsic weaknesses as nation-states and their related inability to develop viable governing institutions. Four of the five lands to the immediate south of

China, all of them former colonies—Vietnam, Laos, Cambodia, and Burma—are extremely fractured countries in terms of national unity. Thailand is relatively united as a nation—and, in that sense, possibly the only real nation in the subregion—but even it has growing difficulties with its northeastern (partly "left-bank" Lao) population, the insurgent minority Meo tribesmen of the north, and the southern or peninsular Malays (who may actively seek union with neighboring Malaysia at a future date). North Vietnam appears to be even more united than Thailand, partly as a result of the unintentional American stimulation of Vietnamese nationalism through a vigorously prosecuted war effort, but "North Vietnam" is still only "North Vietnam" (half a country) and may stay that way for some time to come, possibly even indefinitely. Cambodia's division is almost wholly political and could be fairly quickly repaired if one or the other of the contending military forces could score a victory. Laos and Burma, however, are divided both ideologically and in terms of the various minority peoples who inhabit their high country. Burma is also split between its soldiers and civilians, as are Thailand, Cambodia, and South Vietnam. South Vietnam, besides also being only half a Vietnam itself, is further divided, not only between Buddhists and Catholics, as well as soldiers and civilians, but also in terms of the Communist- and non-Communist-ruled portions of the territory south of the 17th parallel. Even the Communist-controlled areas of the south, moreover, are differently governed; Hanoi itself administers the northernmost part of South Vietnam just below the so-called demilitarized zone, while the rest of the Communist-held territory in the south is ruled by the "Provisional Revolutionary Government."

It is inconceivable that workable governing arrangements and supporting political institutions can be established in such fought-over soil. The strongest government today, and the one most likely to prevail indefinitely, is that of the "Democratic Republic of Vietnam," whether it rules only North Vietnam or all the country. Among the non-Communist governments, that of Thailand seems the most secure in the long run, whatever institutional shape it settles into. Thailand has a popular monarchy (one that has shown itself able to adapt through the years) and a widely and genuinely supported Buddhist faith; yet, it, too, must put its new political house in order, as it has begun to do, and effect a reconciliation between newly emergent power centers and the previously ruling armed forces, which remain potentially very powerful politically. Power will have to be shared by Thailand's new civilian leaders with the soldiers, as the military shared it previously with the civilian bureaucracy and, to a lesser degree, the throne. Burmese leader Ne Win's new constitution, on the other hand, merely institutionalizes and attempts to legitimize existing authoritarian practices. What kinds of political institutions South Vietnam, Cambodia, and Laos have in the future will probably depend on developments on the battlefield; no peace, present or future, is likely to be lasting in any of these three lands (unless it is the enforced peace of Communist military triumph).

These twin weaknesses, national disunity and largely ineffective and frequently changing political institutions, are internal in their origin, stemming from domestic histories that usually include fairly recent experiences under foreign, or colonial, rule. Both types of weaknesses, however, have been exploited since World War II by outside forces—and not just the big powers. The mainland countries may never in the lifetime of their present populations overcome either of these weaknesses, but, if they do not, they will continue to be "sitting ducks" for both neighboring (and distant) interventionist forces.

3

The Insular Lands

Insular Southeast Asia—Indonesia, Malaysia, Singapore, and the Philippines—is the "other Southeast Asia" of which the world as a whole knows so much less than it knows of Vietnam, Laos, and Cambodia. Like the lands to their immediate north, however, the island-states have also experienced insurgencies, frustration with democratic institutions, government changes by force, restrictions on freedom of speech and other liberties, the military's rise as a politically important group, and the failure of ethnic or religious minorities to accept the leadership of ruling majorities. In at least one country, Indonesia, there has also been a large amount of bloodletting, not in the battlefield manner of Vietnam but in the form of the anti-Communist rampage that followed the Communist attack on the country's military leadership in September, 1965. (More than a quarter of a million persons lost their lives in a violent political backlash.) But there has not been a big war, involving foreigners fought on the soil of any insular Southeast Asian country (as there was in Vietnam); there are no Chinese troops on the territory of any of the insular lands (as there are in Laos and Burma); and no local government has sent large numbers of its own soldiers into a neighboring country (as the North and South Vietnamese and the Thai have done in mainland Southeast Asia).

Yet, many of the things that have happened in mainland Southeast Asia have also occurred in the insular region to its south—in miniature. British, Australian, and New Zealand forces aided Malaya (later expanded and renamed Malaysia) in its fight with Communist insurgents even after colonial Britain gave up its governing responsibility for the country—although foreign participation in the war, or the magnitude of the conflict, never compared with that in Vietnam. While no Southeast Asian country ever experienced invasions of its soil of the order of the Communist Vietnamese presence on Laotian and Cambodian territory, Indonesia did land a few paratroopers and send some marines ashore in its short and undeclared war, under Sukarno, against Malaysia in the mid-1960's. A few Filipinos also played a part in American-organized support activity of internal uprisings against Sukarno's government in Indonesia in the previous decade. And the United States provided tactical guidance and other aid to the anti-Communist Philippine government in the late 1940's and early 1950's when it faced a Communist rebellion that threatened Manila itself for a time (but no more than advice and equipment was needed from Washington—unlike in Vietnam, Laos, or Cambodia).

Historically, insular Southeast Asia has exhibited far greater regional harmony, and even unity, than the lands to its near north. It is not alone the greater distance from China that has given the southern island-world a larger degree of tranquillity and cooperation; it should also be noted that, in the late 1960's and first half of the 1970's, it was the island-countries that dominated the membership of the pioneer cooperative regional institution ASEAN (Association of Southeast Asian Nations) to which all of the insular lands belonged (but only Thailand of the mainland countries). It was almost as if conflict was for some reason heightened on the mainland and softened in the island-world, or that greater value was placed on cooperation among the insular countries than the mainland states.

Why has there been this seemingly greater tendency toward cooperation among, and even within, the insular Southeast Asian countries? A review of the recent political development of the countries of this island subregion should help to answer this question.

INDONESIA

The modern Indonesian state owes its territorial form to Dutch colonial rule, which united the peoples of the sprawling archipelago in a single political framework as never before in their history. The Netherlands established its first foothold in the islands in the late sixteenth century but did not complete its conquest of the Indonesians until the first years of the twentieth century. Parts of Indonesia, however, were under Dutch rule for 350 years and most of the country for more than a century and a half before independence was regained in 1949 (after four years of frequently intense fighting). Before the Dutch arrival, various indigenous sultanates and kingdoms jockeyed with one another for political predominance, and in the eleventh and thirteenth centuries major kingdoms established sufficiently strong governmental bases to extend their economic influence into the far reaches of insular Southeast Asia and to the shores of the mainland. But there was never a single political state embracing all of present-day Indonesia, and the trading community of the Madjapahit era (thirteenth and fourteenth centuries) had been shattered before the coming of the first profit-seeking traders from Holland.

There was, however, a degree of cultural unity in Indonesia, particularly among the coastal peoples, even before the establishment of the Dutch colonial presence. Most of the lowland coastal areas, especially on the main islands of Java and Sumatra in the western part of the archipelago, had felt the impact of Indian cultural contact through successive waves of Hindu and Buddhist influence. By the time the Netherlands attempted to bring various parts of the islands under its control, most of Indonesia had experienced yet another major cultural intrusion—also from India—which established Islam as the predominant religious faith throughout the archipelago. The different Indonesian languages, moreover, were closely related to one another, and traders along the coasts of the islands were able to communicate in a single common tongue, that of coastal (or bazaar) Malay. The political structures of the different local sultanates, in addition, were largely the same throughout the islands, and Indonesian common (or *adat*) law regulated relations among people throughout the archipelago in similar ways.

But it took the administrative framework of the colonial Dutch East Indies to provide a political structure for this slowly coalescing cultural community. The Netherlands also organized Indonesia into a single economic unit, differentiating the islands from other territories beyond their shores and making the parts dependent on one another. The exploitative presence of the tall and fair Dutchmen also gave Indonesians throughout the archipelago a common foe; the unity of the different parts of Indonesia became more apparent in the setting of white Dutch colonial rule. But nationalism gave shape to a political community that had deeper roots than mere opposition to the unwanted foreigner. And, when Japan conquered Indonesia from the Dutch in 1941–42, it found a formidable nationalist political elite already in being.

It was during the World War II years of Japanese occupation that the Indonesian nationalist movement developed its military arm (with Japan's cooperation), and the spread of coastal (or bazaar) Malay took place to such an extent in the same years that it became the *de facto* language of most of Indonesia. The quick defeat of the seemingly superior European Dutchmen by the army of another Asian nation, the Japanese, encouraged the nationalists after the war to believe that they, too, could defeat the Netherlanders. The anticolonial struggle that followed was a hard-fought and bitter one; it ended with the Dutch relinquishing their prized Southeast Asian colony in 1949, after four years of struggle against the Indonesian nationalists, who had declared their independence in 1945 (the same year as the Vietnamese under Ho Chi Minh).

Indonesia, like most other European colonies the world over, began its newly regained independence with the proclaimed intention of governing itself through democratic institutions. Its preparation and experience for doing so, however, were extremely limited. Popular participation in national ruling institutions had no historical roots in Indonesia, while autocratic Dutch colonial rule hardly prepared Sukarno and the other leading Indonesian nationalists for governing the country, democratically or otherwise. On the eve of World War II, the colonial government of the Dutch East Indies, as Indonesia was then called, was an extremely authoritarian one. Holland ruled a country fifty times bigger than itself from half a world away—with the only "representative" institution being the *Volksraad*, in which Dutchmen held more than

half the seats, although they constituted less than one per cent of
the population of the islands. No Indonesian by 1940 had served
as governor of a province, and only one had been head of a de-
partment of government. The Indonesian nationalists' experience
was in the area of opposition and agitational politics, which emphasized plotting and conspiracy rather than policy-making, con-
sensus-building, or program-implementation. Only 637 persons,
in a population of about 70 million, were attending college or university in the last year before the outbreak of the Pacific phase of
World War II.

Indonesia's government during the first half-decade of resumed
national freedom (1950–55) was surprisingly good, given the lack
of preparation for either independent government or the democratic version thereof. But, even in those early days of relatively
tension-free politics, the warning signs were there of the difficulties ahead. In 1948, even before the anticolonial war against the
Netherlands was won, the Communists staged their own uprising
to take over the nationalist movement. They were defeated (and
quite handily), but the appeal of Communism in the land, particularly given the manner in which first President Sukarno was
to waste so much of the national wealth, would continue, and the
Communists would become the single strongest political organization in the country by the mid-1960's. Sukarno and the soldiers
also clashed early in the postcolonial period, and a 1952 incident
that brought their differences to a head resulted in the resignation
of the Defense Minister, the Sultan of Djokjakarta, a popular nationalist figure who was to become the country's second Vice-
President in the regime of President Suharto after Sukarno's passage from the Indonesian political scene.

The four-cornered rivalry among the fiery nationalist Sukarno,
the Communists, the army, and rival Muslim religious parties was
to dominate Indonesian politics until Sukarno's fall from power
in the mid-1960's. But this four-way power struggle might never
have reached its subsequent proportions if it had not been for
other important factors. Probably foremost among these was the
already mentioned general Indonesian inexperience in self-rule.
Although there were important ideological differences among the
primary players in the Indonesian political game after independ-

ence, party alignments, leadership, and strategy seemed more
often than not to be largely personal. More than two dozen political parties jockeyed for power, sixteen of them winning more than
a single seat in the 1955 parliamentary elections. It was the resulting vacuum that accorded the politically skillful Sukarno the
opportunity to augment his own power as President far beyond
the original intentions of the country's "founding fathers," of
whom he himself was one. Sukarno was able by 1959, only a
decade after the Dutch had reluctantly acquiesced in Indonesian
independence, to announce the death of "inappropriate" Western-
style parliamentary democracy and the establishment of "guided
democracy." Sukarno drastically altered the nature of the Indonesian political process by playing on the weaknesses and divisions
of the other participants in that process, the country's various
would-be democratic political parties and personalities who, up
until the mid-1950's, were still more important than either the
Communists or the military.

Indonesia's first national elections—free, fair, and totally lacking in demonstrated national consensus—were held in 1955, the
same year in which President Sukarno hosted the historic first
Afro-Asian conference, at Bandung, of the leaders of the newly
independent lands of these two great continents. The occurrence
of these two events in the same year was significant—and unfortunate. It reflected the strong disposition of Sukarno to play a leadership role on the international political stage before Indonesia
had really even begun the task of trying to solve various of its
pressing internal problems. Sukarno subsequently moved to consolidate—indeed, expand—his personal domestic political power.
But never, in the years from 1950 to his complete fall from power
in 1967, was he to provide the leadership in domestic problem-
solving that he was to attempt to assume, largely unsuccessfully,
on the international scene, mainly among other underdeveloped
lands.

The government of President Suharto that succeeded Sukarno
was to charge, as others had earlier contended, that there was
"too much politics" and "not enough economics" during the Sukarno era. The accusation was an accurate one, in the sense that
it rightly identified political posturing, ideologizing, and jockey-

ing for power as major shortcomings of the first decade and a half of Indonesia's resumed independence. On the other hand, there was probably too little of the politics of reconciliation, as contrasted with the politics of confrontation, during the Sukarno years. It was less a question of too much politics and more a matter of not enough of the right kind of politics: nation-building, consensus and reconciliation, and problem-solving politics. Ironically, given Sukarno's ardent and vain desire for a strong leadership role in international politics, it was his personal tendency to confrontation and his lack of interest in problem-solving international cooperation that caused his foreign policy to be so lacking in real content and accomplishment.

Yet, at the same time, Sukarno may have been the most appropriate leader for Indonesia in the early years of independence in a number of very important ways. He was a patriot and nationalist of unquestioned identification with his country, and he provided a national symbol—and colorful style of leadership—that held the country together when it might otherwise have become fragmented. He greatly heightened the Indonesian sense of identity— no small accomplishment in a big, backward island-nation with eastern and western extremities farther apart than New York and Los Angeles. And there was a stronger, more visible, and more penetrating national governmental apparatus when Sukarno's rule ended than there had been at its start, something on which General Suharto and his soldier and civilian supporters could attempt to build their "new order." Sukarno, in addition, contained several separatist revolts, thus strengthening the country's political infrastructure for his successors.

The way in which the long-ruling Sukarno fell from power, like the ouster of Cambodia's Prince Norodom Sihanouk, illustrated a major deficiency in the various national political processes in postcolonial Southeast Asia. There was no other way to remove a ruler who had lost the confidence of either the people or the other members of the political elite. At least some Communists—supporters and would-be successors of Sukarno—feared in the mid-1960's that the anti-Communist military leadership might ultimately seek to prevent their coming to power upon Sukarno's death or retirement. Accordingly, they moved, together with par-

tisans in the armed services, against the top military figures in
1965—with extraordinarily destructive consequences for themselves. Six ranking generals were slain, but a comparatively
unknown soldier, General Suharto, seized the leadership of the
anti-Communist resistance, held the government against the Communists, and ultimately succeeded Sukarno as the country's political leader. Hundreds of thousands of Indonesians, most of them
alleged Communists, were slain in the subsequent bloodbath, as
anti-Communist Muslims, political opportunists, debtors, and
others went on a largely unchecked rampage, with the tacit
support of Suharto and the other anti-Communist soldiers. Could
not Sukarno's would-be Communist successors, the most formidable force in the country except the army, have been kept from
power in a less horrifying way? And could not the Communists
themselves have sought to aid their future political position without their own initial—and so costly—resort to force?

The years after 1965, in which Sukarno was gracefully eased
from power (to die shortly thereafter), were for Indonesia years
of political reorganization, realignment in international affairs,
and consolidation at home on several fronts. General Suharto, who
first became acting President, was made President in his own
right in 1968. The military dominated the new administration,
although Suharto maintained that his was not a "soldier government." Communism was outlawed. Economic development was
emphasized and "politics" de-emphasized. Technocrats (particularly economists) were given enhanced responsibilities and accompanying status, private foreign investment and government
aid were actively solicited, and relations with China were "suspended" and those with the United States greatly improved.
Between 1966 and 1968, Indonesia did an almost complete about-
face in terms of some of its economic policies and the pattern of
its international relations. It made peace with neighboring Malaysia, against which it had warred under Sukarno, and showed
unprecedented interest in regional cooperation with other Southeast Asian states as well as a strong desire for American military
aid. Inflation, worse even than that of South Vietnam, was checked;
food supplies were increased, though not without recurring problems; and ordinary Indonesians were able once again to buy tex-
tiles at prices they could afford.

But the new Suharto government did not mark a return to the attempted democracy of the first years of Indonesia's resumed independence. National elections, the first since 1955, were held in 1971, but they also were very much "guided," though in a more limited and indirect manner than Sukarno's highly ballyhooed "guided democracy." To begin with, one hundred of the seats in the 460-member House of Representatives were appointed ones, 75 of these for members of the armed forces who were otherwise prohibited from standing for election while still in uniform. Even more important, a new government-formed party, *Sekber Golkar* (or "Functional Groups"), enjoyed strong official support as well as a wide range of advantages and won 220 of the 360 elected seats in the legislature. President Suharto, however, unlike Sukarno, who tried to divide (and, thus, control) his opposition, sought to consolidate the rest of Indonesia's legally permitted political parties into two "groups" (or *de facto* new parties). One such group, the "Unity Development" group, comprises the country's Moslem political parties, such as the *Nahdatul Islam* (Moslem Teachers), while the other, the "Democratic Development" group, includes the old "Nationalist" party (of which Sukarno was one of the founders in the 1920's) as well as the Christian parties and the Proletarian Party. In 1973, President Suharto himself was re-elected to a second five-year term by the People's Consultative Congress, made up of the members of Parliament and regional delegates as well as even more "functional representatives" (workers, farmers, students, and others). And Hamengku Buwono, the Sultan of Djokjakarta, longtime adversary of Sukarno's authoritarianism, became Vice-President, a position vacant since the 1950's. Indonesia was by no means yet a democracy, but it seemed to be headed that way at least.

There were still similarities, however, between the Sukarno and Suharto governments, particularly in terms of their desire to control their immediate political environments, which meant definable limits to press and other freedoms. In foreign policy, on the other hand, the two regimes could not have been more dissimilar. Sukarno leaned increasingly toward the revolutionary Communist camp, led by China, and by 1965 was Peking's top non-Communist ally and cosponsor, with the Chinese, of the "have-not U.N.," the "Conference of New Emerging Forces," which was to have been established in Jakarta. Indonesia's fiery first President was also anti-American, patronizing toward his immediate neighbors, regarding them as "little countries," and eager for a personal position on the world stage akin to that of Mao Tse-tung, Nehru, Nasser, and Tito. President Suharto, besides fearing China and courting America, has become a leader—some would say *the* leader—in Southeast Asian regional cooperation (mainly, but not exclusively, through ASEAN). The "have," and technologically advanced, lands of Japan and Australia are also among Indonesia's present-day friends—a reflection of Suharto's realization that Indonesia needs capital, markets, and technology.

MALAYSIA

By the early 1970's, Malaysia and Indonesia, neighboring Malay-majority lands, were the best of political friends and increasingly seeming to resemble one another in terms of governmental goals and other political values. Yet, only a decade earlier, they had been bitter antagonists, possessed very different kinds of governments, and pursued quite dissimilar policies. Why had they once been such opposites, and what happened to make them more alike and to draw them closer together?

The answers to these questions are to be found in different areas of the experiences of the two Muslim Malay lands. Indonesia, as already noted, was not at all prepared for independence by its Dutch imperial rulers. The Netherlands's economic exploitation of its former colony, moreover, resulted in the succession of a highly socialist-oriented indigenous political elite. The Indonesians also had to fight four years against the Dutch for their independence. And, since Indonesia is big and rich in resources, there has always been the temptation for its politicians, like Sukarno, to try to play a leadership role in international politics.

Malaysia, on the other hand, gained its independence in 1957, as the smaller state of Malaya, without having to fight its British rulers. In the decade preceding independence, moreover, Britain did all that it probably could to help the Malays, Chinese, and Indians of multiracial Malaya to succeed politically after independence. National elections for an all-indigenous Parliament were held in 1955, and, on the eve of independence, the Malayans ran much of their own government. The Malays, who monopolized political power (which was not shared with the country's Chinese minority of 36 per cent of the population), were of princely, or upper-middle-class, origins and fairly conservative; socialism, accordingly, had no great appeal for them. Nor were they all that opposed to British economic interests, which did not seem to them to have exploited their land all that selfishly. And, unlike naturally well-endowed Indonesia, Malaya was not, and could not become, self-sufficient in food crops or in many other commodities and had to devote much of its attention to the development and management of its economy. Initially, it was almost completely dependent on the twin exports of tin and rubber. Economic neglect, after the fashion of Sukarno's Indonesia, would have had even more disastrous consequences for the Malayans (or successor Malaysians) than for the Indonesians across the Straits of Malacca.

Since the two neighboring states obtained their independence in very different ways, their first years of independence were, as a result, quite differently managed. The Malaysians, on the whole, seemed to accomplish much more with fewer resources. This, in turn, embarrassed the Indonesians, particularly the proud Sukarno, and a feud developed between Sukarno and the also outspoken Malaysian leader, *Tengku* (Prince) Abdul Rahman.

Before the coming of the Europeans, the peoples of the Malay Peninsula, which extends down into the heart of insular Southeast Asia from the mainland, had been ruled by different (and frequently warring) Malay sultanates. Between 1786 and 1914, Britain extended its rule to all the peninsula as well as the island of Singapore (acquired in 1819) at its tip. Although three different kinds of constitutional arrangements existed for the Malayan-Singapore colonial complex, there was, in fact, a single, increasingly coalescing political system, within a common British-governed framework. On the eve of World War II, accordingly, there was such a political and economic entity as British Malaya. It was a prospering colony, with large exports of tin and rubber.

Even as late as 1941–42, however, when Japan defeated colonial Britain and took over Malaya, there was not a truly Malayan nation and, therefore, not a Malayan nationalist movement. But there was a Chinese nationalist movement, with followers of

Chiang Kai-shek and Mao Tse-tung vying for control of it. Such politically active Chinese were concerned with who ruled China itself and did not agitate against British rule, as such, in Malaya. Although there were some Chinese in Malaya before the British, the majority of the Chinese entered the country during the colonial period to carry out economic tasks that the Malays would not, or could not, perform. The result was that over one-third of Malaya's population was Chinese, and it controlled key areas of the domestic economy. The Malays, some of them recent migrants from the island of Sumatra in Indonesia across the Straits of Malacca, constituted only a slight majority in their historic homeland; an additional 10 per cent of the population were ethnic Indians from British-ruled India. If, however, adjacent British-ruled Singapore were added to the population of the Malay peninsula, there would be roughly equal numbers of Malays and Chinese, three out of four persons in more economically advanced Singapore being of Chinese origin.

This is why there was no Malayan nationalist movement on the eve of World War II. The Malays feared the economic power of the Chinese, which might be translated into political power—and so they did not agitate for the end of British colonial rule. The Chinese, for their part, preoccupied politically with the struggle for China proper and eager to continue profiting from their economic position in Malaya, were quite content to have the British rule the country; moreover, they also probably feared that the pro-Malay British would ultimately leave the land with constitutional power rigged in favor of the "native" Malays. This, in fact, is just what the British did in 1957, when they finally ended their governance of the country.

After World War II, the British, who had returned to occupy the country in the wake of Japan's defeat, attempted to unify the differently governed parts of Malaya into a single constitutional structure that would have linked the various Malay states of the peninsula with Chinese-dominated Singapore. The British proposal had the effect of stimulating a new Malay (not Malayan) nationalism, and the result was two political structures, a new (still British-governed) Federation of Malaya and a separate Crown Colony of Singapore. Most Chinese remained political "fence-sitters," but in 1948, the same year that saw the creation of the Malayan federation, the overwhelmingly Chinese-composed Malayan Communist Party raised the standard of revolt against continued British rule of the country. For the next several years, a very serious insurrectionary war raged in the country, but the British and the growing Malayan armed forces, aided by Australia and New Zealand, eventually contained the conflict. The war, however, further divided parts of both the Malay and Chinese communities.

Colonial Britain undercut the Communists' appeal by peacefully granting independence to a coalition of Malay, Chinese, and Indian communal parties in 1957. This coalition, known as the "Alliance," was dominated by the United Malays National Organization (UMNO), but the participation of the most important non-Communist Chinese political group, the Malayan Chinese Association (MCA), and the Malayan Indian Congress gave the "superparty" at least the appearance of intercommunalism. Yet the 1959 federal elections, the first after independence, were fiercely fought, and there were signs of a breakdown in Malay-Chinese political cooperation. Adjacent Singapore, meanwhile, had become internally autonomous and was rapidly moving toward independence. With a possibly pro-Communist as well as ethnically Chinese government, that island-state would have been strongly sympathetic to the People's Republic of China and capable of stirring up Malaya's own very sizable Chinese minority. It was in such a setting that Malayan Premier Tengku Abdul Rahman proposed the formation of a new single state linking not only Malaya and Singapore but also the still British-ruled northern Borneo territories of Sarawak and Sabah. The mainly Muslim, but non-Malay, populations of Sarawak and Sabah would numerically balance Singapore's Chinese, who would otherwise have given the Chinese community numerical parity with the Malays in the new country.

The state of Malaysia came into being in 1963, succeeding the old Malaya and incorporating Singapore, Sarawak, and Sabah. Britain strongly supported Malaysia's formation and encouraged Sarawak and Sabah, neither of which had any previous modern political experience, to participate. Neighboring Indonesia and the Philippines, however, opposed the creation of Malaysia, largely because it precluded them from ever incorporating Sarawak and Sabah into their own national territories. The Philippine Government limited its opposition to peaceful diplomatic activity, but Indonesia, smarting because smaller Malaya had beaten it to the political draw, launched an undeclared and increasingly threatening war, complete with paratroopers and marine landings, against Malaysia. Indonesia's action had the temporary consequence of uniting the Malaysians against a common external foe, and the Malay-led, multicommunal "Alliance" did better in the 1964 national elections than it had done in 1959.

The Malaysian political leadership was surprised by the lack of outraged reaction to Indonesia's attacks against the Malay Peninsula and adjacent Singapore (as contrasted with disputed Sarawak and Sabah) among the other "new states" of the world. Britain, Australia, and New Zealand variously aided the Malaysians, without directly fighting the Indonesians, while the United States clearly favored Malaysia, sent Robert F. Kennedy to Jakarta to try to influence Sukarno, and agreed to sell the Malaysians military equipment. But these were the "oldfos," as Sukarno called them—the "old (colonial) forces" as contrasted with the "nefos," or "new (emerging) forces" (like Indonesia). For the most part, the "nefos," the more politically radical ex-colonies, seemed to support Sukarno, clearly the "aggressor" in Malaysia's eyes, against the Kuala Lumpur government. This was partly the consequence of the shared radicalism of Sukarno and the leaders of such states, as well as of the zealous wooing of their governments by Sukarno ever since the 1955 Bandung conference.

In the eyes of its own political leadership, Malaysia had been the "good country," concentrating on economic development and trade expansion, trying to solve its internal problems by itself, and eschewing external adventurism, which was the image possessed by the Kuala Lumpur politicians of Sukarno's sabre-rattling foreign policy. But the radical new states, more numerous than the conservative former colonies, saw the old Malaya as a "handmaiden" of the colonial British and the new state of Malaysia as the "neocolonial" creation of the Kuala Lumpur government's London masters. Malaysia survived, however, and continues to prosper today, but not solely because of British, Australian, New Zealand, and American support or, for that matter, the ineffectiveness of the Indonesian assault against it. Jakarta itself called off the war because of political developments within Indonesia—the unsuccessful Communist attack on the generals in September, 1965, and Sukarno's replacement by the moderate and pro-Malaysian Suharto. But the lesson of its isolation from a majority of the other "new states" at the height of Indonesia's "confrontation" was not lost on Kuala Lumpur and would later significantly influence Malaysian foreign policy.

Meanwhile, the internal political development of Malaysia continued, despite the half-hearted war against it by the Indonesians. Following the 1964 elections, Singapore's often abrasive Prime Minister, Lee Kuan Yew, "Premier" of his island-state in a Canadian provincial sense, moved to take over the leadership not only of all the Malaysian Chinese but also of the non-Malays of Sarawak and Sabah as well. Sarawak and Sabah, whose absorption into the new state led directly to the Indonesian-Malaysian war, were brought into the federation to balance the Chinese, but this strategy would have back-fired, in the eyes of the peninsular Malays, if Lee had succeeded in creating a new non-Malay majority to succeed the long-ruling, UMNO- led Alliance government. Lee and Singapore accordingly had to go, war or no war! And, in August, 1965, with no prior notice, Lee Kuan Yew's state of Singapore was unceremoniously kicked out of the Malaysian federation, thereby gaining a very quick and quite real independence that it clearly did not want.

The Alliance central government's action in expelling Singapore from Malaysia, demanded by conservative and Chinese-fearing Malay elements, solved the short-term problem of the ambitious Lee Kuan Yew but not the question of long-term Chinese-Malay relations within the remaining Malaysian state. About 36 per cent of Malaysia's inhabitants were still Chinese, even after Singapore's expulsion. And, in the hotly contested 1969 national election, Chinese-supported, though ostensibly multicommunal, parties made their strongest showing ever at the polls, defeating Alliance candidates in all the urban areas of the country, but failing to unseat the Alliance government in Kuala Lumpur.

Chinese and Malay attacks and counterattacks in the wake of the May, 1969, voting brought the two communities face to face in the streets; there was furious rioting, and Malay-dominated police and militia units intervened, with ten times the officially announced figure of 200-plus dead, 9 out of 10 of these Chinese. Parliamentary government was suspended in favor of emergency institutions and practices, and political and other liberties were significantly curtailed. Malaysian democracy was dead, it was widely concluded—outside the country. But it was not, for parliamentary institutions resumed their functioning in early 1971.

The Malaysia of the first half of the 1970's, however, was a new Malaysia, following the bloody May, 1969, rioting, Sukarno's passage from the Indonesian political scene, the emergence of a friendly ruling group across the Straits of Malacca in Jakarta, and the retirement from political leadership of Malaysia's only ruler since independence, Tengku Abdul Rahman, and his replacement by the less pro-Western Tun Abdul Razak. Relations between Malaysia and Indonesia were to grow extremely cordial in the early 1970's, with an unparalleled number of exchanges of government officials, which had the effect of bringing the two countries' public policies more in line with one another. The two governments became formal allies through their common membership in ASEAN, along with the Philippines, Thailand, and Singapore. But the relationship between Jakarta and Kuala Lumpur was closer than that between any of the others, and some said that the Malaysians were "falling" within Indonesia's "orbit."

Internally, Malaysia was more like Indonesia than ever before, too. Tun Razak, like Suharto, sought to reduce internal political factionalism, but, rather than forcing opposition parties to coalesce as new "groups," as Indonesia's leader did, Razak endeavored to draw such parties into a "front"—or, if not the parties themselves, at least their key members. August 1974 balloting in Malaysia, the country's fourth parliamentary election since independence, saw Tun Razek's new UMNO-led "national front" score a decisive victory, but the survival as the chief opposition party of the predominantly Chinese, left-wing Democratic Action Party suggested that ethnocultural differences persisted as a major factor in the nation's political life.

SINGAPORE

The political circumstances of Singapore are unique in all Southeast Asia. To begin with, the diminutive country is the only one in the area with an ethnic Chinese majority; nearly three out of four people in Singapore's population of 2,300,000 are Chinese. Throughout Southeast Asia, there are "overseas Chinese" minorities, some quite sizable, as in Malaysia and Thailand, but nowhere else is there a Chinese majority. The overseas Chinese are generally unpopular, in part because of their economic power and in part because of their unwillingness to abandon their separate cultural identity. They are also feared because of the historical, cultural, and ethnic ties that link them to mainland China. The fear is widespread in Southeast Asia, especially in Malaysia and Indonesia, of a possible future Singapore leadership in alliance with Peking and the impact this could have on their own Chinese communities and, indeed, on their general internal security.

Prime Minister Lee Kuan Yew denies that his country is a "third China." Singapore's people, according to Lee, are "Singaporeans," no more Chinese than Australians and Canadians are "Englishmen" or Americans are "Europeans." Lee is probably right, too, as far as the political and commercial elite of his island-state is concerned, some of whom, like Foreign Minister S. Rajaratnam, an "Indian," are not even ethnic Chinese. But there is also much evidence to suggest that most ordinary Singaporeans, who speak neither English nor Malay and who dress, eat, and otherwise behave like Chinese and speak one or another Chinese dialect, are still probably more Chinese than anything else. Singapore has the highest and fastest growing standard of living in Southeast Asia, and ethnic Chinese in Singapore are hardly second-class subjects as they are in Indonesia, the Philippines, and even Malaysia. But is Singapore, a largely political and economic entity, strong enough a symbol to counterbalance, for even second- and third-generation ethnic Chinese, the powerful pull of Chinese culture, the pride of being Chinese, and the magnetic attraction of a People's Republic of China that is increasingly becoming more respected politically, militarily, and culturally?

Singapore's Chinese and other citizens, on the other hand, may have more to fear from their neighbors than these neighbors have to fear from Singapore. There were those in Singapore in the early 1970's who greatly feared the increasingly close ties between the Malay-led governments of Malaysia and Indonesia, despite Singapore's common membership with these two states in ASEAN. The Malaysian and Indonesian political elites are regarded as antagonistic to the Chinese minorities within their countries, and some Singaporeans believe the Kuala Lumpur and Jakarta governments could some day "gang up" on their country and end its existence as a separate state. This seems extremely unlikely, in view of Malaysia's comparatively recent expulsion of Singapore, the problem of what to do with Singapore's Chinese in such an eventuality in light of both countries' already large Chinese minorities, and Communist China's probable hostile reaction and possible intervention. But such fears exist in Singapore, nonetheless, and give the small island-state a veritably Israel-like "garrison mentality."

Lee Kuan Yew's assertions of a separate "Singapore identity" notwithstanding, it is obvious that the ruling People's Action Party (PAP), headed by Lee, itself fears the appeal of "mother China" to many Singaporeans. The tactical problem confronting Lee, however, is a delicate one. Singapore's often very skillful Prime Minister cannot afford to appear to be "anti-Chinese," given the Chinese ancestry of 75 per cent of his country's population. It has not been easy for the pro-West, anti-Communist, and anti-Peking Lee to avoid appearing too opposed to a government that has given China greater international respect than it has enjoyed in more than a century. On the other hand, if Lee were ever to seem to be pro-Peking, he might well encourage the very Chinese chauvinism that is the chief obstacle to the development of a true "Singapore identity."

Singapore's leaders boast that they are "democratic socialists," though highly pragmatic ones (as one would expect from the commercially and politically skillful Chinese). There was a time when the PAP was a very dogmatic ideological party brooking no compromise with its opposition to capitalism or foreign investment. Such elements, however, are no longer in the PAP, although

some of them survive in the extreme leftist party, *Barisan
Socialis,* consisting of ex-PAP adherents who follow a strongly
pro-Peking and Communist line. Lee Kuan Yew encourages both
local and foreign capitalism, but within the framework of the
Singapore socialist state, which can hardly be called hostile to
capitalism. Lee's socialism is much more like regulated capitalism,
with a very strong—and genuine—concern for the people's welfare
that is reflected in outstanding public housing accommodating in
the early 1970's approximately half the island-state's population.

Lee's compromise with democracy, however, is of less demon-
strable necessity. Even if *Barisan Socialis* and Chinese chauvinist
elements were to pose more of an immediate threat to the government and various of its programs, neither Lee nor the PAP would
seem to require a 100 per cent majority in the national Parliament, which is what they have—after the fashion of Sihanouk's
former Cambodia. Lee has always had a weakness for "overkill,"
and the tight political ship he runs in Singapore today is a good
example of this tendency. Singapore's is probably a good government; it is sensitive to popular feelings and governs on the people's behalf. But it is a one-party state rather than a democracy.
Unrestricted criticism of the government is not tolerated, as evidenced by Lee's near-record performance in closing down newspapers he paranoically suspects of undercutting him. Almost
every area of human activity—from the trade unions to the
universities—is controlled by PAP loyalists. Even Lee's political
friends sometimes shudder to think what might happen some day
if this tight political control apparatus fell into the wrong hands.
This is not likely as long as the still fairly young Lee remains at
the helm. But, then, Sukarno and Sihanouk once looked politically
invincible, too.

Singapore's foreign policy is an important element in Lee Kuan
Yew's strategy to keep Singapore free and economically prosperous. Singapore is an active member of ASEAN and shares the
strong anti-Communism of the Indonesian-Thai wing of the alliance. Lee also places strong emphasis on his good relationship
with the United States, which he has frequently visited. Singapore
seeks the continued presence of American troops in Southeast Asia
and openly asked Thailand to keep U.S. forces on its soil during a

1973 visit by Lee to Bangkok. In fact, Lee would like to do business with all the major states (China alone possibly excepted) to give them all a vested interest in keeping Singapore a separate state.

THE PHILIPPINES

In the first quarter-century of the postcolonial era in Southeast Asia, there was less interaction between the formerly American-ruled Philippines and the rest of insular Southeast Asia than among Indonesia, Malaysia, and Singapore. The Philippines, though a Malay country like Indonesia and Malaysia, is located in the distant northeastern corner of the island-world to the south of the mainland. Unlike Indonesia and Malaysia, which are Muslim countries, the Philippines is a largely (90 per cent) Christian land (with an important and increasingly restless 5 per cent Islamic minority). Governed during the first forty years of the present century by the Americans from across the Pacific, it tended in the late colonial period to look eastward toward the United States rather than westward toward Europe, as did the nationalists of British- and Dutch-ruled colonial territories in Southeast Asia. In the 1950's and 1960's, moreover, the Philippine Government concentrated much of its political and diplomatic attention on the Southeast Asian mainland, where it participated in the Vietnam war, joined Thailand as a SEATO ally, and participated in training, relief, and other activity in Laos.

There was another, and even more important, reason why the Filipinos seemed quite apart from their Malay kinsmen of Indonesia and Malaysia during the first two decades of their resumed independence. This was the nature of their colonial and continuing relationship with the United States and the political pathway and public policies the Philippines sought to pursue in the years that followed the end of the colonial era in 1946. Never a people of great precolonial cultural or material attainment, the Filipinos fell victim to Spanish colonial conquest more than four hundred years ago; subsequently Christianized, they came to resemble in many cultural ways the formerly Spanish-ruled peoples of Latin America. At the turn of the present century, the United States

succeeded Spain as colonial ruler of the Philippines just as Filipino nationalists were about to throw out their Spanish governors.
The Philippine nationalist movement was the most developed in
Southeast Asia at that time, and the Americans, who had qualms
of conscience about their newfound colonial role anyway, quickly
accommodated themselves to the reality of Filipino political ma-
turity and gave their colony greater autonomy than was enjoyed
by any other country in the area. Ultimately, in 1934, the Filipinos
were promised by the United States that they would be given
their independence within ten years.

But Japan conquered the islands in 1941–42, and independence
was delayed until after liberation, coming in 1946. The Philippines was thus the first Western colony in all the world to gain its
independence after World War II and the first in Southeast Asia
ever to do so. Filipinos were genuinely grateful to the United
States for their treatment, took a real liking to American-style political institutions, and tried for twenty-five years to make a U.S.-
type presidential, congressional, and party system work. It did
work, too, much better and for much longer than did comparable
would-be democratic institutions in other ex-colonies. It did not,
however, work perfectly, largely because it came to be the exclusive property of a fairly narrow and very wealthy political elite
that exploited it for its own ends. Officeholders were generally
freely voted in and, by no means less important, out of office. And,
given enough time, there was no reason why propertied class–
dominated Philippine "democracy," institutionally sound enough,
could not have ultimately evolved into a true political—and economic—democracy. The ingredients for such development were
there.

But, just as Indonesia had its Sukarno and Burma its Ne Win,
the Philippines also possessed a leader who valued perpetuation
of his personal power above anything else: twice-elected President Ferdinand E. Marcos, who declared martial law in 1972 as
a prelude to extending his stay in public office beyond its legal
expiration at the end of 1973. Marcos, former war hero, congress-
man, and senator, was elected President in 1965 and re-elected in
1969 (the first such re-election ever!). But, like most Philippine
Presidents before him, as well as most of the national legislators,

he spent the greater part of his time bolstering his own personal political position. This was especially tragic because he was a man of great ability, and his country needed reform leadership. But in the twenty-fifth year of its postcolonial history, when it held a constitutional convention to improve the prevailing governmental and political system, Marcos's main concern was in keeping power for himself.

For twenty-five years, longer than any other former Western colony in Asia (or Africa), the Philippines experienced democratically accomplished change in the Presidential leadership of the country. Two parties (the Liberals and the *Nacionalistas*) alternated in power. Five men served as President before Marcos, but none prior to Marcos was ever able to be re-elected, reflecting the true freedom and fairness of Philippine elections. Congress, with a Senate and a House of Representatives, shared policy-making power with the executive. In 1972–73, however, all this was done away with, and the dangerous first step was taken of involving the army in a directly political role. In September, 1972, in response to apparently Marcos-staged incidents, the President declared martial law, arrested his leading political rival among others, and closed down all the country's newspapers, once the freest in all Asia. A sitting constitutional convention was told how to finish its job of writing a new basic law, and in January, 1973, President Marcos proclaimed the resulting constitution after hasty and illegal "approval" by so-called citizens' assemblies created overnight for this purpose. The new constitution was supposed to set up a parliamentary, or "prime minister–type," government in place of the U.S.-style Presidential system, but Marcos indicated that he would rule for seven years—without elections—pursuant to the new basic law's "interim" provisions. Congress was prevented from sitting, and in July, 1973, the Philippines's new dictator obtained a 90 per cent–plus "vote of confidence" in a national referendum on whether he should remain as leader beyond the end of the year, when his elected second term as President expired. Marcos wanted to make sure that he had some seemingly popular endorsement of his retention of power. The year ended with no new threat to Marcos's survival, and he entered 1974 probably more secure in his hold on power than he had ever been.

Marcos's economic policies, unlike those of other dictators, such as Sukarno's or Ne Win's, were fairly successful, aided as they were by the windfall of the highest prices ever for Filipino exports. Marcos also was highly effective in all but eliminating his country's long-festering Communist insurgency in northern Luzon island, but he was the first Filipino political leader to have to deal with the much more serious problem of a major Muslim rebellion in the south of the island-country. Islam had come to the southern Philippines at the same time that it swept through the Indonesian archipelago, but it was halted in its expansion on the islands by the arrival of the colonial Spanish and their proselytizing zeal on behalf of Christianity. If the Spaniards had come upon the scene even half a century later, the Philippines might have already become a Muslim country. The Spanish conquest thus had the effect of halting Islamic expansionism on the islands, but neither the Spaniards nor their successor colonial rulers in the Philippines, the Americans, were ever able to integrate the Muslims effectively into the national life of the country. The present problem of Muslim insurgency, however, derives less from any irreconcilable gap between Christianity and Islam in the Philippines than from the "land-grabbing" and general exploitation by unscrupulous settlers from the north of the Muslims of the big southern island of Mindanao and the adjacent Sulu archipelago. Rebellion began in the late 1960's and held down as much as half of the 65,000-man Filipino Army by 1974.

The Muslim problem was probably both an economic and an identity one. But there was also a larger Filipino identity problem that had its roots in the unusually close Philippine-American colonial relationship of the first half of the century. The persistence of this problem was reflected dramatically in 1972 in a movement of several million Filipinos to make the Philippines the fifty-first state of the United States. Five per cent of the Philippine gross national product, moreover, comes from American spending, mainly military, in the country where the United States has its largest military base outside North America. Filipino political leaders, including President Marcos, have also seemed to feel through the years that they had to have American friendship as a primary means of legitimizing their rule. Even in the 1970's, more than a quarter of a century after independence, probably too many Filipinos judged too many things—including political performance—in terms of American values and standards. The Marcos decision for dictatorship, however unfortunate otherwise, could be the beginning of an important change in this respect.

CONFLICT OR COALESCENCE?

There has always been, in the most general sense of the term, political interaction among the rulers and peoples of insular Southeast Asia. Before the European colonial era, there were Malay powers, based on Java and Sumatra in present-day Indonesia, that possessed political as well as economic influence throughout a large portion of the island-world, including the Malay peninsula. Historic western Malaysia (the former Malaya of the peninsula proper) and the east coast of Sumatra were more closely linked in precolonial times than Sumatra and Java; it was an accident of history that their modern development took place within different European colonial frameworks. Malaysia and Singapore were under common British colonial rule and were even part of the same country for a while after colonialism.

The resumption of greater interaction between the Malaysian-Singaporean, Indonesian, and Filipino political spheres—largely nonexistent during the heyday of Western imperialism in the area —began in the late colonial period. The American promise to the Philippines of independence by 1944 had an extraordinary impact on Indonesian nationalists in the 1930's, especially in view of their own Dutch governor-general's declaration that Holland would still be ruling the archipelago in another three hundred years. Filipinos like postcolonial Foreign Secretary Carlos P. Romulo had visited the Dutch East Indies in the late 1930's, and Indonesians who met with them could not see why Filipinos should be allowed to resume their self-governing ways but not they themselves. Some of the very first Malay nationalists in British Malaya at the war's end wanted their country to join the newly proclaimed independent nation of Indonesia across the Straits of Malacca.

In subsequent years, however, there was often more conflict than cooperation, let alone coalesce. Indonesia's Sukarno pursued a foreign policy quite different from that of neighboring states, and some of the leaders of both Malaysia and the Philippines feared possible Indonesian imperialism. Indonesia did, indeed, wage war against Malaysia; the Philippines conspired with the American CIA against Sukarno's Indonesia; both Jakarta and Manila contested Malaya's peaceful expansion to become Malaysia; and Singapore and Malaysia more often than not feared the intentions of their frequently personally feuding political elites. In 1959, when Malayan Premier Tengku Abdul Rahman was the state guest of Philippine President Carlos P. Garcia in Manila, the two Malay leaders proposed a "pan-Malay union." Indonesia's Sukarno, however, refused to join, so they formed instead the "Association of Southeast Asia" (ASA), forerunner of ASEAN, with mainland Thailand as the other member.

Since the mid-1960's, the trend has been in the direction of expanded cooperation, deeper understanding, and even greater resemblance between the various insular governments and the political systems of which they are a part. Indonesia not only stopped its war against Malaysia but also joined, and became a leader of, ASEAN, particularly wooing alliance partner Malaysia. Both Indonesia and Malaysia have made major efforts to thwart the Arab Muslim nations from making political capital out of the Philippines's Muslim-Christian differences. All four island-countries, together with Thailand, belong to ASEAN; exchanges of visits are at an all-time high, and present-day points of friction at a new low. This is partly a result of growing wisdom and experience, but it also reflects the fact that three of the four insular lands are Malay countries that feel real bonds of kinship toward one another. No less important, perhaps, is the fact that their political elites today are more like one another than ever before; the democrats have become less democratic and the dictators less dictatorial, and the differences among the four island-world political systems are smaller than they have ever been.

III

Political Patterns

4

Complicated Legacies

In the nearly 20 years between 1946 and 1965, all the Southeast Asian countries faced the challenge of getting started again as independent states. Even Thailand, which had never been a Western colony but had experienced a partial occupation and serious restriction on its freedom of action by "friendly" Japan during World War II, had to select, establish, and begin to operate new political institutions by which the country could be governed. The first of the former Western colonies to regain its independence was the Philippines (1946) and the last was Singapore (which ceased to be a British colony and became a constituent state of the Malaysian federation in 1963). Between 1946 and 1965, Burma (1948), Indonesia (1949), North and South Vietnam (1954), Laos (1954), Cambodia (1954), and Malaya (1957) became independent countries.

Although the governing institutions and political processes of these lands underwent major changes as a result of the transition from dependence to independence, none of the countries in question truly started afresh. Each built on its particular heritage, and, while some of the new ruling elites broke more dramatically with parts of that past than did others, not one was able to escape completely from the complicated legacies that were the "gift" of history. These legacies were of different sorts, ranging from the political ideas and attitudes of Southeast Asia's new rulers and their followers to the physical state of their lands. Some of the legacies represented restrictions; others offered opportunities.

COLONIAL RULE

All the countries of Southeast Asia except Thailand had been Western colonies for at least half a century; some of them had not been independent for three hundred years or more. Even Thailand lost territory to Britain and France, had to endure extra-territoriality on its soil, and was occupied by Japanese troops during World War II. It would have been extraordinary, therefore, if the experience of having been European colonies had not left a substantial legacy for the successor independent lands of Southeast Asia. On the other hand, France, Britain, Holland, Spain, and the United States—the major colonial powers in Southeast Asia in modern times—were very different countries themselves, acquired their colonies in different ways at different times for different reasons, and governed their dependencies in often very different fashion. The Philippines was almost completely self-governing on the eve of World War II, while Indonesia and Vietnam enjoyed practically no autonomy (thereby gaining little experience in self-rule). It is necessary to distinguish, therefore, between the region-wide legacy of colonial dependence as a general experience and the particular consequences of having been a colony of a specific imperial power.

Throughout Southeast Asia there is the legacy of Western political institutions. Before colonialism, everybody in Southeast Asia was governed by authoritarian and arbitrary emperors, kings, and sultans. In the Philippines prior to the Spanish conquest, the territorial unit of government was fairly small, but it was no less autocratic by virtue of its diminutive dimensions. Where there was government of a considerable territorial extent, it was unable to "penetrate" society; it was, so to speak, "surface government," rule from a distance that ordinarily limited itself to tax collection and conscription—and even these activities were sometimes performed for it by intermediary agents.

The European colonial rulers, whatever their many shortcomings, gave colonized Southeast Asia truly "national" government, the apparatus of a public administration, and the idea, if not always the experience, of democratic political institutions. Only in

Burma was the old monarchy actually ended altogether, but even elsewhere, where kings and sultans survived, the institution of hereditary and constitutionally unchecked government was thoroughly disgraced, largely because of its defeat and humiliation. When independence came after World War II, all the new states of Southeast Asia created governing institutions in emulation of the West, usually, initially, after the model of the home government of the particular power that had ruled them. Even the Communist Ho Chi Minh, proclaiming the independence of the "Democratic Republic of Vietnam" in 1945, sought to justify the Vietnamese case for self-government in language lifted verbatim from the American Declaration of Independence. Thailand, too, attempted right after the war to establish parliamentary government, although the effort was to be a short-lived one. When democratic political institutions were subsequently put aside in many of the countries of the area, the attempt was still made to justify the succeeding arrangements in terms of popular government, as in the Philippines in 1973, when Marcos proclaimed a new constitution, however irregularly, and convened "citizens' assemblies" to legitimate it.

Most but not all of the political institutions to be found in the independent lands of Southeast Asia in the first quarter-century after independence were derived from, or were in imitation of, Western models: elections; political parties; interest groups; a political press; a would-be independent judiciary; "state" governments; and even "special branches," "national security councils," and "central intelligence agencies." The Communist Party and the whole Communist apparatus—parallel state and party organs, party congress, politburo, and all—of North Vietnam were a direct outgrowth of the former French colonial connection, Ho Chi Minh having been a founding member of the French Communist Party in 1920. The concept of legislated rules for the regulation of society and the structured allocation of resources among groups, however represented in government, for the good of the nation rather than the glory of king and religious faith owe their origins to colonial rule.

Colonial rule itself, however, was nonrepresentative; it was purely the governance of one people by another as a result of armed conquest. Especially in French Indochina and the Dutch East Indies, government in the era of enforced Western rule was arbitrary, neither sympathetic to nor representative of the popular will. Even in the Philippines under twentieth-century American colonial rule, the people, who were accorded progressive participation in the government of their land, ruled at the sufferance of the United States rather than as a matter of right. Because the governor—indeed, the whole "governing class"—was foreign and "exotic," Southeast Asians developed often ambiguous attitudes about power and politics. The fact of colonial rule, however, was everywhere essentially autocratic government, whatever the differences in form. This legacy was to influence confused and contested leadership elites after independence. The "good old days," when government was "above politics," were to appear very attractive in the postcolonial period, when everything the new rulers did seemed to be challenged by one opposition element after another.

The appeal of regained self-government to nationalists in the 1930's and 1940's, as well as before, had been in the restored opportunity to make decisions themselves about, and for, themselves. It was not always realized, however, that most such decisions carried costs in terms of money, manpower, alternative activities, and personal, or mass, living standards. The foreign-governed populations of Southeast Asia observed only the exercise of power; they did not, for the most part, perceive the price of power. For example, in the Philippines, for the first quarter-century after independence, the very wealthy indigenous elite that succeeded the Americans as rulers taxed themselves hardly at all and paid only a small percentage of even such taxes as were due from them. Self-government involves unpleasant as well as gratifying decisions and choices, but colonial rule did not prepare the Filipinos, Burmese, Indonesians, and Cambodians, among others, for the unpleasant decisions that are often fraught with political, economic, social, and psychological consequences.

The first generation of Southeast Asian political leaders should not be faulted too strongly for such shortcomings of leadership. Inexperienced as so many of them were in self-government, it would have been extraordinary if they had really understood the subtleties of power and its exercise. What most of the new rulers knew about government, they knew from observation or study, not from experience. The pool of educated persons in economics, management, agriculture, foreign affairs, and other fields on which such leaders could draw, moreover, was meager, especially in Indonesia, Laos, Cambodia, Vietnam, and Burma. This legacy of limited experience and education did not bode well for success after independence.

Attitudes. There were, to be sure, some Indonesians, Burmese, and Vietnamese, among others, who benefited from and even enjoyed colonial rule. But, increasingly, the intelligentsia of Southeast Asia came to hate the imperial presence and everything it stood for. Because the colonial powers were capitalist countries, many of the nationalists became anticapitalist, accepting, often uncritically, the Marxist explanation that colonialism was an inevitable outgrowth of capitalism. Because the colonial powers were Europeans, some of the nationalists became emotionally anti-Western and, blaming the West in general for their past subjugation, displayed friendship for the adversaries of Western nations, often just because they were adversaries. Because the former colonial powers were democracies at home if not in their colonies, there developed in Indonesia, Burma, and even the Philippines antidemocratic sympathies as a reaction to the former colonial presence, or such doctrines became credible to potential followers for this reason. And, of course, almost every person of any political consequence—including followers—was anticolonial, generally supporting anticolonial liberation movements elsewhere. The Communist Ho Chi Minh enjoyed the backing of non-Communists among the Indonesians, the Burmese and even, initially, the Thai. A wide range of behaviors on the part of the European nations and the United States were interpreted as colonial or "neocolonial" in intent or effect even when they were not.

This array of anticolonial, anti-Western, anticapitalist, and antidemocratic attitudes, held by some leaders and many of their followers, was—and is—a legacy of the Western imperial presence in Southeast Asia. Like other legacies of this historic era, however, it is a complicated one. In no two countries of the region is the combination of these attitudes the same. Some of them, moreover, like anticapitalism, were stronger in the first years of independence than they are today, although Burma's anticapitalism increased, rather than diminished, with the years. Antidemocratic feelings, on the other hand, have grown with time almost everywhere, in previously largely democratic Malaysia and the Philippines no less than, say, Burma or Indonesia. (Indonesia, however, is probably less "antidemocratic" today than it was in the political heyday of the late President Sukarno.) The feeling—even in Malaysia and the Philippines—is that the departed imperial power left its former colony with particular political institutions, probably "too democratic" in some respects, that were not appropriate to the "realities" of the land, "realities" that range from the imperfect integration of its various ethnic minorities to just the ambitions of its political leader!

Predictably, these attitudes have changed in the last quarter of a century, and they were never perfectly possessed anywhere; Filipinos and the post-1947 Thai leadership never apparently sympathized with the aspirations and demands of the anticolonial liberation struggle in Vietnam as led by Ho Chi Minh. But elements of all of these attitudes persist down to the present time, however modified. Indonesian President Suharto may sympathize with the continued, if reduced, American military presence in Southeast Asia, but large numbers, possibly a majority, of his countrymen do not share his outlook, but are prevented from expressing their feelings by a more autocratic than democratic soldier-dominated regime. North Vietnam's remarkable staying-power in the war with the United States between 1964 and 1973 is largely to be understood in terms of the intensity with which nationalist feelings are held in that land. Even leaders in Thailand, which was never a Western colony, display various of these attitudes from time to time, though not to date in the chronic form of some present as well as past rulers of Indonesia, Burma, Cambodia, or even Malaysia.

Economy and Society. The legacies of the Western colonial period for the peoples of Southeast Asia were by no means limited to the world of politics. Indeed, some of the other legacies, in the areas of the economy and society, for instance, may be even more important in the long run. Such legacies may be expected to set limits to the politically possible in programs and policies in the years ahead. On the other hand, the colonial powers did much that was highly beneficial by advancing the "modernization" of the territories in their temporary charge, whatever their reasons for doing so. And one can argue, although few nationalists would, that Southeast Asia is a better place for the experience of colonial rule.

Economically, Southeast Asia was a series of small, largely subsistence economies at the beginning of the European colonial era four hundred years ago. There was trade with other parts of the world, particularly centered in the Indonesian islands, but most of the people and kingdoms did not participate in it in the region as a whole. Moreover, it was the Arabs, the Indians, the Chinese, and the Europeans who came to Southeast Asia to obtain its products, such as spices, rather than Indonesians, Burmese, Vietnamese, or others who themselves sought out overseas trading partners. The Europeans came to trade, especially the Dutch and the British, but they stayed to govern and developed local economies to serve the interests of various of their nationals. These economies were largely agricultural or extractive, very much dependent on the purchases of the colonial and other "advanced" countries, and managed by, and in the interests of, foreigners. Extremely low wages were paid, and working and living conditions were unhealthy and depressing. Moreover, labor was brought in from both China and India to perform those tasks that the European would not do, and which, it was said, the Indonesian, Malay, or Burmese could not do.

The result of such efforts was the establishment of a dependent economy and the creation of a "plural society," that is, one in which different segments of the population performed distinct economic tasks and otherwise lived apart from other population groups in the same land. In every country in Southeast Asia, including never-colonized Thailand, there is a substantial Chinese minority, usually performing economic tasks previously handled by neither the Europeans nor the indigenous peoples. The Chinese, however, are not the only "class" apart from the main body of society that came to its present position as a direct conse-

quence of colonial rule. Everywhere there is also a body of nationals of the country that is different from the majority of the
population as a result of its Western "modernization" or "ac-
culturation." This "class" is to be found in government service,
business, education, the professions, communications, and the
military. It is to be distinguished from other groups of Indonesians, Cambodians, or Thai, for example, by the fact that its members usually speak English, have gone to college, may have trav-
eled abroad, and have almost invariably adopted some aspects of
the European life-style. They probably question privately many
of the religious and other traditional beliefs and practices of their
countrymen. Because this group has a much higher standard of
living than other people in the country, it generally looks down
upon the majority of its fellow nationals, and also possesses a
vested interest in the economic rewards of the society as they are
currently allocated.

Thailand, of course, demonstrates that a country did not have
to become a European colony to acquire an economy and society
with various of these characteristics (although the Thai were
much more intimately touched by colonialism than they would
like to admit). The point, however, remains that these economic
and social conditions have their roots in the immediate past, in
which the colonial powers predominated in the region as a whole.

Boundaries and Minorities. The very boundaries that separate
the several Southeast Asian states are a direct legacy of the colonial era, and they do not always accord with ethnic, linguistic, or
other realities. Fairly sizable ethnic groups, such as the Shans of
northern and eastern Burma, are separated from the majority
population of an adjacent country (Thailand in the case of the
Shans) with whom they have more in common than the predominant people of the land in which they are located. The Muslims
of Mindanao and Sulu in the southern Philippines are separated
from Muslims in neighboring Indonesia and Malaysia. There are
peoples on both sides of Burma's long land frontiers with China,
Bangladesh, and India who have more in common with one another than with the ethnic, cultural, and political majority of the
land in which they live. And, for the most part, the boundaries
that compound, if not cause, this confusion were drawn in the

colonial era as a reflection of the power at a particular time of the rival European colonial rulers; the purpose of such frontiers was primarily to divide Southeast Asia among the Dutch, British, and French; it was not to draw a rational ethnic, linguistic, and cultural map of the region.

On the other hand, the colonial powers also did consolidate political units, to the probably lasting advantage of the indigenous peoples of a good part of Southeast Asia. The Indonesian archipelago was pulled together administratively by the Dutch as it had never been before in history, and it is worth noting that today's Indonesia includes West Irian (or western New Guinea), whose people are very different ethnically from the rest of the Indonesians and who were never previously ruled by any Indonesian government, because West Irian was part of the former Dutch East Indies. Similarly, the Spanish united the Philippines—spiritually as well as politically, nine out of ten Filipinos being Christians, the vast majority of them Roman Catholics. Like Indonesia, the Philippines would seem to be a natural geopolitical unit, although the question of whether Mindanao or Sulu "naturally" belongs with the rest of the Philippines is an open one, in view of the failure of more than four hundred years of Spanish, American, and Filipino rule to integrate the southern Muslims into the social and political fabric of the larger country. The Filipinos themselves, however, have been much more successful in this respect than the two Western colonial powers that previously ruled the islands, which is why the Muslims have been in revolt since 1969. Their "culture," in a real sense, is at stake today—more than under former artificial Spanish or American rule—just as non-Burmans in Burma see the ruling Burmans as threatening their very identity.

Malaysia, perhaps as much as any other state in the region, reflects the accomplishments and the persisting problems of the imperial powers' efforts to divide and consolidate the people and territories of the area during the colonial era. Modern Malaysia, comprising the lower portion of the Malay Peninsula and northern Borneo, represents a direct political result of the former British imperial presence in "middle Southeast Asia"; the Malaysians succeeded to all of what used to be British territory in insular

Southeast Asia, even though this territory had never been ruled by a single local power before its British conquest. The British even took away some of Thailand's southernmost Malay Peninsula provinces, with their majority Malay population, thus rationalizing the ethnopolitical map of central Southeast Asia. But some Malay-populated territory seized previously by the Thai remained in Thai hands, creating a potentially major irredentist problem. And the British permitted the migration of so many Chinese and Indians as to threaten the Malays' majority in their own historic homeland.

The insular countries were probably left a better legacy in this respect than their mainland neighbors to the north. No land in the southern island-world has the problem of minorities with ethnic kinsmen across several of its national frontiers that Burma has—and one of Burma's neighbors, actively exploiting this situation, is China. Thailand has Malay, Lao, and Meo minority problems partly because of the way in which the territorial "carving up" of Southeast Asia influenced it. Lowland Laos has historical, ethnic, linguistic, and general cultural links with the neighboring Thai—and might well have ultimately ended up as part of Thailand but for French absorption of the land into that colonial artificiality called Indochina. Part of the unwanted French legacy in Cambodia was a Vietnamese minority that took advantage of common French rule over all Indochina to migrate to Khmer territory, pretty much as more economically aggressive Indians entered Burma from India when both lands were governed by Britain.

World War II. European colonialism ended in Southeast Asia as a direct consequence of World War II, particularly the comparatively easy Japanese conquest of the area, the failure of any of the imperialist states to make a serious attempt to defend its colonial territory (except for the Americans, who, ironically, had promised the Philippines independence in 1944), and the stimulation Japan gave to local nationalism during its occupation (especially after it became apparent that the Japanese would themselves be ousted from the area). Independence undoubtedly would have come to the Indonesians, Vietnamese, Burmese, and others in time, but possibly not for another generation. World

War II accelerated the process of European decolonization of the area, and peoples gained their freedom under less than the most auspicious of conditions.

World War II wrought much destruction for large parts of Southeast Asia. Burma and the Philippines were especially. badly hit, as the result of the wars, first during their conquest and then during their "liberation." Indonesia was not as seriously damaged as these two lands, but the exploitative Japanese occupation was followed by four years of fighting the Dutch, a war that probably would not have taken place when and as it did except for Japan's ouster of the Netherlands from control of the "Indies" in 1941–42. For almost a decade, therefore, there was no development, and much destruction, waste, conflict, and confusion, in Indonesia.

The war was the final phase of the European colonial era and betrayed for all to see, including local nationalists, the weaknesses and political bankruptcy of the Western imperial presence. The Europeans could not even defend the territories they denied to their local, historical, and proper rulers and inhabitants. The conflict, however, did other things that were to plague the "new states" of the region in the years after independence had been obtained. An uninterrupted, peaceful transition from dependence to independence was prevented in the case of the Philippines—with consequences that perhaps did not become apparent until Marcos's 1972–73 termination of Filipino democracy. As a direct result of the war, a quite different and less experienced elite succeeded the British as Burma's rulers than probably would have otherwise; the prewar local elite lost out to a younger and more radical group of leaders as a consequence of the power base the latter built up during the Japanese occupation. Communists gained guns and a start as jungle-fighters during the war, and moral values in general were grossly compromised throughout the region, with visible political effects after independence. Most important of all, time was lost that might have been used to lay a better groundwork for independence in all the lands.

PRECOLONIAL LEGACIES

Precolonial governments in Southeast Asia were universally autocratic, and most of Southeast Asia's postcolonial regimes in the

1970's were also authoritarian. What, if anything, was the relationship between these pre- and postcolonial regimes?

For countries like Burma, Cambodia, and Vietnam, the establishment of colonial rule over all the country was recent enough, occurring as it did in the second half of the nineteenth century, that there were those among the anticolonial nationalists before the war who had personally known preimperial governance or were children or grandchildren of members of the former indigenous ruling elites. Indonesia and the Philippines, on the other hand, were at least partly governed by Westerners for three or more centuries—and yet Sukarno was still able to rejoice in the recollection of Indonesian accomplishments in the ages of Srivijaya and Madjapahit, and Philippine President Marcos in the early 1970's tried to revive the *barangays,* or local councils, of the pre-Spanish era.

Few actual institutions of governance survived the age of colonialism in Southeast Asia as a whole, the exceptions being the Khmer and Laotian monarchies, the emperorship of Vietnam (terminated in 1945), the Malay sultans, and, of course, the Thai King. By the 1970's, only the Thai and Laotian monarchies (of some influence but no real power) and the Malay sultans (of some continuing but limited authority) persisted. But history-stimulated memories of great emperors, kings, and sultans survived, along with the example of "strong leadership" that they manifested.

The first "choice" of all the Southeast Asian lands after World War II was "democratic" government. Even Vietnam's Communist Ho Chi Minh seemed inclined in 1945 to establish governing institutions that were more democratic than Communist in character (though how long they would have lasted is another question). With the "failure" of democratic government, however, the leaders of various Southeast Asian lands such as Cambodia and even the Philippines looked to the past for inspiration and found it in the tradition of former autocratic rule. It is not just that authoritarian government was the tradition of the countries in question, although this is also important in itself, but that this tradition had never been broken by the European colonial rulers, who were very much themselves autocrats in Southeast Asia. The emperor, the sultan, and certainly the god-king in Cambodia were remote ruling figures given to arbitrary and often capricious decisions and actions. To many ordinary Indonesians, Burmese, and Vietnamese, the colonial governor (or governor-general) was no less exotic, distant, or arbitrary. The colonial governors thus kept alive an executive, or ruling, style that embodied and communicated the essence of traditional rule in the colonized lands, even though it simultaneously served as a vehicle for the transmission of new ideas, practices, and models of behavior.

The legacy of the indigenous past was not restricted, however, to the secular side of government. Thailand's King was historically protector of its Buddhist faith, as were the monarchs of old Burma. Former Burmese Premier U Nu's attempt to re-establish Buddhism as the state religion derived from the precolonial legacy of a partly religious state; the reversal of Nu's action by his military usurper-successor, General Ne Win, should not be interpreted as meaning that the political role of Buddhism in Burma has been finally ended, although undoubtedly Ne Win's intent in cracking down on the Buddhist clergy in the 1960's was to destroy their political influence. The question of the official status of Islam remains a major issue in religiously as well as ethnically divided Malaysia, although non-Muslims are not permitted to discuss it, while Muslim rebels have fought the central governments of Indonesia and the Philippines to establish a theocracy in the first instance and possibly to break away and set up a separate state in the second. A Malay Muslim religious-ethnic uprising of major proportions—possibly aided by Malaysia—is a future possibility in southern peninsular Thailand.

Historic Rivalries. The European colonial occupation of most of Southeast Asia ended—only temporarily, as it turned out—age-old rivalries among various of the peoples of the region. One of these rivalries involved the dynamic and expanding Vietnamese of the Indochinese coastal region and the once-powerful but contracted kingdom of the Khmers (or Cambodians). The Khmers had formerly ruled nearly all of mainland Southeast Asia, as far west as Burma possibly, but had been replaced by the intruding and more aggressive Thai from southern China in the central or middle mainland region. In the nineteenth century, the seemingly tired Khmer monarchy was losing ground to the aggressive Vietnamese to the east and southeast as well. The post–World War II effort of the Communist Vietnamese to expand their control to Cambodia as well as Laos was probably as much a reflection of this revived local imperialism as it was of Communist expansionism.

Such rivalries and imperialist urges were also part of the complicated legacies that confronted the various Southeast Asian peoples with the resumption of independence after World War II. Historically, the Burmese and Thai kingdoms warred almost without end, and, while there have been no new wars since colonialism ended, the Thai variously have supported rebellions against the Burmese government. The Thai have also sent troops into neighboring Laos and into Vietnam as well to fight against the Communists; they would have sent them into Cambodia in the early 1970's, too, but for the fear of a hostile popular reaction in that land. Likewise, Vietnamese have fought in Laos and Cambodia in a similar revival of historic tensions among neighbors. And Indonesians have warred against Malaysians and, when Sukarno was still their leader, sent agents into the southern Philippines to stir up the Muslims. Filipinos have aided rebellion in Indonesia, and some Malaysians, if not the Kuala Lumpur government, have assisted Islamic insurgents in Mindanao and the adjacent Sulu archipelago.

Related to such rivalries, and, sometimes, the cause of them, have been the "imperialistic" dreams of some of the leaders of postcolonial Southeast Asia. Former Indonesian President Sukarno is said to have dreamed of dominating all the territory that was once included in the old loosely structured Indonesian "empires" of Srivijaya and Madjapahit. In a less immediate and more indirect fashion, Thailand aspired, after the departure of the British and French, to regain "lost territories" of the preimperial age from both Laos and Cambodia and even Burma to its west. Almost all Southeast Asian leaders have sought to restore the glory, real or imagined, of a much-celebrated past by controlling as much of the formerly ruled territory as possible. Some politicians, however, notably Prince Norodom Sihanouk and Lon Nol in Cambodia, have had to content themselves with simply maintaining their countries' present boundaries.

Migrations. In colonial times, greater attention was accorded the new migrants—the Chinese and the Indians—than the older ones, who from time immemorial have made their way down through the mountain passes from southern China and out across what are today the Indonesian and Philippine archipelagoes. Almost all the "new" migration ended with colonialism's termination; in Burma's case, in fact, there has been a reverse movement of Indians from Burma back to India since General Ne Win took over in 1962. Most of the legal migration of Chinese, moreover, ended by the 1930's, owing in part to the great depression of those years.

But the "old" migrations continue: out of China into Burma, Laos, Thailand, and Vietnam and throughout the insular portion of Southeast Asia from the Indonesian island of Sumatra across the Straits of Malacca to western and peninsular Malaysia as well as back and forth among eastern Indonesia and Malaysia and the southern Philippines. These older population movement patterns preceded Western rule and continued, with little attention, during the colonial era. They have probably increased since independence, in part because of generally unfortified frontiers, coastal as well as land. The increase of Kachins and Chins in northern Burma in the last quarter-century has been much greater than natural growth would explain; members of these minorities from China have crossed the border into Burma in unprecedented numbers since World War II. Among other factors, improved methods of transportation, the greater, if still limited, availability of cash, and expanded awareness of opportunities elsewhere have played a part in increased population movement in and about insular Southeast Asia.

The longtime legacy of such migration has at least two political consequences. Such population movements cannot help hindering national integration, involving as they do new peoples who may not identify with the ethnic or religious majority in their new lands of domicile; such migrants provide possibilities for greater border problems and their exploitations by extraregional powers.

Religion. Religion is a primary force in the lives of most people in Southeast Asia. This would not cause serious problems if everybody in the region, or its constituent countries, were of the same religion or even of closely related religions; but they are not. Most Filipinos are Christians, the only Christian majority nation in all Asia; but about 5 per cent of Filipinos are Muslims, and many of them are today fighting the central government. Religious as well as ethnic, linguistic, and other differences divide Malays, Chinese, and some Indians in Malaysia, and they seem most unlikely to disappear in the future. The Thai look down on all non-Buddhists in their kingdom, and this includes the Muslim Malay minority in southern or peninsular Thailand; this religious dichotomy has both domestic and international political implications. Fear of Burmese Buddhist domination played a part in the rebellion of various Burmese minorities, particularly the partly Christian Karens. In South Vietnam, Buddhist-Catholic differences underlay some of the opposition to the late President Ngo Dinh Diem, and new Buddhist-Catholic clashes will surely occur in the future.

All Southeast Asia's religions established themselves in the area before European colonial rule—except Philippine Christianity, which was a consequence of Spanish conquest and conversion. Since independence, however, many of these faiths have experienced veritable revivals, and there have been religiously inspired clashes in most of the countries of Southeast Asia. Some of the modernized leaders of governments, however, are only nominal Buddhists, Christians, or Moslems, and it may be that such persons will be able to avoid conflicts caused by their different religions. On the other hand, nationalism has heightened the sense of religious identity in the minds of many people in Southeast Asia. And the masses, whom the leaders must take into account, even in authoritarian countries, are more rather than less religiously conscious today than they were under colonialism.

POLITICAL IMPORTANCE

Many factors influence political behavior and development, including geography, resources, and external intervention. History is only one of these. But the particular kind of history the Southeast Asian lands have experienced—not least of all recent colonial rule and the escape from it—is peculiarly pervasive in the ways in which it seems to influence so many areas of their societies. Even when old wounds are healed and bitter memories are forgotten, as they are already in some lands, the legacy of prior historical experiences will still remain, in the form of particular economic systems, disputable national boundaries, and inadequately integrated societies. The past has bequeathed contemporary Southeast Asia a multidimensional legacy and, therefore, a complicated one.

5

Ideas and Attitudes

Three major sets of ideas and attitudes have dominated the outlook of the leaders of the Southeast Asian countries, as well as those who would succeed them, in the years since independence. These have concerned the questions of identity (or definition of the state and its membership), form of government (and resulting means for mobilizing the human resources of the state), and strategy and method for development and distribution of the natural wealth of the country. Other types of ideas, including religion and even astrology, have also influenced the politics of some, if not all, of the lands of Southeast Asia. But the ideas that have moved men and influenced nations have been those of nationalism, democracy, socialism, and their various alternatives.

This is not to say, however, that all political activity in Southeast Asia can be explained in terms of ideology, however defined. Much that has happened since independence can be explained in terms of personal ambition, often narrow and unprincipled, opportunism, improvisation (when action was required and there were no relevant ideological or other guidelines), foreign intervention, and even historical accident. But even the ambitious and opportunistic, and those forced on the spot to respond to an unexpected crisis, act in accordance with the ideas and attitudes they are familiar with and believe in. Some of these ideas and attitudes are widely shared; others are not. Both types of philosophical perspectives have been important in the politics of Southeast Asia since independence.

NATIONALISM

Nationalism—defined as a people's awareness of their common heritage and destiny, combined with a desire to constitute a separate state distinct from all other states—is probably the single most important political idea in all Southeast Asia, as it is, indeed, elsewhere in the world. The quality of being Thai, Filipino, or Khmer is probably more important today to most Thai, Filipinos, or Khmers than what kind of government they have or how their economy is organized. The primary objective of the Indonesian, Vietnamese, and Burmese nationalist revolutions was the ouster of foreign rulers so that Indonesians, Vietnamese, and Burmese could be free to organize their societies, economies, and political systems as they wanted. As the pre–World War II Philippine nationalist leader Manuel Quezon once declared, Filipinos would rather be ruled "like hell" by other Filipinos than "like heaven" by Americans. His emphasis was nationalist—not democratic, socialist, or capitalist.

There was, however, a time—very recently in the case of some of the countries of Southeast Asia—when only a very few people thought in nationalist terms. In the immediate pre–World War II years, for instance, most Indonesians did not think of themselves as Indonesians at all; and still today many Malays and Chinese in Malaysia think of themselves primarily as Malays and Chinese, rather than as Malaysians. Similarly in Laos, the sense of nationalism is probably less strong than the local cultural, linguistic, and other identities of that land's various peoples.

But most—if not all—Vietnamese, Thai, Indonesians, Filipinos, Khmers, and Burmese think of themselves mainly as Vietnamese, Thai, Indonesians, Filipinos, Khmers, and Burmese. Whether most Malaysians and Singaporeans, let alone Laotians, similarly view themselves is not only an open question but also one with potentially politically destabilizing consequences if the answer is in the negative. Malaysia, for example, could yet be forced to endure new communal rioting that could be at least as weakening as the troubles of Northern Ireland and might possibly invite some sort of future Chinese or Indonesian exploitation or even intervention.

Translated into institutional and policy terms, nationalism in its contemporary Southeast Asian manifestation means that peoples who endured the subordination and humiliation of colonial rule, and who fought in some cases to end that rule, wish to retain full control of their "national" domain, including its economy. Strong efforts by foreigners to get the leaders of such lands to adopt policies not of their own choosing have been, and will continue to be, resisted. Americans can well testify to the difficulty of getting the Diem and Thieu regimes in South Vietnam to do things they did not want to do. Burmese leader Ne Win's wholesale expropriation of his country's large Indian ethnic minority, previously the dominant business group in Burma, revealed the intensity with which the political elite of that land wished to regain control of its "national" economic birthright.

National Security and Welfare. Among the government goals in both mainland and insular Southeast Asia today, national security and the welfare of the region's inhabitants are paramount. Although there have been leaders who have thought mostly of their own personal survival, or the survival of the elites to which they belong, most of Southeast Asia's leaders since independence have shown a genuine concern for the social and economic welfare of their countrymen. Conspicuous among them have been Singapore's Lee Kuan Yew, the "Alliance" leaders of adjacent Malaysia, President Suharto and the other leaders of post-Sukarno Indonesia, the North Vietnamese Communists, and even Burma's Ne Win, despite the economic dislocation that his otherwise good intentions brought to his once rice-rich land. They have all recognized that national security depends not only on safe borders, however, but also on a populace convinced of its government's interest in, and serious efforts to grapple with, their problems.

Even when national leaders have not been genuinely concerned with the welfare of their countrymen as a whole, they have given lip-service to the nationalist objective of improved living standards for all who live within the nation. The Philippines' very wealthy, and often greedy, political-economic elite of the 1950's and 1960's mouthed all the slogans of improved popular welfare but did very little to advance the lot of most of their poverty-stricken countrymen. Similarly, the soldier-elite that governed

Thailand from 1947 to 1973 was concerned enough with national security—too concerned, some would say—but it appeared much more interested in advancing various of its own interests than those of the Thai peasantry in general. Even Prince Sihanouk, when he ruled neighboring Cambodia between 1954 and 1970, was more show than substance when it came to improving the welfare of his countrymen.

The twin concerns of national security and popular welfare are the inevitable consequences of true nationalism. "*National* security" means the political-military preservation of the nation, and Southeast Asia has not known a single leader since independence who has not given highest priority to this objective. U Nu and Ne Win may have been bitter political rivals for the leadership of Burma, and the civilian-democratic and military elites they headed may have been strongly opposed to one another, but both leaders and both elites feared Chinese infringement of Burma's independence and placed prevention of such a possibility above all other objectives of public policy. Ho Chi Minh, wrongly deemed a Chinese puppet by a generation of American leaders, clearly regretted his great dependence on adjacent China, historically chief foe of the Vietnamese people; but, because the United States posed a more obvious and immediate threat to Vietnamese independence—as Ho saw it in the 1960's—he reluctantly acquiesced in a subordinate relationship with Peking. Similarly, "popular welfare" as a policy objective flows naturally from nationalism as an idea or from a nationalist movement manifesting that idea. The colonial foreigners had been ousted so that the country might be ruled in the interest of the whole people. But that noble end would fail of attainment if the local elite that replaced alien rule proved itself equally contemptuous of the popular interest, as it did in some cases.

It has been variously held that nationalism in its Southeast Asian setting was mainly *anticolonial* nationalism. This, however, was not true even of the several nationalist movements operating in the days when the colonial powers still ruled most of this part of the world. That it is also not true today is partly evidenced by the fact that most of the former colonial powers enjoy more than ordinarily close relations with the governments of the territories they formerly ruled, the Dutch in Indonesia and the British in Malaysia, for example, as well as the United States in the Philippines. Nationalism as an ideology in most of the Southeast Asian countries is concerned with maintaining a generally hard-won independence and making life better for the vast majority of ordinary people. Attainment of these twin goals has not always been possible, but that such aims are part of the attitudes and ideas that govern the outlook of most leaders and followers in recent and present-day Southeast Asia is beyond question.

Communalism. The main reason why there is no real "Malaysian" nationalism today—more than a decade after the country's creation in 1963—is the "communalism" of its Malay and Chinese populations, and, to a lesser extent, of its far less numerous Indian minority and various Borneo peoples as well. The frame of mind that keeps Malaysia's Malays and Chinese apart is called communalism because it reflects both the self-image and the actual condition of the two ethnocultural groups as distinct "communities." Communalism differs from nationalism in two respects primarily: Nationalism ordinarily involves more people than communalism (though not always), and nationalism also almost invariably seeks a separate political structure for those who are united in such a common sense of identity, that is, it wants a state of its own. Malaysia's Chinese, because they are physically interspersed with Malays and Indians in the country's larger cities, cannot be separated territorially from Malaysia's Malays; they could not become a Malaysian "Bangladesh," even if they wanted to do so (and there is no evidence that they want to do so). As for the Malays, Malaysia is their historic home—the country's very name reflects their leading role in it—and they form a slight majority of the land's population. In the years ahead, the Malays may further identify with ethnically related Indonesia and want to become part of it; the Chinese, on the other hand, may develop a more strident form of promainland "Chinese nationalism" and become more loyal to China than Malaysia, just as many Malays fear. But neither Malay nor Chinese communalism is likely to become the kind of nationalism that expresses itself in separatism, whereby either or both of the two groups seek to form a new state.

Communalism as a force is unquestionably stronger in some of the lands of Southeast Asia in the 1970's than it has ever been before in their postcolonial histories. No country provides a clearer example of the destructive capabilities of communalism than Burma, where almost every minority ethnic group—Karens, Shans, Kachins, Chins, Mon, Arakanese, and several even smaller population groups along the Chinese border—has raised the standard of revolt against the central Burmese Government in Rangoon, which is dominated, as these minorities see it, by the nation's Burman majority. Three-quarters of the Burmese population are Burmans, but non-Burmans inhabit about half the country, largely, but not exclusively, its peripheral or frontier areas. Some leaders of the minorities have sought a separate state for themselves, primarily the Karens in the early postindependence years. But most of the non-Burman ethnocultural minorities have feared the obliteration of their distinct cultural identity at the hands of the majority Burmans more than they have sought a state of their own. But when such communal groups seek a separate state, they clearly have made the transition from communalism to nationalism; if, however, their goals are constantly frustrated, as those of Karen nationalists have been, then they may perhaps more properly become "subnationalists."

Subnationalism. Subnationalism is a potent force in most of Southeast Asia today, seriously rivaling nationalism. In a real sense, it is an "alternate" nationalism—ordinarily involving a smaller number of people than the larger nationalism that brought such countries as Burma, Indonesia, and the Philippines to independence. In Burma today, a second generation of Karen and Shan rebels battle the Burman government of ex-soldier Ne Win, indicating the powerful pull of the idea of the distant subnational identity of Karens and Shans. The question in Burma, as elsewhere in Southeast Asia, is whether a man may think of himself as belonging first to the "national" group and then to the "subnational" group, or whether those who profess primary "subnational" identities and goals should be allowed to pursue them as state-seeking "nationalists" in their own right. In most instances, the nationalist majorities will strongly resist such a solution to the problem, not just because their nationalism itself demands it but because of the danger that such new, small, and probably more easily influenced states would pose to the "parent" nation's own continued survival. It is for such majorities a significant matter of "national security," the highest goal of the national state as such.

Separatism. Separatism, the movement to detach people and territory from a state of which they are a part, is also a strong force in contemporary Southeast Asia and likely to become stronger in the years ahead. It is surprising, perhaps, that separatism, as such, has not been more important in Southeast Asia so far in the years since independence. In 1958, for example, when a Sumatra-based rebellion threatened the Java-based regime of the late Indonesian President Sukarno, no attempt at all was made to take Sumatra or any part of that large and resource-rich island out of Indonesia. The insurgents merely wanted to unseat Sukarno, not to separate from the rest of Indonesia and set up a new state of their own.

Separatism, however, as an idea and frame of mind, is a potent force in Southeast Asia, despite its comparatively modest political impact on the area. Burma's Shans were constitutionally eligible to separate from Burma proper in 1958, and some of their leaders talked about such a move then and later. General Ne Win maintained in 1962 that he unseated U Nu as Premier for the second time because he feared that the forces of separatism were gaining ground and would fragment the country. A decade later, half of the armed forces of the Philippines were battling a Muslim rebellion in Mindanao and the Sulu archipelago in the southern part of the country, some of the leaders of which sought a separate existence apart from the rest of the land. The leader of the easternmost Malaysian state of Sabah was reported to be aiding Filipino Muslim insurgents with a possible eye to detaching at least the Sulu archipelago from the Philippines proper and setting up the wholly new state of "Sabah-Sulu." To do this, however, would require that Sabah itself separate from the larger Malaysian state, between whose central government (on the Malay peninsula) and itself there was no small amount of tension.

Burma's Karens excepted, most separatist movements that developed any political steam at all in Southeast Asia during the first quarter-century after independence did not seek a new separate state wholly by themselves. Some of the Shans of Burma wanted union with their ethnic cousins the majority Thai in next-door Thailand, some of the Philippines's Muslims would apparently like to join with fellow followers of Islam in neighboring Malaysia or perhaps even Indonesia, and Thailand's southern peninsular Muslim Malays clearly would prefer union with Malaysia to a new state of their own. As an idea, however, separatism remains potentially very powerful in Southeast Asia; it is, in a sense, an alternative to both nationalism and subnationalism. It is almost inconceivable that Southeast Asia could go another quarter-century without feeling the greater impact of this force.

SOCIALISM

For many politicians in Southeast Asia before and since independence, socialism has been the economic expression of nationalism. In Indonesia and Burma, the two lands in which nationalism has found its most extreme expression since the end of colonial rule, socialism has been viewed as the main means to regain control of the national economy as well as to establish a more equitable economic order. Not only was nationalism in those particular countries strongly anticapitalist, but there was a widespread belief among the political elite that succeeded the former colonial rulers that only state development and direction of the national economy could attain the various goals they had set for their newly independent nations. Given the key role of Chinese minorities in the economies of both lands (and of Indians, too, in Burma), it was firmly believed that the handful of indigenous capitalists could not possibly develop the economy rapidly enough or perhaps even control it. Socialism, accordingly, would accomplish for the country economically what nationalism had done for it politically: the ouster of the foreigner as controlling agent of the land's natural resources and the development of the country's natural and human wealth for the benefit of its inhabitants.

Socialism in its Southeast Asian setting was frequently, and often explicitly, combined with other ideas or philosophies. When

U Nu was Prime Minister of Burma in the 1950's, he sought to justify his government's socialist policies in terms of Buddhist values; Nu's socialism, therefore, was often referred to as "Buddhist socialism." Nu's self-proclaimed successor, General Ne Win, offered his countrymen a more extreme, and quite ill-planned, type of socialism combined with nationalism and called the "Burmese Way to Socialism." A political contemporary of both Nu and Ne Win, Cambodian Prince Norodom Sihanouk called his ardently articulated but otherwise half-hearted brand of socialism "Khmer (or Cambodian) Socialism." In both Burma and Cambodia, despite the support for socialism of most members of the political elite, it was still necessary to interpret this economic ideology in terms comprehensible to those in the country who either did not understand or were not moved by socialism as an idea by itself. Moreover, many of those who professed to be socialists—particularly Ne Win and Prince Sihanouk, and even, to a lesser extent, U Nu—had themselves only a very limited and highly simplified understanding of socialism.

Practically all members of the new political elites of Burma and Indonesia were supporters of a socialist state in the first years of independence. If anything, Burma in the 1970's was more socialist in outlook than ever before, certain limited concessions to "free enterprise" notwithstanding; while Indonesia's leaders, though no longer as emotional in their identification with socialism as the late President Sukarno had been, still sought the ultimate establishment of a socialist economic order. Singapore's Premier Lee Kuan Yew and his People's Action Party remained very much socialists in theory and purpose; and Lee, in fact, hosted an important gathering of Asian and Western Pacific socialist leaders in his island-country in mid-1972. But, as in Israel and Sweden, two of the world's most successful socialist states, Lee's booming socialist order had sufficiently accepted local as well as foreign private initiative and investment to justify its classification as a "mixed economy."

Elsewhere—except in Communist-ruled North Vietnam—socialism as a set of ideas has had only a limited number of followers. In Thailand and the Philippines, "socialists" are largely equated with "communists"; while in Malaysia they are thought to be political allies of Singapore's Chinese Premier Lee Kuan Yew, and so "suspect" for this reason. Yet, in both Malaysia and Thailand, many policies were pursued that were clearly "socialist" because state direction of the economy was a logical outgrowth of their nationalism (or, in the case of Malaysia, of the ruling Malays' desire to develop the economy to the advantage of the non-Chinese sector of the population). The fact that there is no significant Vietnamese socialist movement is largely the result of the division of the country already into left-wing North and right-wing South.

Communism. The ideological pull of Communism in Southeast Asia remained strong in the first half of the 1970's, despite the fact that among the governments of the area only the Hanoi-based "Democratic Republic of Vietnam" was openly dedicated to it. Ne Win's "Burmese Way to Socialism"—which was hardly "democratic socialism," with its one-party monopoly of political power— was clearly "communist" with a small "c"; yet in foreign policy it showed no partiality toward either the Soviet Union or the Chinese People's Republic. Burma's orthodox Communists, with strong support in the 1970's from Peking, had fought a civil war against the Rangoon government for more than a quarter-century by 1974, with conspicuous lack of success. On the other hand, the Communists of both Laos and Cambodia were stronger in the first half of the 1970's than they had ever been.

The examples of Laos and Cambodia, as well as the seemingly contradictory one of Indonesia, illustrate why Communism has persisted as a formidable political force in Southeast Asia in spite of far more failures than successes. As a means of gaining political power, the first quarter-century after independence in Southeast Asia would seem to indicate that Communism is far from a sure formula. But it has inspired—and continues to inspire—men and women to hold out against seemingly insurmountable odds in support of the values it manifests and articulates. Communists in Southeast Asia may have treated their enemies with great brutality (of which they have no monopoly) and have even employed extraordinary disciplinary measures against their own followers, but they are, perhaps more than anything else, idealists. Although the Communist Pathet Lao in Laos, with its strong support from adjacent North Vietnam since 1954, may not have spent long years in the political wilderness, the Khmer Rouge (Red Cambodians) in neighboring Cambodia struggled for years to retain their identity and even to remain alive. Before his ouster in 1970, ex–Khmer leader Prince Norodom Sihanouk had sought to destroy the Khmer Rouge—with whom he later was uneasily to ally himself. The Khmer Rouge survived to enjoy new political importance in the 1970's because of its leaders' passionate belief in Communist ideology.

So undoubtedly is it today, too, with Indonesia's several million persisting, if undeclared, Communists. The anti-Communism of the largely soldier-regime of President Suharto has not yet destroyed Indonesian Communism, as the government itself readily admits. It will take another decade or so, the soldiers say; but can ten years even of suppression of an ideology wholly destroy it? The appeal of Communism in Southeast Asia lies in the fact that it offers a plausible explanation of history, a means of serving the nation and even humanity in general, and procedures for using as well as holding power once it is obtained. The young men who fought the Marcos government as the so-called Maoist New People's Army in the Philippines in the late 1960's and first half of the 1970's failed in their short-term objectives, but there will be more "Maoists" (or other Communists) in the Philippines in the future. They, too, may be defeated, but they also will try again—for an idea.

"PROGRESSIVISM"

There are many "capitalists" in Southeast Asia—especially in the Philippines, Thailand, and South Vietnam as well as among the area's omnipresent "overseas Chinese," but "capitalism" as an ideology is not an important political force. The "free enterprise" approach is still extolled by chambers of commerce and similar groups in the once American-ruled Philippines, though less than formerly, but nowhere else is a market economy and private initiative supported as economic or political doctrine. Capitalist business practices are reluctantly tolerated on the part of the Chinese merchants of the region, partly because neither state nor indigenous businessmen are yet able to take their place and partly because of the capital such Chinese bring into the country from Chinese sources elsewhere in the area as well as in Hong Kong and Taiwan, available only to themselves. In the ordinary business of nearly all the countries of Southeast Asia, except North Vietnam and Burma, the capitalist method predominates and involves far greater sums of money and numbers of people than state enterprises, but it persists for practical rather than ideological reasons. Indeed, even in strongly socialist-inclined Indonesia under Sukarno (as well as in the more mildly socialist Indonesia of the present day), state agencies "hired out" many of their responsibilities to private entrepreneurs, usually Chinese.

If capitalism as an idea is relatively unimportant politically in Southeast Asia, this does not mean that capitalism as a practice is lacking in an ideological foundation. Throughout the area in countries like Malaysia with "mixed economies," there is a strong belief in the inevitability of progress, or primarily economic development. This area-wide belief in progress, which is particularly conspicuous as part of the outlook of the leaders of Malaysia, Singapore, Thailand, the Philippines, and Indonesia, contrasts sharply with the sense of despair that hangs over some of the drought-ridden and otherwise afflicted "new states" of recently decolonized Africa. Such "progressivism," lacking in a formal set of "how to do it" principles or any specific intellectual or moral rationale, is at least as important ideologically or politically in the area today as either socialism or communism.

The reason for the intensity of such a belief in "progressivism" is the largely pragmatic character of the men who have ruled those Southeast Asian states that have shown the greatest economic development in the last quarter-century: Singapore (where Lee Kuan Yew's socialism seems to have more to do with public housing and other types of welfare activity than with state-run production facilities), Malaysia, Thailand, and the Philippines. The leaders of these countries, on the whole, are not ideologues; even their nationalism is subdued compared with that of the late Indonesian President Sukarno, Burma's General Ne Win, or Cambodian Prince Sihanouk. Eclectic in ideological orientation, politicians like Premier Tun Abdul Razak of Malaysia are concerned more with getting results than with proving philosophical points. Their objective is success, and their belief in the reality of progress has been fortified by their quite consistent success in developing their own national economies. "Progressivism," if such it may be called, is the far greater "enemy," ideologically, of Communism in Southeast Asia than is capitalism. As an idea of any genuine political importance, capitalism just does not exist, partly because of its past link with exploitative colonialism—not least of all in the eyes of the area's nationalists.

Socialism, Communism, and "progressivism" are the chief economic ideologies, or sets of ideas, of major political importance to be found in Southeast Asia today. By themselves, the ideas will not settle the future of this vast—and resource-rich—region. Yet, they will play a part in shaping tomorrow—just as they have already helped to make the area what it is today.

DEMOCRACY

The number of democratic governments in Southeast Asia was at a postcolonial low after 1972, the year in which President Marcos signed the death warrant of Filipino democracy. Malaysia's was the only competitively elected regime remaining in a region where all of the former colonies, except Communist North Vietnam, began independence with democratic constitutions and declared intentions of governing themselves democratically. Nonetheless, despite the demise of half a dozen democratic governments in the quarter-century following World War II, the democratic idea, and ideal, is very much alive in the area today, however paradoxical this may seem to be.

Democratic government suffered in Southeast Asia in the quarter of a century that followed World War II from region-wide lack of experience; internal war that was often internationalized; and the assault upon it by several skillful demogogues like Sukarno, military dictators like Ne Win, Nguyen Van Thieu, and Lon Nol, and power-perpetuating politicians like Ferdinand Marcos. Popular support for democracy, however, did not falter through these years—in the Philippines, Burma, and Indonesia in particular—and dedicated democrats like Burma's U Nu and the

Philippines's Raul S. Manglapus struggled in exile to restore government to the people in their homelands. Even the dictators themselves, from Ngo Dinh Diem to Marcos, felt it necessary to try to justify their stolen or manipulated power by means of managed "popular support." Vietnamese elections under Diem (or Thieu) were far from free or fair, while Marcos's mid-1973 referendum on behalf of his unconstitutional continuance in office was more blatantly rigged than the balloting even in Communist countries.

The survival of democracy as an idea in lands where it has been much abused in practice is not difficult to understand. The whole point of the "nationalist revolution" was self-government. Democracy was much invoked by nationalist leaders like nondemocratic Sukarno and Sihanouk in the era of agitation against colonial rule and won much ideological support from lesser political actors and enthusiastic elements of the population as a whole. In a very real sense, democracy is to the relations among the people of a nation what national self-government—or nationalism achieved—is to relations among nations. It is "self-rule," and the will to self-rule (or democracy) within Burma, the Philippines, or South Vietnam has no more died because of local suppression than the desire for national liberation was killed by former foreign tyrants.

What is the role, then, of democracy today in a setting of near region-wide authoritarianism in Southeast Asia? Its function is severalfold. It exists, first of all, as an alternative to autocracy, which is why General Ne Win, with all his troops, so visibly feared U Nu, who had only a modest number of insurgents fighting for him, in the years 1969–73 before Nu went into seeming political retirement in India. In addition, the democratic ideal forces Southeast Asia's several nondemocratic leaders to justify themselves and their rule in democratic terms, and this has probably blunted the edge of their tyranny a little. And, finally, democracy as an idea serves as a sustaining link between suppressed democratic elements in authoritarian-ruled countries and fellow democrats elsewhere in the world, as during the years of Sukarno's dictatorial rule in Indonesia.

Antidemocracy. Antidemocracy, too, is a force of some political importance in Southeast Asia today. Like "anti-Communism," however, which also exists in Bangkok, Jakarta, and other capitals of the area, it is weaker than the force it opposes because of its essentially negative nature. "Antidemocrats"—Burma's soldier-leaders and Thailand's former military rulers were explicitly "anti-democrats"—believe, or profess to believe, that their peoples are incapable of governing themselves. The Burmese soldiers argued that democracy was not possible in their land because it allowed the politicians who exploit it to divide the land—an argument used by Indonesia's Sukarno as well. Thailand's army politicians called their country's civilian parliamentarians "irresponsible" and termed the people "naive" for following them. All the area's dictators have advanced alternative philosophies to guide their countries, from Sukarno's "guided democracy" to Marcos's "constitutional authoritarianism." But each of them, without exception, has been weak in inspiring ideology and strong in dictatorial behavior.

"Antidemocracy" is not so much a set of specific alternative ideas to democracy—indeed, usually it is not that at all—as it is a frequently inconsistent collection of objections to the way democracy has been operating in practice in the country in which the dictator has been "forced" to "assume control." Burma's Ne Win, for example, was highly critical of democratic politics under the ousted U Nu, although Nu and his fellow civilian politicians in fact achieved more successes than Ne Win's own later "Burmese Way to Socialism." Autocrats of the ilk of Ne Win, Marcos, and Sukarno will persist in the politics of Southeast Asia into the indefinite future, and they will invoke antidemocratic ideas in their support. But few will follow the antidemocracy of these nondemocrats when they fall from power.

Free Speech. The idea of free speech—and, relatedly, of freedom of the press—have yet to throw down real roots anywhere in Southeast Asia (except for the Philippines, where the press is severely controlled today, though possibly only temporarily). Before President Marcos's personally motivated proclamation of martial law in September, 1972, the Philippines had the freest press in all Asia, if also one of the most irresponsible. Today's Philippine newspapers, as well as television and radio, are run along the lines of public media in totalitarian countries; they repeatedly extol the virtues of the great leader and stifle genuine criticism. But the Philippines has known a free press, and this tradition of free speech will probably outlive the man who currently suppresses it.

The freest press in all Southeast Asia today is that of Thailand. Criticism of the government in Thai newspapers is greater than any found in the newspapers of, for example, Malaysia and Singapore, where there are strong restrictions on freedom of speech and the press. Even Indonesia's press, enjoying a rebirth after the stifling climate of the Sukarno years, may have more freedom to express itself today than does the press in Malaysia and Singapore. In none of the other countries of the area is there really any free speech at all, or true freedom of the press, although brave men speak out courageously from time to time—and subsequently pay a high price for doing so. It is odd, indeed, that the idea of democracy has not been accompanied by greater awareness of how essential free speech is to the functioning of democratic government. But this is only one of the ideological contradictions to be found in present-day Southeast Asia and is presumably to be explained largely in terms of the newness of democracy in the area.

Elitism. In the days of nationalist agitation against European colonial rule, nearly all the politicians in Southeast Asia stressed their ties with, and roots among, the people. There is still much mouthing of democratic slogans even in the most undemocratic political processes, but there is also a widespread belief among leaders in the area that the people do not understand the problems facing the nation and that, therefore, a small group of men must make the decisions at this crucial point in history. Such a belief in "elitism," while lacking formal ideological structure, is a major force in the area today, if only because most of the political leaders espouse it and foster it.

Soldier Superiority. Among the military men of the area, particularly the soldier-elites of Indonesia, Burma, and South Vietnam (and, formerly, Thailand), there is the related belief that men in uniform are better than the civilian politicians who had their chance and failed. These soldiers apparently believe that they are superior to civilians in intelligence, skills, patriotism, and morality, and that they are entitled to rule because of their heroic struggle against the old colonial rulers and Communist insurgents and other foes of the nation. Military elites believe that there has been "too much politics" in the past and, accordingly, limit "divisive, partisan political activity" in the lands they rule. These views, of course, are self-serving, but, in Indonesia and Burma particularly, they appear to be genuinely believed by those who hold them; and, since those who hold them, though a minority, are politically important, the views themselves assume extraordinary importance.

Cooperation

Ideas of cooperation are exerting unparalleled influence in Southeast Asia. Internally, in democratic and nondemocratic lands alike, there is great emphasis on "pulling together." In Indonesia, for example, President Suharto has strongly encouraged the country's surviving Sukarno-era political parties to "come together" in pursuit of the various goals of the Indonesian nationalist revolution. Similarly, in Malaysia, Premier Tun Abdul Razak has actively sought, "on behalf of national unity," to assimilate into a "front," or coalition, different parties and personalities previously opposed to one another. The objective of Burma's new constitution, which came into effect in 1974, is to "unite" the country and thwart possible future "fragmentation."

Such cooperative thinking has also influenced the conduct of foreign policy in the area. In the early years of independence, it was every nation for itself—with or without a foreign patron; only a handful of far-sighted leaders advocated "regional cooperation," and even they did so with the ulterior motive of seeking their country's pre-eminence. Since the late 1960's, however, regional cooperation, or unity, in international affairs has acquired new advocates and registered solid accomplishments. Creation and growth of the "Association of Southeast Asian Nations" (ASEAN) is the most important development in this respect. Such international cooperation among governments of the area reflects the growing belief in leadership circles that the survival of the new states may be possible only in such patterns of partnership. Like growing internal cooperation, such international partnership represents the widespread feeling that the alternative to "working together" may well be the loss of all that was sought and obtained in the "nationalist revolution."

Neutralism. When neutralism, or nonalignment, was first espoused as a valid foreign-policy option by a Southeast Asian country, newly independent Burma, it was not generally regarded as a means for drawing various third world countries into a relationship of closer cooperation. Neutralist lands would not align themselves with any bloc, even a bloc of other also nonaligned countries, and no government in all the world has pursued such a policy more scrupulously than Burma through the years. Five South and Southeast Asian countries, however—Indonesia, India, Pakistan, Ceylon, and Burma—did consult together as the so-called Colombo Powers in the early 1950's, and out of their meetings grew the 1955 Bandung conference of independent Asian and African political leaders, hosted by Indonesia. The subsequent conferences of leaders of nonaligned countries that began in the early 1960's, and the most recent of which took place in Algeria in 1973, were a logical follow-up to the 1955 Bandung meeting.

Indonesia under Sukarno was a very vocal participant in international meetings of the nonaligned countries, even though some of them, like Sukarno's own Indonesia, were not truly nonaligned. Cambodia, when Prince Sihanouk headed its government, also took an active part in such conferences. In the 1970's, however, the new political elites of Jakarta and Phnom Penh have displayed markedly less interest in meetings of the avowedly nonaligned governments of the world—Indonesia merely endeavoring to keep a foot in this important political camp, and Cambodia seeking unsuccessfully to prevent such nonaligned nations from recognizing exiled Prince Sihanouk as the true voice of his country. The Malaysians, on the other hand, have never been more interested in the nonaligned countries as a bloc in world politics; in 1972, the Kuala Lumpur government hosted a preparatory conference of such states. Premier Tun Abdul Razak, however, seems mainly to be seeking to prevent the kind of isolation from other third world countries in which Malaysia found itself in the 1960's, at the time of Indonesian President Sukarno's undeclared war against it.

As an idea, however, neutralism—and even cooperation with other nonaligned governments—continues to enjoy high favor among the political leaders of Southeast Asia. On the other hand, the stronger leftist ideological outlook of the world's other nonaligned political figures and their obvious partiality toward the same kind of international radicalism that once inspired the Indonesian nationalist Sukarno have kept several of the leaders of the reigon from taking a more active role in such international conferences through the early 1970's.

Anti-"powerism." Closely related to neutralism and nonalignment is what may be called anti-"powerism," that is, active opposition to great power domination of weaker countries and, indeed, of world politics in general. This was a dominant theme of the 1973 Algerian-hosted nonaligned conference, and it also underlies one of the key foreign-policy alternatives under consideration in Southeast Asia by the five ASEAN states (Malaysia, Indonesia, Singapore, Thailand, and the Philippines). Malaysia has proposed the neutralization of Southeast Asia, meaning the nonalignment of the states of the region with any of the great powers and the consequent nonintervention of such powers in the affairs of the area. The other four ASEAN governments have thus far been reluctant to support the Malaysian proposal other than in principle, but it is clear that their hesitation derives from reservations about this particular policy and its potential consequences; for one thing, it might give China a possible opportunity for enhanced interest in, and even domination over, the region. But anti-"powerism" as an idea, minimizing great-power domination of world economics and culture as well as politics, is a growing one in Southeast Asia today.

OTHER IDEAS

There are a number of other ideas that are also influencing politics, indirectly in some cases, in Southeast Asia at the present time. Self-reliance, for example, has become a rallying cry in the new Indonesia of President Suharto and his soldier-civilian supporters; "national resilience," as Suharto calls it, refers to the country's capabilities not only for solving its own problems but also for recovering from possible future setbacks. "Do it yourself" economics—and politics—exists in exaggerated form in "lonely" Burma. But self-reliance, as an officially encouraged idea, is also growing in support and importance in Malaysia, Thailand, and the Philippines. Indonesia, indeed, has raised with its ASEAN partners the desirability of developing "strategies of 'national resilience,'" in each of the countries of the alliance.

Nepotism ordinarily would not seem to qualify as an ideology, but there is, in fact, such a widespread belief in Southeast Asia that places high value on helping "members of the family" that it must be considered among the many politically relevant attitudes found in the area. Similarly, the folk-beliefs of spiritism and astrology should also be included among the ideas influencing politics in Southeast Asia today. Such important leaders as Suharto of Indonesia and Lon Nol of Cambodia regularly consult their astrologers and follow their advice. And religious ideas today may be more important politically than ever before in some countries of the area—such as the Philippines, where the Mindanao-Sulu rebels are exclusively Muslims and believe they are fighting a veritable "holy war" against "Christian oppressors."

IMPORTANCE OF IDEOLOGY

The importance of various ideologies ranging from spiritism to Communism notwithstanding, it is probably true that Southeast Asia as a whole is ideologically more free today than it has been at any time since the coming of independence. That is to say, ideology no longer dominates the outlook of so many leaders, as it once did, for example, in Indonesia under Sukarno. To be sure, Burma's Ne Win appears as doctrinaire as ever, but in general the second generation of Southeast Asian political leaders—and most of today's rulers represent a second generation of postcolonial political leadership—are more pragmatic than their predecessors. There are several reasons for this: the demonstrated inadequacy of some of the ideologies that once were highly favored by the rulers of the region, the heightened awareness of the difficult nature of many problems of the present generation of politicians in the area, and the uncertainties of the times, such as the shifting foreign policy of the United States and the other major powers. In addition, most of today's leaders in Southeast Asia are less intellectual than their immediate predecessors, that is, more given to action than ideas. Nonetheless, even such men of action function within the framework of the things they believe in, and today's Southeast Asian leaders still believe in many things. They may, perhaps, be influenced by ideas more subtly than previous leaders, but they are still influenced.

6

Political Elites

When the twentieth century dawned, Europeans governed all but one of the Southeast Asian countries. They were the political elite of the dependent lands of the area, though, in view of their accountability to superiors in distant "colonial offices," far from autonomous actors. Because they were foreigners, moreover, they did not reflect the political ascendency of one local "class," or part, of society over others. As an "imported" governing elite, they did not represent any particular group or groups in the country, although they often favored one or another such group in the decisions they made in both their ruling and related business activities.

This having been said, it was still very much the case that some groups were more important than others politically in colonial times, even though they themselves were neither rulers nor the class from which rulers came. In British Malaya and Dutch-governed Indonesia, colonial power was partly exercised through local sultans or regents who, by sharing in the carrying-out of policy, became the most important indigenous political actors, although they fell short of being a true political elite. The French likewise used the royal houses of Cambodia and of the three historical kingdoms of Laos, their members being the only local persons of any real political importance before World War II.

Indirect colonial rule—in Indonesia, Malaya, Cambodia, and Laos—preserved elements of the traditional political elite in all of these countries, although they were no longer the true ruling groups that they had once been. In the Philippines, Burma, Singapore, and Vietnam, however, the imperial power governed more directly, with the result that the old political elites were almost destroyed. This was particularly the case in the Philippines, where there was no "national" political elite to begin with, and where Spanish rule lasted three and a half centuries before the Americans took over at the end of the nineteenth century. In Burma, the British eliminated the monarchy altogether, packing off the last Burmese King to India in chains; while Singapore, largely lacking permanent human habitation at the time of British settlement, had no existing political elite to be destroyed. The French very much governed Vietnam themselves, but they did use former "imperial" and "mandarin" elements in new administrative roles.

Only in Thailand, at the present century's start, was there a true indigenous political elite—the royal family—which ruled through an elaborate bureaucracy, and from which new political actors regularly emerged. In the first three-quarters of the twentieth century, significant changes were to take place in the Thai political elite structure. But even greater changes were to occur in the dependent lands that were Thailand's immediate and regional neighbors. The emphasis of most writing about Southeast Asia since 1900 has been upon the quest for, and the successful attainment of, national independence. But this momentous transformation of most of Southeast Asia—from dependence to independence—was paralleled by equally important changes in the composition of the political elites of the countries in question. Power was transferred from the departing colonial powers to quite different groups from those who had resisted the forceful establishment of European rule in previous centuries. And the elite structure of these countries has continued to change in the quarter-century since the colonial presence was largely ended.

Old Elites

Three elites existed in Southeast Asia before the coming of the Europeans between the sixteenth and nineteenth centuries. These were the kings and their courts, religious leaders and their retinue (who often exercised considerable political influence over sometimes very superstitious monarchs), and "village headmen" and their "councils," or advisers. The local impact of the last was greater than that of the court because of its physical distance from most of the people. None of these elites, however, ruled or otherwise politically influenced territories as extensive as today's Southeast Asian nation-states. Moreover, Burmans, Mons, Shans, and others were continuously fighting one another in pre-British Burma, as well as their more distant neighbors, and each of these ethnic groups had its own "political elite," sometimes even several as a consequence of chronic factionalism within such ethno-cultural "communities." Similarly, there was not a single Indonesia or Malaya before European rule but, rather, many "Malayas" and "Indonesias" in the form of rival kingdoms, sultanates, principalities, and such, each with its own political elite. The number of such "royal" political actors was fairly large in precolonial Southeast Asia.

The religious and secular spheres of society were generally not separated in historical Southeast Asia, with the result that it was difficult to determine when a King acted as political leader and when he was fulfilling his responsibilities as patron of his realm's religion. Cambodia's monarch was regarded as a veritable "god-king," which made such role distinction even more difficult—and, perhaps, pointless. There were, on the other hand, religious leaders, as such—clergy, as they would be called today—but, while they were not political figures in any direct sense, their non-spiritual advice was often sought by monarchs and sultans. A decision to wage war might well reflect the advice given the King by a particularly trusted (or feared) priest (much as in Europe before the dawning of the modern secular age, although history records no Southeast Asian Richelieus). Priests influenced politics in other ways, too—not least of all through their direction of the education of the young in various of the Southeast Asian kingdoms. In general, people were encouraged by their religious leaders to be loyal—and submissive—to both state and faith.

In a very real sense, court and clergy were mutually supporting rather than rival elites, but were still different elites. They may have tried to influence one another, but each also generally respected the primary role of the other. Of course, both king and priest were more than willing at times to seek to dominate weak secular or clerical figures. The "local elite," on the other hand, the village headman and his "court," belonged to an altogether different world politically. To begin with, it was a far less sophisticated and complex world, being concerned "governmentally" more with adjudication of differences than anything else. Although such headmen and their "councils" were not "elected" in the modern sense, there was popular participation in the selection of new village leaders, primarily when death or sickness necessitated such action; headmen appear to have "ruled" as much by consensus as by any other means. Because of the incomparably greater power of the central courts, local officials ordinarily did their bidding or cooperated with touring officials seeking perhaps taxes or labor. But the two political processes, the local and the monarchical, were only very loosely integrated, if at all. It was the local leadership that most directly touched the lives of most of the people most of the time, and which often sought to help the people fend off the usually arbitrary demands of the "central government."

To varying degrees and in different ways in the many kingdoms and other communities that fell to European colonial conquest, these elites were altered by the loss of their independence to foreigners. Some of them were destroyed altogether even as participants, let alone leaders, of the artificial political processes that emerged in their lands in the age of triumphant imperialism.

Colonial "Rulers"

The "political elite" of British Burma, French Indochina, the Dutch East Indies, and the Spanish Philippines (which were named after a onetime heir to the throne in Spain, Philip II) was the colonial governing class. But it should be noted that they came from the political, social, and economic elites of their own lands. They were often "political apprentices" dispatched to distant territories for experience and maturation. Except for the Philippines, there was comparatively little intermarriage between the ruling foreigners and members of the old indigenous elites or, later, new emerging elites. In the Philippines, however, there were many such unions, not all of them through the institution of marriage, with the result that the Filipino ruling class that assumed control of the country in 1946, after half a century of post-Spanish American rule, was very much of mixed blood and culture.

The Europeans, however, could not govern by themselves in such new, exotic, and little-understood settings as their Southeast Asian colonial territories. Accordingly, in some of the colonies, principally Dutch-ruled Indonesia and British Malaya, they sought to rule indirectly, through local traditional governing elements—the sultans, and their advisers, of the precolonial political process. One consequence of this policy was the perpetuation of this group as a politically relevant, if no longer dominant, one in these countries. Thus, the royal class survived as a potential alternative indigenous elite and supplied some of the ranking political leaders of the lands in question with the coming of independence. Among these were Malaysia's "founding father," first Premier and Prince (or "Tengku") Abdul Rahman, and Sultan Hamengku Buwono, longtime Indonesian nationalist and his country's second Vice-President under President Suharto.

Not all the Southeast Asian colonies were, however, ruled indirectly, and even in those that were the sultans and regents needed help in the colonial administration of the territory they helped to govern. Schools were established throughout the area, though not in large numbers and often of uneven quality, and, especially in the late nineteenth and early twentieth centuries, public administrators, lawyers, and teachers were trained. These were the local persons who would help the foreigners rule their lands. They were a new political class, if not an elite, and out of their ranks a new elite would rise.

NATIONALIST "INDEPENDENCE-WINNERS"

There were two potential indigenous political elites in Southeast Asia on the eve of World War II: One comprised the usually young nationalist agitators against continued colonial rule of their country, and the other was the local civil servant class, which, adopting many of the ways of the foreign rulers, felt that it was the rightful heir to European political leadership. In a few lands, the first group, the nationalist politicians, was further divided into older and younger generations; the latter was usually much more radical and less in the image of the colonial ruling class than the former. The members of these different groups had often attended the same schools and had otherwise similar backgrounds, but some had become administrators, while others became political agitators. One Burmese nationalist put it this way: "The best graduates of the university joined the civil service, the rest of us became nationalist politicians by default." But the late President Sukarno of Indonesia was a good student, who chose the alternative of agitation against Dutch colonial rule.

It was the agitators, and, often, the more radical of these, who were to become the political elite that governed the new nations of Southeast Asia following World War II. The war itself helped them immeasurably in this respect. The old administrative structure was destroyed in most of the Japanese-occupied countries, and Japan chose, probably wisely, not to seek to rule through those who had most faithfully served the ousted European colonial rulers. Moreover, many such indigenous administrators, as well as some older politicians, had fled the country, along with the leading European political figures (who left behind quite a few of their own nationals in Indonesia, Malaya-Singapore, and the Philippines). In Burma in particular, the war and the Japanese occupation served to discredit some of the most prominent older politicians—most conspicuously Ba Maw, wartime leader under the Japanese. Younger and more radical elements, meanwhile, gained experience, confidence, and visibility. When the war was over, they became the country's new leaders after independence instead of the men who might have filled these roles had there been a peaceful progression toward national liberation, as in neighboring India. A political generation was skipped, so to speak, with various consequences—both good and bad—for independent Burma.

In the Philippines and Malaya (later Malaysia), there was continuity in political leadership from dependence to independence. The first leaders of an independent Philippine republic came from the same political elite that had drawn up the constitution in 1935 for promised independence. Malaya's postcolonial rulers also were the same men who had played the most important political roles on the eve of independence; the transition, however, came ten years later for Malaya than it did for the Philippines, and many of these leaders, including Premier Tun Abdul Tazak, remain in power today. In Indonesia, the country's rulers after independence were those nationalists who had been most distant from the Dutch, often in jail for their anti-Dutch politics. But in Vietnam, those who led the fight against French colonialism, the Communists, so far control only the northern half of the country, while the leaders of the south since 1954 have been a coalition of anti-Communist (as well as anti-French) nationalists and former administrative, military, and other indigenous *de facto* allies of the French.

The Agitators. Indonesia's Sukarno, Burma's U Nu, and Singapore's Lee Kuan Yew were leaders who came to power after agitating against the continuance of colonial rule in their lands and suffering, or risking, political detention. All three men trained for and practiced modern professions of engineering, teaching, and law, respectively. The groups they led to—and after—independence comprised mainly men like themselves, though of lesser ability: former political conspirators, for the most part, like their leaders. Neither such leaders nor most of their political subordinates had served any practical apprenticeship as members of executive, legislative, or judicial governing institutions. They came to power because they opposed Dutch or British colonialism, and either they forced the imperial ruler to turn power over to them, as in Indonesia, or the colonial government aquiesced in political change that it recognized could not be avoided, as in Burma.

Of these three leaders, two failed in mobilizing the resources of their countries after independence to improve living standards and generally solve, or at least manage, those problems of government that confront people the world over. Lee Kuan Yew and his fellow Singapore politicians built a veritably model social-welfare state in the years after 1965, but Singapore is a small island-country. Sukarno and U Nu faced far larger problems of internal rebellion, foreign intervention, and greater population size and complexity. Both men, however, perhaps because of their unique personalities, held their nations politically together against great odds and left office with their countries more united because of

their leadership. But neither was even remotely a modern problem-solving political leader, nor did he surround himself with advisers who compensated for his weaknesses. They were nationalist
"symbol-manipulators"—"unifiers" but not policy-makers.

The Administrators. Power is ordinarily shared by politicians
with the bureaucracy. In both Burma and Indonesia, however,
there were very few trained indigenous administrators, to begin
with, and many such civil servants were tainted in the eyes of the
former "agitators" for having worked too closely with the departed colonial ruling power. Two consequences followed from
this circumstance: Senior civil servants were not sufficiently utilized by the new indigenous political elite in its attempted governance of the now liberated lands in question; and, largely because of this, the administrators were in no real position to
threaten the politicians as an alternative elite. When the politicians were later ousted from office in both lands, some of the administrators rallied to the side of the succeeding military elite.

In most other countries—particularly Thailand, Malaysia, Singapore, and the Philippines—the bureaucrats were allies of the ruling elite. In Thailand, for most of the time from 1937 to the ouster
of the military regime of Field Marshal Thanom Kittikachorn in
1973, soldiers, not civilians, ruled the country, but they did so
through civilian bureaucrats who exacted a price in power and
status for the role they played. The predominantly ethnic Malay
civil service in Malaysia is, in a similar sense, the ally of the ethnic Malay-dominated policy-making arm of the government.
Singapore's civil servants, likewise, are loyal to Lee Kuan Yew's
ruling People's Action Party, being thoroughly penetrated, indoc-
trinated, and otherwise dominated by the formidable government
party. Patronage in the Philippines long ago made the country's
civil service the ally, not the rival, of the politicians.

The "administrators" in Southeast Asia have rarely held power
in their own right. But there have been times in the recent histories of some countries when they have rallied to the support of
new elites in reaction to their treatment at the hands of the "independence-winners," the first generation of national political leaders. In this way, they have helped to shape the political elites of
Southeast Asia without necessarily being a part of such elites
themselves.

The Military. Two types of soldiers were to be found in the newly independent lands of Southeast Asia in the first years of independence: those who had undergone professional training and had functioned as soldiers under colonial command before independence, and the nonprofessional freedom-fighters who carried the brunt of the military struggle against the imperial power in the war for national liberation, as in Indonesia. The best-known of the nonprofessional soldiers—that is, those who came into their own militarily and politically without professional training—were Burma's General Ne Win, who seized power and became his country's leader in 1962, and North Vietnam's General Vo Nguyen Giap, "hero" of Dien Bien Phu in 1954 and strategist for the Hanoi regime's military defense against the Americans in the years 1963–73.

The professional soldiers of the Philippines, Malaysia, and Singapore were well trained in the Anglo-American tradition of military subordination to civil authority and played no part in the politics of their countries in the first years of independence. They still do not do so even today in Malaysia and Singapore. French-trained—and once French-commanded—Nguyen Van Thieu of South Vietnam, on the other hand, is the professional soldier very much turned politician, while Dutch-trained General Suharto also managed to become, though not as a result of a conscious strategy, Indonesia's second President. Thai soldiers of the years 1938–73 excepted, most of the military men who have come to political power in Southeast Asia have done so as a direct consequence of challenges to, or involving, the armed forces.

For most of the first years of independence—that is, through the 1950's—the military considered itself an ally and supporter of civilian governors in Southeast Asia. In some countries like Malaysia and the Philippines, the soldiers did not think in political terms at all; in others, such as Burma and Indonesia, the military thought of the civilians as brothers-in-arms in the recent anticolonial struggle. While soldiers were frequently consulted on nonmilitary matters, especially in the latter two states, they were at best an "auxilliary" of the political elite rather than part of that elite. Their political neutrality, however—if such it may be called—ended when they began to question the superiority, loyalty, and wisdom of their civilian leaders.

Religious Leaders. Priests were very much part of the nationalist struggle for liberation from colonial rule in several of the Southeast Asian countries. Monks engaged in various types of demonstrations against British rule in Burma in the 1920's and 1930's, as they were to do subsequently in South Vietnam in the early 1960's, in protest against the alleged partiality to his own religion of Catholic President Ngo Dinh Diem. Muslim extremists desiring an Islamic theocratic state fought a deadly civil war against the secular-oriented Sukarno government in Indonesia in the first fifteen years of independence. And other Muslims, following more peaceful tactics, tried to influence policy-making in the same island-country through two once-formidable parties, the modernist *Masjumi* and the more conservative *Nahdatul Ulama* (or Muslim Teachers).

In general, religious leaders were more important in the first years of independence than later. For the most part, in such countries as Indonesia, Burma, South Vietnam, and Malaysia, they sought to influence the government primarily on religious questions. Their relative decline in the late 1960's and early 1970's is a reflection of the growing secularization of politics in the area.

NEW ELITES

The years since 1962 have seen a steady erosion of the hold of civilian elites on the politics of most of the countries of Southeast Asia. To be sure, military rule was ended by a student uprising in Thailand in October, 1973, but how long the soldiers will remain absent from the highest levels of power in that country remains an open question. Elsewhere, in Burma, South Vietnam, Indonesia, and Cambodia, soldiers have replaced civilians as the country's rulers, while in Laos they have tried again and again to do so. In the Philippines, the military is more politically important today than it has ever been before in the country's history, but it has not yet seized power (although it may still do so).

Why have soldiers replaced civilians as leaders of so many Southeast Asian countries in the last fifteen or so years?

The answer is to be found largely in two areas: the competency, or lack thereof, of civilian elites, and the power (primarily, but not exclusively, military) of the soldiers. Civilian elites in Indonesia, Burma, Cambodia, and South Vietnam in power for periods of nine to sixteen years failed to solve various major problems. In Indonesia and Cambodia, they seemed almost to ignore altogether some of the most important problems, such as inflation and unemployment. In South Vietnam and Burma, civil wars, partly because they required the creation of sizable military establishments, played a major role in setting the stage for an end to civilian government. And in all these (and other) countries of the area, the military has grown in sophistication and ambition through the years, duplicating the increasing politicization of the Thai Army in the 1930's.

But soldiers have been only one element, albeit the most important, in the new political elites of postcolonial Southeast Asia.

Soldier-Politicians. Four Southeast Asian countries—Indonesia, Burma, South Vietnam, and Cambodia—were ruled by soldiers at the start of 1974. In Thailand, an uneasy political truce prevailed in the wake of the October, 1973, student overthrow of the military regime of Field Marshal Thanom Kittikachorn, but the army remained by far the biggest and best-organized political organization in the land. In the Philippines, self-retained President Ferdinand Marcos ruled through the military under martial law, although he himself was a civilian. As recently as 1973, some soldiers tried to topple a civilian government in Laos to block implementation of the February cease-fire with the Communist Pathet Lao insurgents and came closer to succeeding than was generally admitted at the time. Only in Malaysia and Singapore, in all of Southeast Asia, were soldiers not members of the political elites of their lands by 1974.

Some of the soldiers came from privileged backgrounds, but most of them were of more modest, if not actually humble, origin. Armies throughout Southeast Asia have been vehicles for upward mobility, economically and socially as well as politically. Burma's soldiers excepted, those of the rest of the Southeast Asian ruling elites tend to be more conservative than the civilians they have replaced, as well as less liberal with regard to popular participation in government and various political freedoms. Some have been civilian-educated, but most are products largely of service schools. Morally, they appear to be at least as corrupt as their civilian predecesors and no less skillful in legitimatizing the fruits of their corruption (including large houses, foreign cars, and pleasure-trips to Hong Kong and Tokyo). Most important, they are self-perpetuating; that is, in Indonesia, Burma, South Vietnam, and Thailand in particular, they have been extremely skillful in attracting some of the best young men in their lands to their ranks, thus guaranteeing their continuation as a powerful political force for many years to come.

In most cases, Southeast Asia's soldier-politicians did not really seize power but partly "backed into" their present positions of political predominance. Even where they did seem to grab power, they did so incrementally, that is, in steps or stages. The first soldiers to rule in their own right in the independent countries of Southeast Asia were those of Thailand, who imitated, to some extent, in the 1930's the rise to power of the Japanese military, although the reasons behind the emergence of the army as a political force in the two countries differ in several important ways. The Thai military probably came to power in the 1930's for its chief leaders' own aggrandizement, although the most important of its early leaders, Marshal Phibun Songkhram, was also a modernizer in his own right (but no Ataturk by any stretch of the imagination!). Phibun and his soldier-colleagues gained control of Thailand's government in two stages; as allies of certain civilian groups in 1932, when they placed restrictions on a previously unlimited monarchy, and in their own right in 1938, when they took over the leadership of the state themselves.

All the other military elites of Southeast Asia were drawn into positions of political predominance by events—not that they might not ultimately have seized power otherwise. The split among anti-Communist civilian leaders in Burma in 1958 was followed by a dramatic revival of Communist and other insurgencies; this possibly necessitated the caretaker regime of General Ne Win that governed the country for eighteen months between October, 1958, and April, 1960. In 1962, Ne Win declared that he had to seize power again because Burma as a country was in danger of breaking up under Premier U Nu's weak leadership, although many doubted this explanation. South Vietnam's and Cambodia's military leaders came to power as a direct result of the wars that raged in their lands. Khmer leader Lon Nol, however, had actively participated in nonmilitary political decision-making before his March, 1970, overthrow of Prince Norodom Sihanouk. As for Indonesia's soldiers, they had also shared power under Sukarno and ultimately assumed leadership only after Communist plotters had literally decapitated half a dozen generals. In the Philippines in 1972, and subsequently, it was power-seeking (and self-retained) President Marcos who used the army for his personal political purposes; by contrast, Malaysia's civilian leaders were refused when they asked their country's top soldiers to play a larger political role after the May, 1969, postelection riots.

In several of the Southeast Asian countries, the rise to political power of the army was aided by foreign military assistance, training, and perhaps even encouragement. South Vietnam's army was built up by the Americans in the late 1950's and early 1960's, and it moved against President Ngo Dinh Diem in 1963 when it became obvious that Diem had lost American political support. Despite strong overt support by the United States in the same years, General Phoumi Nosavan and other Laotian soldier-politicians failed to retain power for an appreciable period of time. Indonesia's military, though not aided in such fashion by the Americans, had received U.S. training in years gone by and clearly knew that Washington would side with them once they came to power. Such foreign assistance, however, may not be enough to keep a military regime in power indefinitely, as the fall from office of pro-U.S. Thai Army strongmen Thanom Kittikachorn and Prapas Charusathien demonstrated in 1973.

Technocrats. Almost everywhere in Southeast Asia today, whether civilians or soldiers have the upper hand politically, the leaders are aided by the new postcolonial "technocrat" class. In Indonesia, Malaysia, Thailand, and the Philippines—with quite differing governing arrangements in 1974—the ruling regimes were heavily dependent on the technocrats to help them solve, or at least manage, the problems that would permit the regimes' survival and possibly even the survival of their countries. Included in this new politically important class were economists, agronomists, bankers, engineers, health specialists, and other similar types of experts, trained in the world's best universities.

Before independence, such higher education as was available

in the Southeast Asian colonies was largely in the arts. Colleges and universities existed mainly to staff the lower levels of the civil bureaucracy as well as the teaching staffs of the country's schools. Law was the most popular profession among those who were able to obtain higher professional training; but lawyers, from whose ranks many early-generation politicians were recruited, are not trained to cope with problems of agricultural development or fiscal management, for example. Economists, engineers and other such specialists were extremely rare in Southeast Asia before the war, except in the Philippines, where some extremely good engineers were trained during the American colonial period. After colonialism, such skills were in great demand, for the new nations wanted to avoid continued dependence on foreign experts. At first, these experts, few in number, were used only as agents of the power-wielders, but it soon became obvious that their input was also needed at the policy level of decision-making. Without such an input, President Suharto might not have made the strong start he did in the late 1960's in alleviating Indonesia's various economic ills (and also consolidating his own political power). Similarly, technocrats—and their policy-making input—were vital to the survival, let alone the success, of President Marcos's "New Society" in the Philippines after 1972 (even more so perhaps than the army!).

Generally speaking, the technocrats are not really rivals for office of either the civilian-politicians or the soldier-politicians; but they *are* rivals for power. The technocrats will serve the regime most likely to provide them with an opportunity to improve their societies. In this sense, they are very important members of the political elite structure of second-generation independent Southeast Asia.

"*Businessmen.*" Like the technocrats. Southeast Asia's "businessmen" have become a political force only since independence. Before independence, there were few, if any, really local "businessmen" in any of the Southeast Asian countries (except in the Philippines, and not including, of course, the powerful Chinese commercial minorities that could be found throughout the area). The emergence of local businessmen—merchants, investors, bankers, and the like—as a political force has been much slower, moreover, than that of the technocrats (not to mention the soldiers). The reason has been the antibusiness, that is, anticapitalist, bias of the first generation of political leaders in many of the Southeast Asian lands. But, even in Indonesia under strongly left-leaning former President Sukarno, businessmen were an important force; Sukarno's socialist government "contracted out" much of its work to them. Most such businessmen in Sukarno's day were "Sino-Indonesians," Indonesians of mixed Chinese and Indonesian parentage or Chinese migrants and their descendents who had made Indonesia their home; but there were also some "pure" Indonesian "merchants" even in the 1950's and 1960's, and there are more today.

It was in such nonsocialist countries as the Philippines, Thailand, and Malaysia that businessmen were most important in the first quarter-century after World War II, and where, not surprisingly, their political role has been the greatest. In these three lands in particular—but also in Singapore, South Vietnam, and Laos in differing ways—businessmen rendered various services much needed by the political leadership. For the most part, their economic services or contributions were an integral part of the country's development aspirations; in some cases—most conspicuously in the Philippines and Thailand—the "pay-off" from business was part of the economic rewards of those who held political power, whether by election or otherwise.

Like the technocrats, but more blatantly, the business community exacted a price for its services. This price was both in the form of profits and in terms of influence on economic policy in ways favorable to their own interests. Southeast Asian businessmen, as part of the political elite, sought influence, not office, and so could easily serve succeeding types of masters.

Religious Leaders. Religious leaders have largely been important politically since independence as opposition elements: Catholic priests working against Marcos's self-serving "New Society" in the Philippines, Buddhist monks opposed to authoritarian rule in Burma and South Vietnam, and Muslim leaders critical of both Presidents Sukarno and Suharto for their essentially secular outlook and policies in Indonesia. Some Buddhist leaders have bid for power in Vietnam but failed, mainly because of the lack of politically effective organization, their limited credibility as an alternative ruling group, and chronic divisions among the country's amorphous Buddhist "community." Supporters of a Muslim theocratic Indonesia mounted a costly rebellion for the first decade of their country's independence but were defeated and ceased to be of importance politically. In Malaysia, on the other hand, Islam and its spokesmen, whether or not the latter were sanctioned Muslim religious leaders, have become more politically important through the years. And, in the Philippines, Islamic religious leaders, as well as Muslim politicians, were a key instigating force behind the Islamic uprising in the southern part of the country in the early 1970's.

Far too little is known of the political role of Buddhist monks in the Hinayana Buddhist lands of Thailand, Laos, and Cambodia in recent years. Such monks unsuccessfully opposed General Ne Win in Burma. But their political participation in Thailand and the two lesser Indochinese lands has been less overt and probably minimized by observers as a result. At times, however, there have been signs of monk backing for particular persons or institutions in the troubled politics of these three lands: in support of student demonstrators and a prostudent King in Thailand in 1973, in favor of Prince Souvanna Phouma when he was confronted by recurring rightist opposition through the years, and on behalf of Prince Norodom Sihanouk after his overthrow in Cambodia in 1970.

The popularization of politics in Southeast Asia, if it develops, could give new political importance to religious leaders as a secondary, but nonetheless still very important, part of the postcolonial political elites. Thus far, such leaders have declined in importance as members of these elites, but their resurgency is a real possibility, even in would-be modernizing "new societies."

Transition—And Competition

The present years represent a transition period between elites in Southeast Asia. The first generation of postcolonial political leaders—Indonesia's Sukarno, Burma's U Nu, Malaysia's Tengku Abdul Rahman, and even the great Vietnamese Communist Ho

Chi Minh—were very much products of the departed era of imperialism. They owed their positions of leadership to their successful opposition to colonial rule rather than to their qualifications or policies for the redevelopment of their respective national societies. Some of them, however, did a better job than might have been expected in guiding their nations to the selection of strategies and policies of managed change in the first years of independence.

The soldier-successors to the civilian political "founding fathers" in lands like Indonesia, Burma, South Vietnam, and Cambodia reflect, among other factors, the absence of other alternatives to the first-generation political elite of former anticolonial agitators. The political elites of the first half of the 1970's in most of the Southeast Asian states are, in a very real sense, temporary elites. A more "permanent" ruling class awaits the further development of the societies in question and the emergence of new, mature political interests within such societies.

Most of the governments of Southeast Asia, as the area approached the mid-1970's, came to power by force, not through elections. They will probably depart by force, too, as happened to Thailand's increasingly disliked military regime in 1973. The full transition from political elites derived from, and socialized by, the colonial era to truly national political elites, to leaders out of and for really national societies, is far from completed. Fierce competition will probably mark the late stages of this transition, and there could be considerable bloodshed. But, then, the making of nations has never been easy or peaceful. It is surprising, indeed, that the transition thus far in Southeast Asia has been as nonviolent as it has been (the civil wars in Vietnam, Laos, Cambodia, and Burma being more among rival first-generation elites than between old and new elites). Possibly—just possibly—the transition will be completed in Southeast Asia in an age when oldfashioned interelite wars like the American Civil War and the Bolshevik Revolution can be avoided. If so, it will be an almost unprecedented situation, historically.

7

Political Parties

In Southeast Asia, the first political parties, whether in the Philippines, Indonesia, Burma, or the other lands of the area, were established as instruments of opposition to colonial rule. Some of these parties, or their successors, became democratic ruling, or opposition, parties, while others developed along authoritarian lines. But in the beginning they were almost all "nationalist parties." Indonesia's Nationalist Party, for example, was created in the 1920's to replace Dutch rule of the East Indies with a government of Indonesians. The Indonesian Communist Party, the first Communist Party in the European colonies of the area, was founded in 1920 with the proclaimed aim of overthrowing Dutch colonialism. Earlier political, or partly political, movements in the Netherlands's rich island-colony like the largely cultural *Budi Utomo* or the originally economically oriented and anti-Chinese *Sarekat Islam,* were also nationalist in origin, outlook, and objectives, even if they were not really political parties, as such, at their founding.

It was essentially the same almost everywhere else in formerly foreign-ruled Southeast Asia. Political parties, usually modeled after those of the ruling colonial power, were created as a principal means for ousting that power from its colony. With the coming of independence, earlier than had been expected in most cases, these same parties—in Indonesia, Burma, Malaya, and Singapore—assumed the responsibility of governing the new country. Virtually overnight, such parties had to shift from being instruments of sometimes violent opposition to colonial government to directing a newly emancipated government concerned not only with the maintenance of law and order but also with the formation and carrying out of policies of economic and other development, national integration and stabilization, and foreign relations.

Some of the "parties of independence," as they may be called, survived into the 1970's and may continue to rule their countries for more years to come, as in Malaysia and neighboring Singapore. Others governed for several years, with varying degrees of success (or failure), before being succeeded by new political institutions. In Burma, for example, the once all-powerful Anti-Fascist People's Freedom League first split and then was eclipsed altogether as a factor of importance in the country's political life.

This transition from dependence to independence was not an easy one. The question was not initially raised of whether existing political organizations—parties or other institutions—could survive with altogether different functions in the new era of emancipation. The leaders of the parties that won independence assumed the right to lead their lands after the colonial ruler departed. In almost all instances they did so, at least at the beginning. Later, however, most of them fell by the political wayside. The reasons why some political parties survived and others did not throws considerable light on the general problem of political development in the Southeast Asian lands as well as on the strengths, limitations, and prospects for different kinds of political parties in the area.

NATIONALIST PARTIES

Political parties in Burma came into being, for all practical purposes, after World War I, in response to a British decision to make political concessions to the rest of India—of which Burma was then a part—that would not apply to the Burmese. The immediate cause of the formation of Burma's first political parties, then, was to influence a government controlled by foreigners rather than to gain control of that government. The consequence of this political arousal was Burma's first national elections in 1922, in which these new parties participated.

Burma, however, was not typical of the colonies in general in Southeast Asia or of the early role of political parties in them. To be sure, parties played a major part in the politics of the pursuit of independence after the American takeover of the Philippines from Spain at the end of the nineteenth century, but such organizations had previously been secret and conspiratorial under Spanish colonial rule. In Indonesia and Indochina, similarly, parties were either proscribed or very restricted in what the Dutch and French colonial overlords permitted them to do. In both of these tightly controlled colonial systems, political parties almost exclusively opposed the foreign leadership that governed them. They were parties not just of opposition but of overthrow and destruction. They were conspiratorial organizations—by necessity—because of the almost complete opposition of the ruling foreigners to indigenous assumption of political control over these lands, even within a continued constitutional relationship with the metropolitan power.

Several consequences followed from such circumstances. One was the cooperation of otherwise very different political elements within the framework of a single political party. The unity of these disparate groups had its roots in their common opposition to continued colonial rule; there was little agreement, or even serious thought, about what would follow such rule. The anticolonial nationalist parties, in fact, were not really parties at all but, rather, temporary coalitions that called themselves parties or were inaccurately called parties by others. Secondly, such "parties" were, by virtue of experience and purpose, almost wholly opposition in nature; their single aim was to overthrow the ruling colonial power and replace it with a "national" government composed of indigenous personnel. They were not prepared to compromise with this single overriding aim of independence, but they were increasingly willing to employ "direct action," if not outright violence, in pursuit of their purpose. Finally, these anticolonial nationalist parties were highly elitist organizations formed by small groups of intellectuals and reaching out, sometimes almost as an afterthought, for mass support, but neither having nor wanting popular direction or control.

RESISTANCE "PARTIES"

In two of the countries of Southeast Asia in particular, Burma and Vietnam, World War II had an extraordinary impact on anticolonial politics and political organizations. Several different parties had competed with one another in the late 1930's in British-governed Burma following the colony's separation from India in 1937, but none was ever able to gain a majority of the seats in the colonial legislature, partly because of the rivalries among their highly ambitious leaders. During World War II, two things happened to alter the pattern of Burmese political development dramatically: The older generation of political leaders was overshadowed and outmaneuvered by new, younger, and even more uncompromising politicians; and mounting opposition to Japanese occupation, far more harsh and oppressive than British rule had ever been, stimulated unparalleled cooperation among hitherto feuding Burmese political and ethnic elements. The result was the formation in 1944 of the Anti-Fascist League, later renamed the Anti-Fascist People's Freedom League, to work for the overthrow of the hated Japanese.

The AFPFL began as the political arm of the "Burma National Army," the renamed "Burma Defense Army," which had entered the country with troops of Japan in 1941 and then turned against the occupying Japanese in 1944. The AFPFL was not created as a political party in the traditional sense of the term and was not yet a true party even when the war ended. But it was very much a "political" organization, and it did become a political party after the war. Having helped to end Japanese rule of the country, it then sought, less violently, the early termination of restored British governance of the land, and it went on to become the governing party when independence came in 1948.

The AFPFL, when World War II ended, included two different Communist parties within its fold as well as democratic socialists, some "rightists," and every ethnic minority of any numerical size in the country. It was truly a "united front," summoned to unprecedented agreement against a much-hated foreign oppressor in a land of great traditional factionalism and even warring among opposed political and ethnic groups. This "great coalition" began to fall apart almost at the war's end.

The Vietnam League for Independence, or Viet Minh, was created in 1941 for essentially the same reason as that underlying formation of Burma's AFPFL: opposition to Japanese occupation of the country. During World War II, the Viet Minh—Communist-led but not wholly Communist-composed—monopolized resistance to the Japanese and the cooperating Vichy French. When the war ended, it was the only political organization of any consequence in the country, although it, too, was not a political party in a formal sense. Indeed, the longtime nationalist-Communist Ho Chi Minh, chief founder of the Viet Minh, had disbanded the Indochinese Communist Party he had founded in 1929 in order to attract non-Commnstis into the Viet Minh "coalition" during the war. Independence for all Vietnam was proclaimed by Ho in 1945, and in elections held for a "National Assembly" in 1946 the *Lao Dong* (or Workers) Party, the re-created old Indochinese Communist Party, predominated. The Viet Minh was, and continued to be, directed by the leadership of the old Communist Party, which became the leadership of the new *Lao Dong* Party. In this sense, the Viet Minh itself, at least during 1941–45, was an authentic party, however disguised.

Burma's AFPFL was a genuine, though unnatural and temporary, wartime (and postwar) coalition organization and, later, a "party." The Viet Minh was the Indochinese Communist Party in coalition disguise (which means that the Viet Minh was itself a "political party" at least in the historic conspiratorial sense identified with Communist "parties" out of power in many other lands throughout the world). The two political organizations were similar, moreover, in the sense that their core leadership used the war to build a base, within the AFPFL and Viet Minh, respectively, on which to establish predominance in the independence struggle and, subsequently, after independence itself following the war. Aung San and the "democratic socialist" wing of the AFPFL led Burma in 1948 to independence (although Aung San was assassinated in 1947) and governed the country fairly successfully in the first years of independence after the Communists and other groups had quit the wartime coalition. Similarly, the Communists of Ho Chi Minh predominated within the Viet Minh in the form of the *Lao Dong* Party, which was the core of the movement after the war and assumed responsibility for governing North Vietnam in the wake of the Geneva Accords in 1954.

The Burmese-Vietnamese "model" did not apply to all the other nationalist movements and political parties associated with them in Southeast Asia, but there were similarities between what happened in Burma and Vietnam and developments elsewhere in the area. In Indonesia, non-Communist and Communist nationalists cooperated with one another, though secretly, during the war, only to split after the war, in part because the non-Communists had attained predominance in the national liberation struggle and the Communists feared relative political insignificance after independence. In Laos non-Communists and Communists became similarly split; while in Malaysia the Communists were unable to convert their leadership of the wartime resistance into postwar political dominance, because most of the Communists were Chinese, still very much distrusted by the majority Malays in the country.

"INDEPENDENCE PARTIES"

The "parties of independence" were the political organizations that took over control of the former colonies of Southeast Asia with the ending of foreign rule after World War II. These included the Anti-Fascist People's Freedom League in Burma, the "Alliance" in Malaysia, the People's Action Party of Singapore, and the Communist *Lao Dong* Party in North Vietnam. No single party assumed responsibility for governing Indonesia after the Dutch departure, but the longtime anticolonial Nationalists and the modernist Muslim *Masjumi* party shared power with the Muslim Teachers party, a conservative offshoot of the *Masjumi*, and first President Sukarno, who was not really a party politician but played different parties and other groups against one another. The Nacionalistas were the most important preindependence party in the Philippines, but the Liberals won the first postwar election in 1946, the year of freedom from American colonial rule. Yet, the Liberals were formed only shortly before the election to permit Manuel Roxas to try to become the country's first President, which he did do. The Liberals, in short, were really a party of opportunistic, breakaway Nacionalistas.

These were the parties that, as vehicles of political agitation, and sometimes violence, "won" independence for Burma, Viet-

nam, Malaysia, Singapore, Indonesia, and the Philippines. They
had no true counterparts in Laos and Cambodia, where parties,
as such, did not really exist before independence. And, in South
Vietnam, parties such as they were had to be created after independence, the independence-winning Communists being the chief
"enemy" of the post-French regime of Ngo Dinh Diem and, subsequently, of the ruling political soldiers.

By 1974, "independence parties" remained in power only in
North Vietnam, Malaysia, and Singapore. Burma's AFPFL split in
1958, and both factions of the onetime government party were
suppressed after General Ne Win's 1962 military takeover. Indonesia's various independence-winning parties, not only the Nationalists and the reformist Islamic *Masjumi* but also the Communists and the conservative Muslim Teachers no longer existed as
major overt political forces in the country. The *Masjumi* was
never allowed to resume its former influential role in Indonesian
politics after the participation of some of its leaders in a 1958 revolt; the Nationalists and the Muslim Teachers were required by
President Suharto to amalgamate with other parties to form two
new "blocs" in the early 1970's; and the Communists were outlawed altogether after their September, 1965, uprising. In the
Philippines, both the Nacionalistas and the Liberals were eclipsed
in the wake of former Nacionalista (and Liberal) Marcos's declaration of martial law. Both parties "survived" but had no function
in the years after 1972, Congress having been dissolved and elections abandoned.

The countries in which "independence parties" survived—North
Vietnam, Malaysia, and Singapore—were three of the most tightly
controlled political systems in all Southeast Asia, whatever their
ideological, economic, or foreign policy differences. North Vietnam was, and is, a Communist country, where the government
party, the *Lao Dong*, allows no challengers whatsoever to its authority. Singapore is not a Communist nation, but its Premier, Lee
Kuan Yew, and the ruling People's Action Party (PAP), which
Lee himself largely controls, also permit no other party or group
to establish the kind of political bridgehead that might become a
subsequent challenge to the government. Malaysia's governing
"Alliance" is actually a "superparty"—comprising three compo-

nent communal parties: the United Malays National Organization (UMNO), the Malaysian Chinese Association, and the Malaysian Indian Congress. Singapore was expelled as a constituent state of Malaysia in 1965 because of the challenge that Lee Kuan Yew represented to the conservative Malay ruling elite, which, through the "Alliance"-directing UMNO, controls the country's political affairs. This "Alliance" leadership was again seriously but unsuccessfully challenged by a largely Chinese opposition in the 1969 elections, which were followed by the bloody racial rioting of May of that year. Since then, the "Alliance"—which really means the UMNO—has pursued a new partnership with other political groups and personalities as a means of consolidating its hold on power. Its control techniques are not as violent as those of North Vietnam or as restrictive as neighboring Singapore's, but they are real nonetheless, if also vulnerable.

The "independence parties" of Indonesia, Burma, and the Philippines were ultimately eclipsed as real political forces—which is much more serious than merely losing office temporarily—because of their preoccupation with personal rivalries, their inability to develop and carry out policies appropriate to the problems confronting their lands, and their failure to anticipate and so head off the challenge of military or civilian dictators. The independence parties of North Vietnam, Malaysia, and Singapore, on the other hand, have survived because they did not become bogged down in leadership rivalries, have governed effectively, and have been quite effective in checking those who would replace them. Thailand, which escaped becoming a European colony, never had real parties in the years 1945–73—or earlier, for that matter—while the so-called parties of South Vietnam, Laos, and Cambodia were artificialities that were more instruments of support for particular personalities than real political parties.

TWO-PARTY AND MULTIPARTY SYSTEMS

The only two-party system to develop in Southeast Asia in the first quarter-century after World War II was that of the Philippines. It has often been said that the Filipinos modeled their party system, like their Presidential form of government, on that of their former colonial ruler, the United States. To a degree, this may be true, but the Philippine two-party system, even in its heyday, was less of a two-party system than many observers, including its critics, realized. Prewar and wartime President Manuel Quezon, who led the country during the "commonwealth" period of internal autonomy, actually favored a one-party system—or "partyless democracy," as he called it. The Liberals were formed from the Nacionalistas in 1946 wholly to advance the Presidential candidacy of Manuel Roxas. In subsequent years, almost every Philippine politician of note was a member, at one time or another, of both of these two important parties. Marcos, as an example, quit as Senate "majority leader" of the Liberals in 1964 to seek the Presidential nomination of the "opposition" Nacionalistas. In short, the Philippines's two parties were drawn wholly from the same narrowly based elite and represented, more than anything else, the instruments by which rival politicians—power- rather than policy-oriented—sought high political position. The Philippine two-party system collapsed, surprisingly easily, in 1972–73, when President Marcos, who had used the system to become his country's chief executive, abandoned it.

The political systems of Indonesia, Malaysia, and Burma (and possibly even Laos) were multiparty ones in the first years of resumed independence. Twenty-eight parties participated in Indonesia's first national elections in 1955, twelve of them winning seats in Parliament. Three parties made up Malaysia's independence-winning "Alliance," while other parties, both communal and noncommunal, contested the country's parliamentary elections through the years and won a good share of the seats in the national legislature and also gained control of some state governments in the Malaysian federal system. Although the AFPFL dominated Burma's politics from 1948 to 1958, other parties also existed. AFPFL control of Burma's government was as complete as it was largely because most Burmese strongly supported highly popular Premier U Nu and his independence-winning party. As for Laos, its parties were really factions associated with leading politicians, but there was competition, at least within the small Laotian anti-Communist political elite, for control of the government during many of the years after 1954. Even the Communists' above-ground *Neo Lao Hak Xat* (Patriotic Laotian Front) participated in the 1957 elections.

Indonesian democracy, if such it may be called, failed in part because there were too many parties spending too much time and effort jockeying for power—a situation on which autocratically inclined President Sukarno skillfully capitalized. The fall of Burma's party system was the direct result of a military coup, but it was a weak and ineffective system and might have otherwise collapsed of its own weight. Longtime Premier U Nu and his political supporters through the years were much more skillful in winning elections than in subsequently ruling their very difficult-to-govern, insurgency-ridden land. Malaysia, on the other hand, has retained an essentially competitive party system, though with some very important restrictions, primarily because it has so far worked extremely well. On the whole, however, multiple party systems did not function all that successfully in Southeast Asia: they either encouraged political disagreement, as in Indonesia in the 1950's, or were too easily subject to dominant party-manipulation, as in both AFPFL-run Burma and "Alliance"-governed Malaysia.

TREND TOWARD CONSOLIDATION

All the political systems of independent Southeast Asia are less competitive today than they were twenty years ago, with the exception of Thailand, where student demonstrators forced a seemingly entrenched military regime from office in late 1973. There are three basic reasons for this reduction in multiparty interaction throughout the region: There is no longer the widespread belief in the superiority or desirability of party or political competition that there formerly was; jockeying for political influence has proved costly to the countries of the area; and ruling elites have developed an increasing reluctance to turn over control of governments to their opposition. Some, but not all, of the former "party democracies," such as Burma, have become tightly controlled dictatorships or one-party systems.

Not all the political systems of the area, however, are today one-party states, although this would clearly seem to be the trend.

There has been a consolidation of political organizations throughout the region, partly of necessity. Indonesia and Malaysia are examples of this process of political consolidation. Under Sukarno in the mid-1950's, Indonesia had four major political parties: the Nationalists, the liberal Muslim *Masjumi*, the conservative Muslim Teachers, and the Communists. In addition, there were half a dozen other parties of more than local significance, some of whose leaders, like present Indonesian Foreign Minister Adam Malik, were important political personalities. The *Masjumi* was proscribed after the 1958 regional uprising against Sukarno, and the Communists were banned in 1967. In the early 1970's, President Suharto forced the Nationalists and certain smaller parties to form the so-called Democratic Development group—and the Muslim Teachers and other parties to come together as the "Unity Development" group. In addition, an altogether new political institution, the *Sekber Golkar* ("Functional Groups"), was created to fight—and win—the 1971 elections, the first national elections since 1955, for the government. Indonesia, accordingly, had three main "parties" in existence by the middle 1970's: the *Sekber Golkar* and the "Democratic" and "Unity" groups. The *Golkar* however, was much more important than the other two groups, the constituent organizations of which had seemingly lost much of their identity —and thus their following—as a consequence of the consolidation. Indonesia's *Sekber Golkar* and the development and unity "groups" do not direct Indonesia's government. The *Golkar* is clearly an instrument, as well as the creation, of the largely military elite that rules the country today. The two multiparty groups were forced into consolidation by these same rulers, who believe that independent parties generate unnecessary and undesirable divisions.

In Malaysia, on the other hand, the multigroup and increasingly consolidationist "Alliance" party does control the government, or at least the Malay political elite that comprises the leadership of UMNO, senior partner in the "Alliance," controls the government through the "Alliance" mechanism. Since the racial riots of 1969, which were preceded by a strong Chinese as well as noncommunal challenge at the polls, the UMNO-MCA–Indian Congress coalition has sought to draw other parties and personalities to its ranks. The means have been different from those employed in Indonesia's political consolidation, but the end has been the same in the two countries: elimination of "divisive" and "threatening" "factionalism" and an alleged strengthening of national unity. The result in both cases has also been the same: a decline in political competition and a reduction in the meaningfulness of party participation in national political life.

One-Party States

The epitome of political consolidation is the one-party state—of which North Vietnam, Burma, and Singapore are examples, though quite different kinds, in present-day Southeast Asia. The Communist North Vietnamese did permit other parties to exist after establishment of their government north of the 17th parallel in 1954, but these were largely "window dressing" and were in no way important. For more than a decade after his overthrow of U Nu and Burmese democracy in 1962, General Ne Win ran his often inefficient "Burmese Way to Socialism" as a virtual military command. The Burma Socialist Program Party (BSPP) was created early in the Ne Win regime, but it was not until 1974 that a new constitution was adopted that gave the party a legal role in a Burmese political system that had banned all other parties. The 1974 East European–style Burmese constitutional order provided for only one political party: the soldier-created BSPP. Singapore's People's Action Party (PAP) preceded the acquisition of independence following the territory's ouster from federal Malaysia. Other parties have taken part in Singapore's elections through the years, but the PAP has always managed to come up with a 100 per cent majority in the national legislature. Allegedly pro-Communist organizations and personalities have been prevented from seriously challenging Premier Lee Kuan Yew's hold on the government, and there has been no serious opposition to Lee except from the drastically restricted "far left."

Although North Vietnam, Burma, and Singapore are the only one-party systems in Southeast Asia at the present time, there have been other attempts similarly to restrict political competition in the past and more are surely likely in the future. Until his overthrow in 1970, former Cambodian Chief of State Prince Norodom Sihanouk was able to win consistently 100 per cent majorities in elections to the national Parliament for his *Sangkum* (People's Socialist Community) party. The late South Vietnamese President Ngo Dinh Diem, aided by his brother and political adviser, Ngo Dinh Nhu, sought to establish an essentially one-party system in the late 1950's and early 1960's. And soldier-President Nguyen Van Thieu was endeavoring to achieve the same end in the years after the January, 1973, "settlement" in Vietnam; his "Democratic" Party won control of almost all the village councils in elections in all the country's provinces in May and June of the same year.

Some—probably most—of the leaders of these established or would-be one-party systems in Southeast Asia sought to consolidate their personal hold on political power. But Burma's Ne Win, Singapore's Lee Kuan Yew, and the Vietnamese Communists were also moved by their dedication to ideas or goals or their fears of possible threats to the survival of their states. Ne Win has long feared the possible political fragmentation of Burma as a result of foreign exploitation of his country's minority differences; his one-party state is designed largely to contain such differences. Singapore's Lee Kuan Yew is likewise fearful of the pull of a resurgent China upon his country's ethnic Chinese majority. Tight PAP control is intended to prevent an antinational political opposition feeding on such "Chinese chauvinism."

COMMUNIST PARTIES

In the still-colonial years of agitation against foreign rule of their countries, Southeast Asia's Communists were largely nationalist in outlook and objectives, being frequently the overt or tacit allies of the also anticolonial non-Communist nationalists. The classic example of the "nationalist" Communist Party was Ho Chi Minh's original Indochinese Communist Party—and its disguised successor, the League for the Independence of Vietnam (Viet Minh). But Burma's two Communist parties (Stalinist and Trotskyite) and Indonesia's Communists before and during World War II were also mainly instruments of nationalist protest agitation.

There were, however, other types of Communist parties—and

still are today. The original Malayan Communist organization, for example, was called the South Seas (*Nan Yang*) Communist Party and in the 1920's and 1930's was an overseas extension of the Chinese Communist Party. The Communists carried the main burden of wartime resistance in Malaya against the occupying Japanese, but the postwar Malayan Communist Party (MCP), which raised the standard of revolt in 1948, was still an overwhelmingly ethnic Chinese-composed party. Today, the MCP fights a lingering insurrectionary war against the Kuala Lumpur government as the Malaysian Revolution Liberation Army, and, although it has actively sought Malay and Indian members, it remains more Chinese than anything else, like most of Malaysia's overt opposition parties. The MCP is still a communal party, despite its would-be universal ideology.

Because the colonial Americans pledged themselves to Philippine independence before World War II, Filipino Communism has always been more "social justice" Communism than "nationalist" Communism. Thus it was in the 1930's; and, after World War II, economic and social problems were the main focus of the Communist Hukbalahap uprising on central Luzon island. The Maoist "New People's Army," which today fights the Marcos government of the autocratically ruled Philippines, is very much a vehicle of social protest. Similarly, Indonesia's outlawed Communists and the pseudo-Communist *Barisan Socialis* party of Singapore are revolutionary class parties.

Burma's "new" Communists, who took over from the old Burman-dominated Communists of the central part of the country with their almost complete defeat by the Ne Win government in the late 1960's, are a multi-ethnic group coalition that is very sensitive to the Burmese minorities' charge of Burman ethnic majority domination of the country's government. In neighboring Thailand, too, the Communists have sought to play upon the particularistic complaints of the Lao-like northeasterners, the northern Meo minority, and the Muslim Malay community of the south. In Laos and Cambodia, however, the Pathet Lao and the Khmer Rouge—both Communist-led—have sought to portray themselves as popular uprisings against tyrannical regimes and oppressive foreign influence upon those regimes.

Some of the differences among Southeast Asia's Communists, of
course, are tactical. The Communist parties of the region have
adapted their tactics to the problems and opportunities of the
countries in which they exist. On the other hand, Southeast Asia's
various Communist parties are, for the most part, largely autonomous organizations. The nationalist character of Vietnam's Communists, the Chinese coloration of Malaysian Communism, or the
social protest emphasis of the Philippines's neo-Maoists is a natural consequence of the particular political fabric of these countries. Such differences, in short, are not wholly assumed postures.
There really are different kinds of Communist parties in Southeast Asia today.

"Partyless" Systems

Indonesia's Sukarno, Burma's Ne Win, Thailand's various military leaders between 1947 and 1973, and the Philippines's prewar
leading nationalist Manuel Quezon have all spoken out against
political parties as inappropriate to the circumstances of their
countries. And there have been times in the postcolonial histories
of some of these lands when there have not been political parties.

Political parties, for all practical purposes, did not exist as functioning entities in the Philippines in 1974. They were outlawed
for most of the time that the soldiers ruled Thailand between
1947 and the overthrow of that country's military dictatorship—
which may yet return—in October, 1973. And, although the Burma
Socialist Program Party was created early in the Ne Win military
regime that came to power by force in 1962, it was well into the
1970's before the BSPP came to play a real role in Burmese political life, and then it was as a vehicle for government control of national politics rather than as an instrument for direction, Com-
munist- or democratic-style, of the government.

Moreover, many political organizations elsewhere in Southeast
Asia that were called by those who used them "political parties"
were parties only in name. Most so-called parties in Laos were factions directed by traditional ruling families or "political auxilia-
ries" of the chief military commanders. Post-Sihanouk parties in
Cambodia were political parties, at best, only in intention. Yet, it

is interesting to note that in lands like Indonesia and Burma, where military leaders really did not have to create parties or hold elections, they did so in the first half of the 1970's, however non-democratic their intentions. And the purpose of such parties was probably more than symbolic.

CHANGING ROLES

Political parties, which have changed dramatically in Southeast Asia over the past twenty years, also perform quite different functions today from what they did in the first years of independence. In the immediate postcolonial years, when hopes for democratic government were high, parties were the major means of selecting the leading officeholders and determining public policies. Such was the case in the Philippines, Burma, Malaysia, and Singapore at the start of independence. Elections were not held in Indonesia until 1955, five years after victory against the Dutch in the war for freedom, but the main parties agreed to the parceling out of parliamentary seats and formed, and toppled, governments. There were even efforts to create party governments in Laos and Cambodia in the wake of the 1954 Geneva Accords, which brought independence to these two former French Indochinese colonies. Real party government, however, was probably never seriously attempted in South Vietnam nor in North Vietnam except in the particular Communist sense of the term. Nor have parties ever played a major role of any kind in never-colonial Thailand, where soldiers have dominated political life most of the time since the late 1930's.

Besides competing for offices and the right to determine public policies, parties in the democracies of Southeast Asia in the first years of independence were also vehicles for economic and social mobilization, national integration, and mass political education. Malaysia's "Alliance," in fact, still does all these things, as did Burma's AFPFL and Indonesia's major parties in the initial decade after the termination of colonialism. Though not especially democratic, Singapore's People's Action Party is also still an instrument for national development, solidarity, and education. Philippine parties, on the other hand, though long described as democratic, were mainly the means whereby a skillfully slogan-eering—and often selfish—elite maintained itself in power.

The decline of political parties began in the late 1950's; the once-powerful AFPFL government party split in Burma, setting the stage for a military takeover, and the strong-willed Sukarno sought to establish so-called guided democracy in Indonesia un-der which a complex array of institutions were established to wa-ter down the impact of parties on national decision-making. The most recent casualties were Philippine political parties, which survived as long as they did because they aided autocratic Fili-pino politics. When, however, they got in the way of President Marcos in 1972, they were pushed aside.

Only in Malaysia today is there a political party–controlled na-tional government that came to power as a result of essentially free elections. Elections were held in Indonesia in 1971, and the progovernment *Sekber Golkar*, a "party that isn't a party," re-ceived two-thirds of the vote; but the outcome of the balloting was strongly government-influenced, and *Golkar* was created by the military-dominated government to give it control of the re-sulting national legislature. The flow of governing direction in Indonesia, therefore, is almost the opposite of what it is in Ma-laysia. Likewise, the Burma Socialist Program Party, "victorious" in one-party balloting in 1974, is the soldier-administration's tool rather than the force that directs the government. A law legalizing parties was proclaimed in Thailand in 1974, but they have yet to throw down roots in Thai political soil. The People's Action Party does control the government in Singapore, but Singapore politics long ago ceased to be democratic politics.

Political parties in more countries than not—Indonesia, Burma, Singapore, South Vietnam, and Cambodia—are today tools of non-democratically selected ruling elites. In Singapore and Burma in particular—two otherwise quite different countries—such parties are intended primarily to be instruments of national mobilization. In these and most other countries, parties are important means of political indoctrination of the population and an auxiliary instru-ment for control of this population. In most of the countries of the area—North and South Vietnam, Indonesia, Burma, Singapore, the Philippines, and Cambodia—there is no longer open political com-petition among parties or party-like organizations.

The changes of the years 1946–74 have occurred for a number of reasons, but principally the relative ineffectiveness of parties to do the things that were expected of them added to the desire of self-imposed leaders to prevent their own dislodgement from office. Although the years of attempted party government were far from glorious ones, they did provide alternatives that could be peacefully attained to the personnel and policies of the governments of the day. Such alternatives and peaceful flexibility have been largely eliminated, thus appreciably increasing the already strong tendency to political instability in most of the lands of Southeast Asia.

8

Public Participation

There are four main ways in which popular participation has oc-curred in the politics of the Southeast Asian lands since national liberation. The people have taken part in the selection of the chief leaders of their lands, though to a decreasing extent; they have sought, with varying degrees of success, to influence the policies of the governments that rule over them; they have sometimes tried to topple such governments; and they have been the objects of governmental, and opposition, efforts to "mobilize" them for one political purpose or another.

In the first years of independence, such publics, both mass and special interest, probably were more active in trying to control and influence their governments than they were by the mid-1970's. On the other hand, the governmental leaders are probably more aware of the need to keep public opinion in mind today than they have ever been. It is one of the many paradoxes of pres-ent-day Southeast Asia that its nondemocratic regimes are in some ways more sensitive of the problem of public acceptance than a number of the former democratic governments of the area were.

LEADER SELECTION

Most of the first generation of leaders in Southeast Asia—Indo-nesia's Sukarno, Cambodia's Sihanouk, and Vietnam's Ho Chi Minh, among others—were virtual living legends in their lands when independence came. Whether elected or not, they were clearly the popular choices to lead their nations. The basis of their power was the fact that they were mass political heroes because of all that they had done through the years to gain freedom for their countries from colonial rule.

Elections. The first governments of many of the Southeast Asian lands were chosen in generally free and fair elections, particularly those of the Philippines, Burma, Malaysia, and Singapore. But only Malaysia of these four countries still had a government by 1974 that had been freely selected by the people to rule over them. Indonesia's immediate postcolonial government was not an elected one, largely because of the difficulty of holding national elections for the first time in its history of the world's fifth most populous nation. Elections were held in 1955 in Indonesia, though, and, while the parliamentary government formed as a result was shortly thereafter subverted by extremely popular, but never elected, President Sukarno, an effort had been made to allow the people to pick their leaders.

Elections in the other countries of the area were much less important even in the first years of independence—a warning, perhaps, of political things to come in the region as a whole. The turnout was very small in Thailand's 1946 voting for the country's first democratic government ever, a government that, however, was to be overturned within two years by a military coup. Subsequent balloting in the country—in 1956 and 1969, for example— was neither free nor fair; unrepresentative government parties predominated and riggings of various sorts took place. In South Vietnam, under President Diem in the late 1950's and early 1960's and Thieu in the late 1960's and early 1970's, candidacies were controlled, the legal opposition was limited in number, kind, and activity, and many irregularities were reported. Cambodia's elections under both Sihanouk and Lon Nol, Indonesia's 1971 vote, Singapore's balloting since independence, and many, but not all, of the elections held through the years in Laos have been exercises in mass manipulation more than they have been democratic experiences in which the whole citizenry has expressed its preference among different slates of candidates for public offices.

Plebiscites. Plebiscites—in which the public is asked to indicate its choice for or against a governmental institution or activity of one kind or another—have been held from time to time in various countries of Southeast Asia. A few of these votes have been open and honest, such as the 1962 referendum in Malaya and Singapore on the question of the creation of the new state of Malaysia, even though the governments of both territories threw their full weight behind an affirmative answer in the preballoting "debate." Most such referendums, however, have been heavily controlled and intended to legitimatize the hold of particular politicians on public office, often through, or as a result of, changes in the form of government.

One of the earliest of such manipulated plebiscites was then Premier Ngo Dinh Diem's much-managed referendum in 1956 to make the post–Geneva Accords territory of South Vietnam a "republic," so that Diem could become its chief of state as President in place of Emperor Bao Dai. He received an endorsement of more than 90 per cent. President Marcos's 1973 referendum on whether he should remain in office beyond the end of his second term was of the same kind of actively arranged popular approval. The price for not voting in, let alone opposing, the 1973 Philippine referendum was high enough so that most Filipinos, accustomed to chief executives who did what they wanted to do anyway, took the easy political way out and cast their ballots for Marcos by a margin of better than nine out of ten. Burma's 1973 vote for a new "socialist republic" constitution was more like the Diem and Marcos plebiscites than a really democratic exercise in public preference indication. The object of the Burmese balloting was to legitimatize the new one-party order that General Ne Win had created during the nearly dozen years since he had overthrown democratically elected Premier U Nu. But the new basic law did go through several drafts, was taken "on tour" of the country for public discussion of its strengths and weaknesses, and was less a means of maintaining Ne Win in power than of creating the kind of Burma he wanted after his rule had ended. This having been said, however, the Burmese voter in the 1973 plebiscite, or in the first elections for a "legislature" under the new constitution in 1974, had no real choice.

Such plebiscites, like most public-office elections in Southeast Asia by the mid-1970's, involved only formal popular participation. The "citizens' assemblies," hastily convened by Filipino dictator Marcos in early 1973 to "adopt" the new constitution to keep him in power, had no basis whatsoever in Philippine law, as the country's Supreme Court subsequently stated. But Marcos could claim that the "people" had given their "approval." And apparent legitimization, not genuine popular participation, was what the Filipino usurper wanted.

Forced Removal. No leaders have yet been placed in power by popular movements of the street or countryside in postcolonial Southeast Asia. But several leaders have been toppled by this type of popular participation in politics. Thailand's long-governing military-political pair of Premier Thanom Kittikachorn and Deputy Prime Minister Prapas Charusathien was catapulted from office in 1973 by student demonstrations against their arbitrary leadership. The easing from power of onetime nationalist hero President Sukarno in Indonesia in the second half of the 1960's resulted from the initiative of aroused students who paved the way for the more cautious soldiers to take over. Neither Vietnam's Diem nor Cambodia's Sihanouk was overthrown by street mobs, but both had clearly lost the support of many of their onetime followers, particularly in their capital cities, which made them more vulnerable than they would otherwise have been to the forces that actually did overthrow them.

By the mid-1970's little opportunity existed in most of the Southeast Asian lands for the mass of the citizenry to participate in the selection of those who ruled them or to "throw out" leaders who no longer pleased them, as Filipino voters did to *all* incumbent Presidents who sought re-election up to 1969. Such nonparticipation in leader selection was the way it had been in precolonial times and under European rule, of course, and in most countries during most of history. But it was nonetheless a step backward politically and a source of weakness, probably recognized as such by most of the rulers of the area, as evidenced by the comparatively easy ouster of Thanom and Prapas from power in Thailand in 1973.

INFLUENCE ON GOVERNMENT

There are really only two strategies for influencing government. One is to try to get government to change or maintain policies of general applicability in the society; the other is to obtain exceptions from government for an individual or group from the existing law. In the colonial period in Southeast Asia, indigenous interests had only limited opportunity to influence policy formation as such, largely because so much of it took place in London, Paris, or The Hague. The result was that local interests sought to influence the application of the law to themselves more than they tried to change policy. By the mid-1970's, many observers believed that politics in Southeast Asia had again become "exception politics," "administration politics," or "politics for a price," as it had been in colonial times, with the general public, and even particular publics, exerting little real overt influence on policy-making as such.

Elections. Probably no elections in Southeast Asia ever had a particularly profound effect on public-policy development as such, even in the heyday of democratic government in the area. This is because there never really were any head-on ideological or interest clashes at the polls between significantly differentiated major parties. The Nacionalistas and Liberals in the Philippines were "Tweedledum" and "Tweedledee" personified, as indicated by the steady movement back-and-forth across the political aisle of members of the two allegedly "rival" parties. Likewise, many of the parties in Indonesia in the 1955 elections were very similar, being generally socialist-oriented. Only in Malaysia, perhaps, have there been significant differences between major parties contesting public office, and in 1969 the strong showing of the anti-"Alliance" opposition parties may actually have been counterproductive in its impact on public-policy formation. The challenge to the government party, the "Alliance," in that voting probably motivated it to intensify its efforts to aid the economically weaker Malay community in the country. The opposition, however, had been protesting the pro-Malay bias of the UMNO-led "Alliance" government.

In the 1960's, elections either were not held, as in Indonesia, Burma, and Thailand—which went all or most of the decade without such voting—or were not really open and honest, as in South Vietnam, Cambodia, and Singapore. The 1969 election in Thailand, the 1974 Burmese vote for a one-party legislature, and the partly controlled 1971 balloting in Indonesia reflected renewed interest in popular participation in politics through some kinds of legislative elections. But in neither the Burmese nor the Indonesian voting were there really any choices regarding programs and policies.

Interest Groups. Not surprisingly, interest groups—representing labor, business, agriculture, education, and other sectors of society—are the most developed and most influential in two of the more economically advanced of the Southeast Asian nations, Malaysia and the Philippines. They are probably as numerous and diverse in Singapore, too, but there they have come under very strong People's Action Party control, making them far less autonomous than interest groups even under Philippine President Marcos's "constitutional authoritarianism." Singapore's Lee Kuan Yew probably fears for his own ouster from office, but he also clearly fears a "left-wing" takeover of his government—and, thereby, his country—even more. Lee's tight control over trade unions, professional and economic associations in general, students and professors, and other groups is designed to prevent Communists from gaining control of any of these areas of society via the organizations that "represent" them. Marcos, on the other hand, is moved mainly by personal ambition. The Philippine leader can afford, accordingly, to permit the fairly free interplay of major interest groups because, as he sees it, they do not threaten him personally.

South Vietnam and Thailand also have experienced the emergence of a substantial number of interest groups in the last ten to fifteen years—despite the preoccupation of their political elites with security and foreign-policy questions and, in Thailand, the limitations on the activities of many such groups, such as labor unions. It may, indeed, be the case that the historian of tomorrow will rank the chief contribution of the Americans to Vietnam in the years 1954–73 to have been the incidentally forced modernization of the country. More new interests, and, hence, interest groups, developed during these years than in any period of similar length in the country's history, including the period of French colonial rule. Thailand's military regime fell in 1973, partly because such interests had been denied meaningful participation in the country's political life. It was not that labor, business, and other such interests conspired against the government, but they did nothing at all to aid the autocratic army regime when it was threatened and were, in fact, visibly pleased to see it go. South Vietnam's strong-armed soldier-rulers may yet experience a similar fate—which could be much more bloody and costly, given the complexity of the partitioned country's "mixed" modern-traditional society and economy.

Some of Southeast Asia's most important interest groups are "institutional" ones—"government groups" like armies, civil servants, university professors, and the like. These groups, too, are competitors for influence on government decisions in contemporary Southeast Asia. Both types of interest groups, "institutional" and "associational," may be more important politically today than they have ever been.

Press. The press was once influential in the shaping of public policy in some of the independent lands of Southeast Asia. Newspapers, weekly magazines, radio, and even television were important political forces in the Philippines, a country in which the growth of "modern" communications probably outstripped the development of the nation in general, before President Marcos's imposition of martial law in September, 1972. Likewise, in the first fourteen years of Burma's independence, the press, principally the great *Nation* newspaper but also the rival *Guardian,* influenced the two governments of U Nu and the intervening eighteen-month Ne Win military caretaker regime more than any other institutions or forces in the country, possibly even including the insurgents. Both countries' press featured communications from concerned citizens and vividly reported popular actions disapproving of government policies, such as rallies, demonstrations, and the like.

Individual newspapers and, to a lesser extent, other periodicals in Indonesia, Thailand, and even South Vietnam have espoused public causes or opened their columns to spokesmen for such causes at times in the past. But the press in Malaysia and Singapore has been largely nonpolitical in the postcolonial period, surprisingly in light of still-functioning Malaysian democracy and Singapore's former democratic vitality. The explanation is to be found perhaps in the licensing controls exercised by government in these two lands as well as the unwillingness of highly profitable business ventures to run the risk of being shut down.

Thailand's press was probably as free as it has ever been in the mid-1970's, but elsewhere in the region the press was not a main vehicle for the transmission of public or other nongovernmental opinion and thus hardly a major influence on policy formation.

Demonstrations. Suspension of elections, limitations on interest-group organization and activity, and controls on the press and limited freedom of speech in general seriously restrict opportunities for the public to speak out in behalf of policy or other interests it may have. It is for this reason, surprisingly little understood by the leaders of the various Southeast Asian governments through the years, that students, workers, followers of different religious faiths, and others have been forced into the streets to draw attention to their demands or objections and to seek to influence public-policy formation. Widespread opposition to Japanese policies toward Thailand were obvious in that country for years, but army leaders who may have profited personally from such policies ignored such opposition almost altogether, apparently believing that they were above such public opinion. The 1973 demonstrations against visiting Japanese Prime Minister Kahuei Tanaka, following, actually, the overthrow of the unpopular Thanom-Prapas regime, emphasized the nonavailability of other means in still politically underdeveloped Thailand for such opposition to be expressed.

The Japanese leader was greeted by even bigger demonstrations in the Indonesian capital of Jakarta later on the same "goodwill" tour of Southeast Asia. The Indonesian demonstrators, mainly students, were protesting not only Japan's economic policies toward their country but also the Suharto regime's obliging acceptance of these policies and the use of hated Chinese businessmen as the local representatives of Japanese economic interests. The protestors also decried widespread corruption in the Indonesian Government and its unresponsiveness to public opinion in general. President Suharto subsequently effected a major shake-up in his military-dominated administration, the reported eleven deaths in the streets accomplishing what a more open political environment might have done much easier and earlier.

International Pressure. The Philippine Muslim insurgent initiative in February, 1974, that led to the nearly complete destruction of the southern Filipino city of Jolo and hundreds of deaths in a week's fighting indicates, more than any other recent political event in Southeast Asia, the degree to which the countries of the area have become part of an international political process. The Filipino Islamic political warriors renewed their attacks on government forces, provoking retaliation, though not necessarily on the scale on which it took place, to attract the attention to their plight of Muslim Presidents, Premiers, and Foreign Ministers about to meet in an international conference in Lahore, Pakistan. Lacking the means to influence the Philippine Government, with which the rebels did not identify anyway, the Islamic insurgents sought to induce the government to come to their terms through an appeal to a body of opinion outside the country believed to be sympathetic to their cause. (Libya's Colonel Quaddafi had previously supplied the rebels with some arms and ammunition; an earlier Muslim conference had dispatched an inspection team to the Philippines, and there was a possibility of influencing the Arab oil countries to cut off the flow of vitally needed petroleum to the Manila government).

Others have also sought to influence their governments through appeal to international opinion, the United Nations, or the various major powers, but few have done so quite as dramatically as the Filipino Muslim insurgents in February, 1974. The "Jolo affair" clearly indicates the plight of minority or other nonfavored elements confronted with a nonresponsive and, indeed, outright hostile government.

INSURRECTIONS

Insurrections have come to be regarded as such a distinct political activity in their own right that it is often overlooked that they are a form of popular participation in politics. Not all uprisings, of course, necessarily fit this framework, but most do. The 1948 rebellion of the Indonesian Communists at Madiun at the height of the armed struggle of the nationalists against the Dutch was an oldfashioned "power play." But it was a different case when the

Philippines's Communists were forced underground after independence; elected legislators were denied their seats because they were Communists and the Filipinos who voted for them were denied their representation in Congress. The Hukbalahaps, or "Huks," took to the bush, in part because other means of political participation were closed to them, as they were to be closed in more subtle manner to the young men and women who became the Maoist "New People's Army" in the same land in the late 1960's. French policy forced many anticolonial Vietnamese into the Communist-led Viet Minh after World War II. Indeed, the Vietnamese Communists' resort to force in the late 1950's was a direct and probably inevitable consequence of South Vietnamese and American opposition to the Geneva-mandated 1956 elections. It is also open to question whether there was really a possibility that non-Communist leaders in Laos and Cambodia, Prince Souvanna Phouma and Norodom Sihanouk no less than Marshal Lon Nol, would ever have permitted the peaceful acquisition of control of their governments by the Communist Pathet Lao or Khmer Rouge.

Communists, however, have by no means been the only groups to resort to insurrectionary activity to get what they wanted politically in Southeast Asia since national liberation. Some of Burma's minorities impetuously took to the bush in the first years of independence, particularly the Karens, but others resorted to rebellion, especially after U Nu's second ouster in 1962, only when there appeared to be no other means available to them to make their political points. The Philippines's Muslims and some of Thailand's Muslim Malays and Meo tribesmen are other groups involved in insurrections partly because their political systems would not hear, or help, them.

PASSIVE PARTICIPATION

Voters, members of political parties and interest groups, journalists and writers of letters to newspapers, and, not least of all, insurrectionists are all *active* participants in politics, men and women taking action to get what *they* want from their governments (which may even include the replacement of such governments or the separation of some people and territory from the country over which the government rules). In all the countries of Southeast Asia, however, most of the people have been *objects* of politics rather than active participants in politics most of the time since independence.

Objects of Politics. Although there were spontaneous acts of popular reaction against the foreign presence in colonial times, even the nationalist movements that won independence for most of the Southeast Asian countries made an organized effort to mobilize the general population for purposes believed to be important by leaders. Since independence, such leaders have continued to "use" the people for purposes of national mobilization or even their own continuation in power, as Philippine President Marcos through his "citizens' assemblies."

Both the Communists and the Saigon regimes that opposed them used ordinary Vietnamese as "objects" of actions related to the higher ends to which they were dedicated. The democratic U Nu and the soldier Ne Win, who followed him as Burma's leader, sought to mobilize their countrymen with appeals to Buddhism or to the proclaimed benefits of the Burmese socialist order, hoping to rally resistance against the country's persisting Communist insurgents. Former Indonesian President Sukarno tried, with less than his usual success, in the early and mid-1960's to induce his countrymen to identify with his strategy to break up newly formed Malaysia. But most Indonesians saw no reason why they should be opposed to their religious and ethnic kinsmen, the neighboring Malays, and Sukarno's "crush Malaysia" campaign might have collapsed even if the anti-Communist soldiers had not eased him from power.

Victims of Politics. Not only have the vast mass of ordinary Southeast Asians been *objects* of politics, as happens more or less in all political systems, but some of them have also been *victims* of politics. Particularly has this been so of millions of men and women in the hundreds of villages over which Communists and anti-Communists fought in Vietnam or of those parts of North Vietnam that the Americans bombed in the same war. Such Vietnamese, like Filipino Muslims, were used, with little apparent concern for their humanity, by those who killed them or set them up to be killed. Involuntary participants in politics for the most part, such "victims" nonetheless played their part, and payed their price, in the bloody postcolonial politics not only of Vietnam but, in lesser numbers, of most of the other lands of the area as well.

The overseas Chinese, however, have probably been the most frequent "victims" of politics in Southeast Asia since independence. In the May, 1969, Kuala Lumpur rioting, nine Chinese died for each Malay who was killed in the disturbances in which the police and security forces were largely Malay. Under old-style Filipino "democracy," many wealthy Chinese found it difficult to qualify for citizenship—because they would then be less vulnerable to the politicians' threat of deportation if they did not give generously to the campaign war chests of both parties. Through the years, likewise, Indonesia's leaders under both Presidents Sukarno and Suharto kept just enough pressure on local Chinese businessmen to satisfy anti-Chinese ultranationalist elements, but not so much as to drive away badly needed entrepreneurial capital. In nearly all the Southeast Asian countries, in fact, the Chinese have been a favored political "whipping boy"; subversion, inflation, unemployment, and almost everything else could always be blamed on them to take the heat off the government politicians. Thousands of Chinese have lost their lives as a result of the animosities caused in this manner over the past quarter of a century, most dramatically in the anti-Communist bloodbath in Indonesia in 1965–66.

RULERS AND RULED

So much do ruling elites monopolize power in many of the Southeast Asian countries today that there are almost no competing or autonomous centers of power—voting power, economic power, or other types of power—except the various insurgencies. As a result, popular participation in politics has tended to be increasingly on the government's terms, that is, on the terms of the elites that control such governments. In some countries, even trade unions, student groups, and the like are extensions of government or party power, as in otherwise different North Vietnam and Singapore. Nonetheless, even autocratic rulers like those of Indonesia and Burma have seemed to feel the need for symbolic popular acceptance of their rule. This, however, should not be confused with the reality of popular politics, which may be at a postcolonial low in Southeast Asia at the present time. Burma's and Indonesia's most recent elections did involve popular participation in politics, but much less so than in earlier years. Likewise, in the Philippines, Singapore, Cambodia, and even Malaysia people participate spontaneously in their countries' political life less than they once did. But in these lands, as in the two Vietnams, they still do participate, though often as objects and even victims, of the political wills of others.

9

An Authoritarian Trend?

The political trend in Southeast Asia from the mid-1950's through the 1960's was clearly in the direction of authoritarian government. The two Vietnams, Indonesia, Thailand, Burma, Cambodia, and Singapore were all essentially autocratic regimes by the end of the 1960's, with soldier-administrations that had come to power by nonelectoral means prevailing in South Vietnam, Thailand, Burma, and Indonesia. The Philippines joined the ranks of the region's nondemocratic governments early in the 1970's, but the long-ruling Thai military regime fell in reaction to student agitation against it. Even in Malaysia, Parliament was suspended for a year and a half following the May, 1969, Kuala Lumpur riots and, though reconvened in 1971, has subsequently functioned with greater restrictions than previously. As for Laos, its government in the 1960's and early 1970's was neither democratic nor dictatorial, although it probably would have been more autocratic if the Communist Pathet Lao had been allowed to come to power, or if the U.S.-restrained military on the anti-Communist side had been left to itself.

Although the Philippines and Cambodia moved in the direction of greater authoritarianism in the first half of the 1970's, Burma and Indonesia held their first elections in fourteen and sixteen years, respectively. Was the authoritarian trend of the late 1950's and 1960's beginning to reverse itself, or were the Burmese and Indonesian elections largely symbolic efforts to legitimatize existing autocratic regimes? Perhaps Thailand's new political freedom was only a political breathing spell between past and future military dictatorships.

Toward Autocracy

The democratic constitutional orders with which most of the Southeast Asian nations started their resumed independence were out of step with many of the political, social, economic, and other values and circumstances of these countries. Political behavior was never as democratic in the Philippines or Burma, for example, as the institutions of government appeared to be. Many Filipino politicians did not really regard their often impoverished and illiterate countrymen as equals, family and other personal relations were highly autocratic, and most of the country's rigidly run schools probably did more to stifle than to encourage democratic values and behavior. Likewise, many Burmese political leaders in the era of U Nu and the independence-winning AFPFL may have been democratically oriented themselves, but their supporters away from the capital often behaved as if they were the unlimited rulers of the areas in which they represented the government party. Nowhere in Southeast Asia, indeed, was politics as democratic in practice in the first years of independence as it appeared to be in form.

Attitudes. There has probably been less change in the ways leaders have regarded their countrymen in Southeast Asia over the last twenty years than is generally appreciated. The Philippines and Burma, again, are good cases in point. Some democratically oriented Filipino leaders excepted, most politicians in that country between 1946 and 1972, when President Marcos declared martial law, looked down on most of their countrymen, regarding them as subjects rather than the source of their privilege to rule. Some governors and congressmen practiced gross brutality, including murder, in their local fiefdoms; their provinces and districts were almost literally personal political estates, in which hundreds of thousands of plantation workers and other peasants were mercilessly exploited without any evident concern on the part of such leaders. Similarly, the behavior, though by no means as brutal, of many Burmese politicians before the military seized power in that land was difficult to reconcile with the democratic ideas they professed. The ruling Anti-Fascist People's Freedom Party went ten years without holding a national convention, AFPFL candidates for Parliament were forced on districts that did not want them, and even democratic Premier U Nu went four years without addressing the Chamber of Deputies, to which he was formally responsible.

All these years Filipino and Burmese politicians spoke publicly of their devotion to democratic ideas, but the behavior of many of them indicated that such ideas were more than modestly mixed with some of the values of political authoritarianism. The non-democratic ideas articulated by President Marcos in the Philippines after 1972 were much more consistent with pre-1972 Filipino political behavior than the high-sounding oratory of the same years. Likewise, Burma's Ne Win's autocratic political ideas are more in tune with the political realities of pre-1962 politics than were the articulated ideals of that era. Articulated political values, in short, in becoming more authoritarian through the years in many parts of Southeast Asia, have caught up with the behavior and practices of the real-life politicians.

Institutions. The institutional changes of the same years have actually been much more dramatic. In 1955, the Philippines, Burma, Indonesia, South Vietnam, Cambodia, and Laos all professed to be democratic governments or seemed to be headed in that direction, while Malaysia and Singapore were becoming more democratic as they moved toward independence from British colonial rule. Only Communist-ruled North Vietnam and soldier-governed Thailand were autocracies twenty years ago.

By the early 1970's, the Philippines, Burma, Indonesia, South Vietnam, Cambodia, and Singapore had all ceased to be democracies. A new "parliamentary" constitution was proclaimed in the Philippines by Marcos in 1973, but no Parliament was subsequently established, and Marcos vowed to rule for seven years without new elections. Burma had no constitution at all between 1962 and 1974 under General Ne Win's strong-armed rule, and the one it got from its never-elected leader in the latter year permitted only one political party to operate and gave the new legislature no effective checks on the executive. The Parliament elected by Indonesia in 1971 in the first national voting in the country since 1955 was dominated by a party (*Sekber Golkar*) that was created by the military-dominated government to fight the elections on its behalf and by a hundred soldier-members appointed by that government; these parliamentarians, together with additional appointed members, also made up the superparliamentary "People's Consultative Congress," which "re-elected" President Suharto in 1973. Elsewhere, South Vietnam's President Thieu was "re-elected" in a one-candidate election in 1971, Singapore's Lee Kuan Yew's People's Action Party held a 100 per cent parliamentary majority, the main opposition parties declined to contest Cambodia's 1973 voting, and the Communist *Lao Dong* Party showed no signs of relaxing its rule in North Vietnam.

Practices. Even Malaysia, probably the most democratically oriented of the Southeast Asian governments in the early 1970's, was less liberal in practice than it appeared to be in form. Following the reconvening of Parliament in 1971, it was illegal to discuss publicly matters of race, religion, language, or Malay constitutional privileges (and, while the decree prohibiting such discussion could always be repealed, such a repeal could not easily be discussed, even in Parliament, without violating the law!). The decree forcing the integration of Indonesia's Nationalist and Muslim Teachers parties with smaller parties into so-called democratic and unity groups was designed to reduce even further their once formidable opposition potential; and their leaders complied for fear of having their political organizations banned altogether. In the Philippines, the country's second most important political personality on the eve of the declaration of martial law in 1972, Senator Benigno S. Acquino, Jr., widely expected to succeed Ferdinand Marcos as the nation's next leader, remained in jail in 1974; Marcos did not dare to release him for fear that he might mount a successful opposition to the President's pseudoconstitutional retention of power.

These three types of behavior—restrictions on freedom of speech, forced alteration of existing political organizations, and detention of opponents—were widespread in Southeast Asia in the first half of the 1970's. They were used more extensively than a decade earlier—a reflection of the continuing trend toward autocracy in Southeast Asia.

WHY AUTOCRACY?

There are several reasons why authoritarian rule has come to be so widely established in Southeast Asia. Those who head the autocratic regimes of the region emphasize the magnitude and complexity of the problems confronting their countries. Indonesia's Suharto, Burma's Ne Win, and the Philippines's Marcos have all stated that only the undistracted and united effort of the whole people of their lands can solve such problems. One of these problems, in particular, however, is probably more of a real reason than some of the others for the trend toward authoritarianism in the region: the inadequate integration of the national societies of the area. Karens, Kachins, Chins, and Shans still fight Burmans in Burma; pro-Communist elements probably remain a threat among some of the unassimilated ethnic Chinese of Singapore; and Communist, Muslim, and other political factions could yet cause serious political disunity in Indonesia. The leaders of these three lands (Burma, Singapore, and Indonesia) as well as of others believe that their internal political divisions could be exploited to the disadvantage of their long-pursued national freedom. Authoritarian rule is justified by such leaders, and may, in fact, be really necessary, to keep such factionalism in check until true national unity exists.

It has also been argued by authoritarian rulers from Ne Win to Marcos that democracy will not work in their lands. Such dictators cite, with some justification, the extremely imperfect performance of previous democratic regimes. Unfortunately, however, democracy was tried first and, in a probably genuine sense, was found to be wanting. If, on the other hand, authoritarian government had been attempted first, it, too, would probably have been found to have shortcomings. This is because most of the Southeast Asian countries' leaders, and followers, lacked experience in any kind of self-government, not just the democratic variety, when independence came. It is also true, however, that Southeast Asia's various ex-colonies also lacked the "political infrastructure" to make democracy work in the first difficult years of independence: a literate and otherwise educated population, opportunity and time to learn about alternative policies and leaders, a responsible and objective press, and the quantity and quality of politicians sufficient to staff both a government *and* a loyal opposition (and who would accept ouster from office as part of the nature and risks of politics).

The men who seized power from the democrats, or who manip-
ulate it today in far from democratic ways—such as Marcos,
Thieu, and Lee Kuan Yew—are as ambitious as they are qualified. Probably no Filipino politician ever pursued the Presidency
of his country with a determination quite like that of Marcos.
Similar ambition underlay Lee Kuan Yew's attempt in 1963–65 to
become the leader of all Malaysia that provoked the central government of that federation to expel Singapore. Even those leaders
who did not scheme to become their countries' rulers, such as Indonesia's General Suharto, subsequently displayed great skill in
holding on to office (and little interest in really restoring democratic government). Taking advantage of the inexperience and
inadequate preparation of their countries for democratic government and responding to problems that virtually cried out for solution, Southeast Asia's new leaders came to power as a result of
both their ambition and their perception of themselves as men
indispensable to their lands in an hour of national need.

The trend toward authoritarianism in Southeast Asia has also
probably been much influenced by the impact of perceived, and
often actual, foreign threats. South Vietnam created an army to
hold off the assaulting Communist Vietnamese, recognized by
Peking and Moscow as rightful rulers of all of the country in
1950, and this army in turn subsequently seized power in Saigon.
The same thing happened in Burma, where U Nu built up a military force to defeat foreign-aided Communist and ethnic minority
insurgents, only to have this army—or its leadership—oust him
from office and jail him. Both U Nu and his successor, General Ne
Win, feared Chinese exploitation of Burmese disunity, and Ne
Win's new one-party order is largely rooted in this fear. It may be
open to question whether Indonesia is "China's number-one enemy in Asia" (as contended by some Jakarta generals), or that
China, Indonesia, and Malaysia threaten in any immediate way
Singapore's government, but there is no doubt that the Suharto
and Lee Kuan Yew regimes do, in fact, see such "threats."

Foreign friends as well as foes have also influenced the trend
toward authoritarianism in Southeast Asia. The United States provided millions of dollars' worth of military aid to Thailand through
the years and even more such assistance to South Vietnam, giving

these regimes the means to stay in power and also legitimatizing them in the eyes of some of their countrymen. Philippine leader Marcos endeavored after 1972 to convince the United States of his friendship, and worth as an ally, and to persuade his countrymen of U.S. acceptance of his autocratic government. Both Burma's and Indonesia's soldier-governments also were aided in retaining power by U.S. military sales, or aid, to them.

AGAINST AUTOCRACY

The first years of the 1970's did see some liberalization of politics in a couple of Southeast Asian countries, but the trend toward authoritarianism has probably not yet been reversed. The most important anti-authoritarian political development was the ouster of the Thai military regime in 1973, which was followed in 1974 by the legalization of political parties and efforts to draft a new and more democratic constitution. But there are still some very important unanswered questions about the ease with which the Thanom Kittikachorn army regime was overthrown in 1973. The ouster of Thanom, who kept postponing his political retirement, was very much in the interest of younger military elements. And it remains to be seen whether such soldiers continue their support of, and neutrality toward, the democratic trend in their country.

If Indonesia and Burma held elections in the first half of the 1970's, the Philippines joined the ranks of the authoritarian countries of the area, Cambodia became more autocratic than it had ever been under Sihanouk, the Pathet Lao consolidated their hold on most of Laos, and Malaysia limited some of the freedoms of its democratic political system in significant ways. The Indonesian and Burmese voting, moreover, seemed more symbolic than anything else. Neither election influenced the question of who governed the country, the way in which the land was governed, or the policies that were pursued by the government.

IV

Prime Problems

10

National Integration

The politics of the Southeast Asian countries, as we have seen, are partly dictated by the histories, social and economic groups, and relations with various foreign powers of these lands. But they are also partly determined by the kinds of problems these lands face, how they choose to approach these problems, and what the results of these approaches are. The relationship is very much a two-way one: The setting influences the approach to the problems and the results thereof, but the types of problems and how successfully or unsuccessfully they are managed may also decisively shape the very nature of a country's political process. The problem of Burma's imperfectly integrated multiple ethnic and social communities is an outstanding case in point; it was probably the single most important factor underlying the forced termination of democratic politics in that country, the subsequent dozen years of dogmatic military rule, and the formal establishment in 1974 of a new, noncompetitive, one-party political-economic order.

The major problems of the independent lands of Southeast Asia during the past quarter-century have included those of modernization (or socio-economic development), foreign relations (or the maintenance of political and economic independence and the improvement of the nation's international economic position), human liberties (and the extent to which they must be curtailed in the interest of allegedly larger national interests), and competition and criticism (or the degree to which alternative policies, and leaders to enact them, may be openly and freely considered). Perhaps the most important problem of all, however, underlying many of the others, has been that of national integration. It may be the problem on the solution, or at least management, of which hinges the very existence of nations and all the great gains of the historic struggle for emancipation from foreign rule.

The problem of national integration is essentially that of the development of an enhanced sense of national unity, the country-wide, deeply rooted feeling of oneness and belonging to a common society and culture that accords the nation the highest priority among the loyalties of the men and women who inhabit it. By the mid-1970's, there was probably only one country, or half a country, in which national integration as such appeared not the number-one political problem. This was North Vietnam—considered a single country by itself. Vietnam as a whole, however, may have had the most exaggerated problem of national unity in the whole region.

COMPETING LOYALTIES

The forces hindering the full attainment of national integration in the various Southeast Asian lands are multiple and of differing degrees of intensity from country to country. Most of these forces, however, are to be found in nearly all the nations of the area, though in often quite distinct patterns or combinations.

Ethnic Identification. Most people who are legally Thai or Filipino are also ethnically Thai or Filipino and identify, accordingly, with the Thai and Filipino nations. Some inhabitants of Thailand, however, and probably an even smaller number of people making their home in the Philippines, do not think of themselves as primarily Thai or Filipinos. Even more people in Burma do not regard themselves as "Burmese," considering themselves rather Shans, Karens, Chins, Mons, Arakanese, or other of Burma's multiple minorities. The problem of primary identification of members of such minorities with the ethnic group to which they belong, which exists in its most exaggerated form in Burma, is a major obstacle to the attainment of national integration throughout the area.

Burma's many minorities; the Lao, Meo and Malay populations of northeastern, northern, and southern Thailand; the hill-peoples of the two Vietnams and Laos; the indigenous inhabitants of the eastern Malaysian states of Sarawak and Sabah, who are ethnically distinct from the majority Malays of the country; and, not least of all, the "overseas Chinese" to be found in all the Southeast Asian lands are examples of peoples throughout the area who have resisted complete—or, in some cases, even partial—identification with the majority, or main national, community of the country.

Besides being ethnically distinct, members of most such minorities ordinarily possess culture and language that are their own and different from the life-style and language of the ethno-political majority.

Religious Minorities. Some, but not all, of the ethnic minorities also profess a different religion from that of the majority of the population in their country. Many of Burma's Karens, including most of the leaders of the land's twenty-five-year-old Karen insurgency, are Baptist Christians, converted in the colonial period, who fear the fate of their religion in a Buddhist majority state. Similarly, Thailand's Malay minority are Muslims in a Buddhist country and regard themselves as different from the overwhelmingly majority Thai religiously as well as racially. But not all religious minorities are ethnically different from the majority of the population of the country in which they live. The Philippines's southern Muslims, for example, many of whom were engaged in a very deadly civil war with the Manila government in 1974, are of the identical ethnic stock as the country's Christian majority. The immediate causes of the war that began in earnest in 1969 were probably economic and political as much as they were religious, but the struggle was increasingly perceived in religious terms by the Muslim insurgents.

Not all religious minorities pose integration problems of a conventional kind, moreover, and some of them have not posed real problems at all. Indonesia's Christian minority, for example, identifies with Indonesian nationalism as much as the country's Islamic majority apparently. And South Vietnam's Roman Catholic minority is among that otherwise troubled state's most assertive nationalists, with an influence on politics disproportionately strong for the 10 per cent of the population it constitutes. In the future, however, the country's Buddhist majority could well become dominant politically, and its religious-cultural nationalism could cause very serious problems for the Catholics. Although this would be a case of a religious majority belatedly asserting itself rather than a minority refusing to identify with the nation, tomorrow's Catholics could find it difficult to identify with a vigorously Buddhist South Vietnam.

"Overseas Chinese." Southeast Asia's omnipresent "overseas Chinese," who numbered an estimated 15 million in the mid-1970's and who constitute an overwhelming majority of Singapore's total population, are both an ethnic and, to a much lesser extent, religious minority in the area as a whole. There are extremely few Muslim Chinese in Indonesia or Malaysia, for example, although many more Chinese have become Buddhists in Thailand or Christians in the Philippines, possibly a majority of them. Southeast Asia's Chinese, however, are viewed by the other peoples among whom they live as primarily a "national minority." As we have noted, they are also considered an "economic minority," holding power over the commercial and manufacturing sectors of the economies of the countries in which they live out of proportion to their numbers.

It is the status of such Chinese as a "national minority"— allegedly possessing a higher political loyalty to another state, the increasingly important and mammoth People's Republic of China —that particularly concerns the majority populations and the governments that rule over them in Southeast Asia today. There have been occasions when some Chinese have taunted local political leaders with the prediction of ultimate Chinese domination of the region, but most Chinese have been political fence-sitters and fearfully discreet in this respect. Some "left-bank Lao" in northeastern Thailand and the Malay Moslem minority in the latter land (and Cambodia's remaining Vietnamese population) have also identified with other nations, but the Chinese are by far and away the area's most important "national minority."

Regionalism. In sprawling island-countries like Indonesia and the Philippines, primary identification with major regions of the nation have posed persisting problems, though not so far unsettling ones, for their national and nationalist governments. Sumatra is probably the wealthiest of Indonesia's many islands in terms of known and developed natural resources, but two-thirds of the country's population is located in the smaller and poorer island of Java, whose majority inhabitants, though also Malay and Muslim, differ nonetheless culturally from the different subcommunities of Sumatra. Many in Sumatra have believed from the resumption of independence that their island has not been getting its fair share of the rewards of its resources and their export, including oil; they believe that Java is living off Sumatra.

Similarly, many Filipinos identify with the region of their, or their families' origin, such as Cebu in the Visayan or middle islands of the country. There are many Filipino dialects, and such linguistic differences are largely a consequence of the geographical fragmentation of the island-country. To non-Filipinos, the Philippines appears to be a culturally homogeneous country, with the exception of its southern Muslim minority. But the country's leaders are aware of the regional differences that distinguish their island-land—as evidenced by the failure to date of non-Tagalog-speaking Filipinos to use the allegedly syncretist national language "Pilipino," which is mainly the Manila dialect of Tagalog.

Village Loyalties. Most Southeast Asians are village-dwellers, not urban residents. And, although such cities as Jakarta, Manila, and Bangkok seem to be teaming with millions of excess people from the countryside, the rural areas are still where an overwelming majority of Southeast Asia's people are to be found. The figure runs as high as 95 per cent of the total population in some lands.

For this majority of Southeast Asia's people, the village is their world and the focus of their identification and loyalty, not the comparatively new notion of nation. Most villages are probably not antigovernment as such, but in some countries postcolonial governments appear to them to have taken away more, in the form of taxes or artificially low state prices for their agricultural output, than they have given. Wars that the peasants little understand, but which have taken enormous tolls among them, as in Vietnam, Laos, and Cambodia, have undoubtedly alienated millions of people from the Saigon, Phnom Penh, and Vientiane regimes, which have not been able adequately to protect them.

Of fundamental importance is the emotional and psychological attachment of the peasant to his village. It is here that he was born and here that his grandparents and possibly his parents are buried. There is also probably a local "god," or spirit, that protects and otherwise aids him in his village setting. The transistor radio, new schools, expanded roads, previously unknown consumer goods that induce the villager to identify with buyers of his products elsewhere in the country, and the flow of young men and women to and from the national capitals have broken down some of the historic parochialism of the Southeast Asian peasant. But the village, even in the mid-1970's, was still a rival with the nation for the primary identification of the ordinary rice-roots farmer of the region.

Family Ties. Family ties are generally strong throughout Southeast Asia, and often the welfare of family businesses and other activities is placed above that of the nation. Trading with the Communist Vietnamese for a family profit in Cambodia, before the Vietnam war dramatically spilled over into that country, is a case in point. Malay politicians in Malaysia have claimed that local Chinese also put family above country, preferring short-term gain of improved or sustained family status to the long-term economic improvement of the nation. The late South Vietnamese President Ngo Dinh Diem may have been a true patriot, but his brother and sister-in-law worked largely for family, not state.

For many, even today in Southeast Asia, family poses the same problem as the village does for the rural peasant. It is very difficult, if not impossible, for some people in nearly all the countries to place the general welfare above the personal and so to put the nation above the family in terms of primary identification and loyalty. The point is not that family members are loyal to one another in various personal matters, but that they are loyal to one another in matters that are in no genuine way personal. They sacrifice for the family, as men and women elsewhere have done for the nation, at the expense of the nation. And often even the families of leaders like Thailand's ruling soldiers Sarit and Thanom have profited immensely at the expense of the country itself and its people.

Ideological and Political Loyalties. Although most of Southeast Asia's Communists are also nationalists, Communism is a competing ideology with nationalism and a rival for primary loyalty with the nation-state. Burma's Communists, for example, are apparently willing to accept some tactical guidance, perhaps in exchange for arms and ammunition, from the adjacent People's Republic of China. Some Southeast Asian national leaders have been similarly influenced by non-Communist foreign governments, too—but not Burma's! Burma's almost xenophobic nationalist leaders through the years, earlier civilian Premier U Nu no less than this antiforeign soldier-successor Ne Win, have never apparently accorded even partial loyalty to an alien ideological or political cause. Burma's Communists claim to serve two masters—the nation *and* Communism—but U Nu and Ne Win served only one: Burma.

The Burmese case is perhaps the most extreme one of this sort in Southeast Asia. Burmese nationalism has been as uncompromising as any in the area—but the behavior of Burma's Communists has been more typical. Indonesia's Communists, likewise, were probably more influenced by considerations related to their ideological identification than by their national loyalties at the time of the September, 1965, uprising. Similarly, the Communist insurgents of both Laos and Cambodia seem to identify as much with the cause of Indochina-wide Communism as with their own nations as such.

Communism, however, may not be the only political loyalty competing with the nation-state for support and identification in contemporary Southeast Asia. "Political Islam," the increasingly strong bloc of Muslim countries and their rulers, may tempt Malaysian leaders, for example, to emphasize the nonreligious importance of the faith of the Malay majority of the country over the interests of the 36 per cent Chinese minority. And some Filipinos are clearly more attracted to things American than to things Filipino, as evidenced by the huge numbers of citizens of the Philippines who annually migrate to the United States, a phenomenon that has no parallel anywhere else in Southeast Asia.

GOVERNMENT RESPONSES

Governments in Southeast Asia have responded in different ways to the problem of the obstacles posed to national integra-

tion by conflicting loyalties to ethnic group, religion, foreign nations, region, village, family, and ideology. They have sought to
woo minorities possessed of such competing alternative loyalties,
and they have battled them with the gun. They have tried to
draw them into active participation in the nation's political life,
and they have held them at more than political arm's length. And
they have been successful in some instances, not so successful in
others, and outright failures in still others.

Full and Equal Political Participation. The former Burmese
constitution, overthrown by power-seizing General Ne Win in
1962, provided for a federal union based on ethnic considerations
and ethnic minority, or communal, representation in the Chamber
of Nationalities, the second house of the original bicameral national legislature. The 1974 constitution, however, provides for 16
districts within a unitary structure of government and has no
ethnic representation as such in the People's Assembly. The aim
of Burma's new political order is full and equal participation of
all Burmese, those who accept "socialist democracy," that is, in
the nation's political life as Burmese (not as Burmans, Shans,
Karens, or other ethnic groups). Whether, however, the politics
of the "socialist republic" of Burma will result in the more effective integration of the country's various minorities remains to be
seen.

Singapore's People's Action Party government of Premier Lee
Kuan Yew has long pursued a policy of such equal participation
of all ethnic groups—Chinese, Malays, and Indians—in its political
life. Other governments, however, have limited the participation
of ethnic, religious, and ideological groups of one kind or another.
Malaysia's ruling Malay political elite is not yet probably willing
to share power fully with the country's large Chinese minority;
Indonesia's secular soldiers have sought to restrict the role of
Muslim parties, as such, in the country's politics, despite the
fact that they are themselves Muslims, and in South Vietnam, the
Philippines, and elsewhere Communist resort to force has been
partly occasioned by the political leadership's unwillingness to
permit the Communists to take part as equals in the country's political life.

Suppression. All the governments of the area have employed suppression as a means of forcing the integration of political, religious, and ethnic minorities in their countries. In Burma, the Ne Win government almost seemed to welcome the 1963 failure of peace talks with various rebels in order that it might return to the "less risky" policy of military action against the insurgents. In the first half of the 1970's, the Marcos regime in the Philippines employed all-out force against Muslim insurrectionists in Mindanao and Sulu. And anti-Communist administrations in Saigon, Vientiane, Phnom Penh, Rangoon, Bangkok, Kuala Lumpur, Jakarta, and Manila have all fought Communist insurgents to force an end to their armed opposition.

When attacked, a government presumably must strike back. But such a policy of counterattack has a tendency to become self-motivating—and, often, to persist beyond the time when it is really necessary (or desirable).

"Wooing." The Communist North Vietnamese have pursued a policy of "wooing"—or seeking a favorable response through rewards or promises thereof—toward the hill tribes in their part of the divided country. When Malaysia was being formed in the early 1960's, the Kuala Lumpur government of initiating Malaya offered the non-Malay peoples of still British-ruled Sarawak and Sabah, which possessed the theoretical option of separate independence, development funds and other benefits if they would join the federation. Ex-Burmese Premier U Nu, who both wooed and fought various of his country's minorities, was giving serious thought to conciliating the Shans and other non-Burman peoples by accepting their proposal for a revision of Burma's federal governing arrangements to give the ethnic group-based states increased powers when he was overthrown by General Ne Win in 1962.

Other governments—like those of Thailand and the Philippines—have also wooed minorities to draw them into the national political family but usually only after alienation had led to revolts among the Lao-like northeasterners in Thailand or the Filipino Muslims of the south.

Education. Malaysia, Burma, and Thailand, among other governments, have employed education as an instrument for helping to integrate their plural societies. The Malay leadership of Malaysia has sought the expanded and preferential teaching of the Malay language and has emphasized the teaching of Malay history and culture, while simultaneously seeking to restrict Chinese-language education. Similarly, Burma's government under both U Nu and Ne Win used the Burmese language and culture to unify the politically and ethnically divided country. The object was to educate the many peoples of Burma to think of themselves as one people, and various national days and other occasions were utilized for this purpose. Such efforts in both Malaysia and Burma and among the Filipino Muslims and various of Thailand's minorities have been somewhat counterproductive, at least in the short run, for some minorities have regarded such education as actually designed to terminate their distinct cultural identity.

Economic Development. Economic development has been pursued for its own sake throughout the area, but it has also been consciously used on behalf of greater national integration. Malaysia's leaders, for example, apparently believe that a true Malay-Chinese national partnership can exist only when the Malays, a slight majority, possess economic skills and power comparable with those of the country's large Chinese minority. Hence, a development policy partial to the majority Malays is perceived as bridging the economic gap between the country's two chief ethnic groups and aiding sociopolitical integration.

Thailand's use of economic means to foster national integration —among the northern Meo tribesmen, for instance—had had the initial consequence of upsetting traditional behavioral patterns and provoking very substantial resistance and here, too, fostering alienation rather than integration. The Philippines's Islamic minority, which was grossly exploited by individual non-Muslim Filipinos before it was ever offered any major economic development assistance by the Manila government, has so far been less conciliated by such aid than it has been further alienated by the Marcos regime's bombing and other military activity.

Control. The strategy of control has probably been employed, at one time or another, by all the Southeast Asian governments to isolate political, ethnic, and other minorities; integration is thus aided by preventing the spread of disunifying influences. This policy of "internal containment" is less heavyhanded and potentially counterproductive and much less bloody than suppression. Lee Kuan Yew's Singapore government has "controlled" the far-left opposition by detaining and later releasing various of its members. Similarly, Burma's Ne Win—after 1962—sought to "control" the civilian politicians he unseated by soliciting their participation in his new order and, when some of them refused, he jailed them. Many did respond affirmatively, however, and still others followed them after their release from detention. The object in both Singapore and Burma was to control a potentially troublesome political minority, the left-wing opposition in the case of Singapore and the old political elite in Burma, so that it would ultimately die off from nongrowth or insufficient replenishment.

Denial of Means of Expression. The policy of such "control" has ordinarily been accompanied by a related strategy of denying such minorities—ethnic, political, and ideological alike—adequate means of political expression. Burma's 1974 constitution, for example, proclaims the principle of full participation in the country's political life for all who accept a one-party, secular, socialist, unitary, "Burmese national" state—which excludes the country's Communists, many members of various minorities, and the remnants of U Nu's former democratic front. Underground newspapers and political plotting in churches in the Philippines are the direct result of the policies of Marcos's "constitutional authoritarianism"—which severely restricts the means of political expression of both the majority and such minorities as the "Christian democratic left" and the southern Muslims. The Islamic uprising, it should be noted, flared anew in the wake of Marcos's 1972–73 "constitutional takeover."

Denial of the means of political expression is designed partly to enhance national unity by limiting opposition that weakens the nation. Its effect, however, may be just the opposite.

THE RESULTS

After a quarter of a century of resumed independence, the problem of minority alienation persists throughout Southeast Asia, and the results of various policies of national integration are uneven. Some countries may be more united than they formerly were, others less so. Those that are more united and, thus, seemingly more successful in this aspect of their nation-building efforts would seem to be North Vietnam in the territory it rules (which is much less than all of Vietnam), Indonesia, Burma (for all its persisting insurrections), Malaysia, and Singapore. Seemingly less united than in the past, but not necessarily wholly unsuccessful in integrationist policies, are the Philippines, Thailand, South Vietnam, Laos, and Cambodia. Laos, however, could move dramatically and quickly to greater unity, possibly under Communist rule, while South Vietnam is probably more united today in the territory it rules than ever before (but it does not rule all of South Vietnam!).

The lesson to be learned from the different policy approaches to the problem of inadequate national integration in Southeast Asia is primarily that this key dimension of nation-building is a slow process. It may well be that conscious policies of forced or even encouraged integration may not work *because* they are conscious policies. Inadequately assimilated minorities, political and ideological as well as ethnic and religious, may not truly feel a part of the nation until they have a "stake in the society" as the nationalist majority would see it manifested. And this could take a great deal more time, at least the remainder of the twentieth century in all likelihood.

But majority leadership must still be aware of the problem of imperfect integration. All other policies and behaviors must be reviewed and sometimes altered to avoid further alienation of the minorities in question and a worsening of the problem. And some very drastic political and territorial surgery may still be necessary, such as the detachment of the southern Malays of peninsular Thailand, who probably should be part of Malaysia, or the redrawing of the map of eastern insular Southeast Asia to include the Filipino Muslims in Indonesia or Malaysia (or even to give them a state of their own). The trouble with such an extreme solution, which is not advocated publicly by any government in the area, is that any such change could increase the problem of minority agitation for altered political status throughout the area.

11

Modernization

The object of the nationalist revolution in all of the former colonies of Southeast Asia was to obtain freedom from foreign rule. "Modernization," one of the primary goals of the leaders of these nations after independence, has sought to reduce the *economic* dependence of such countries upon the major and more advanced states of the world. Full independence did not really follow the lowering of American, British, Dutch, or French flags over ex-colonies in Southeast Asia, because none of these lands was any less economically dependent on other countries of the world as a result of the transfer of legal sovereignty. Through various policies of modernization, the governments of the Southeast Asian countries have subsequently endeavored to attain, if not full economic independence, at least much less dependence on the so-called developed and primarily capitalist countries.

Modernization has also had other objectives: a higher living standard and a generally richer and fuller life for the ordinary men and women of the Southeast Asian countries, the development of human skills through expanded educational opportunities, the improved health and longer life expectancy of the population, and, not least of all, victory in the "population race" between man and resources through both more productive employment of human and natural riches and population control.

GOALS

Not all the Southeast Asian governments have pursued modernization goals with equal dedication, skill, or success, but all have sought to develop their national economies, improve the well-being of their inhabitants, and stimulate a sense of greater pride through accomplishment in the hearts of their citizens. Diminutive Singapore and energetic, but not especially resource-rich, Malaysia led the lands of the area by a large margin in accomplished modernization through the mid-1970's. Their economies are the most modern, their growth rates are the most impressive, and their dedication to the syndrome of goals symbolized by the term "modernization" is the strongest and most genuine. Considerable progress has been made by the Philippines and Thailand, too, although their growth has been more sporadic and the results have been more uneven. Indonesia has also moved with determination, skill, and a fair amount of success since the late 1960's, when General Suharto, his soldier supporters, and the technocrats took over, but much time, energy, and resources had previously been wasted by President Sukarno, who talked on behalf of development but did much to hinder its occurrence.

Far less has been achieved in the modernization of the economies—and life in general—of the two Vietnams, Cambodia, Laos, and Burma. The reasons, in general, are the same for all five lands located in the turbulent mainland portion of the region. Vietnam and Burma, in particular, are very resource-rich countries, but their energies have been absorbed in the politically motivated wars that have gripped their lands since the late 1940's (as have the talents and resources of Laos and Cambodia in more recent years). Reunification has been the main objective of the North Vietnamese Communist leadership since the French departure from the country. And Burma's Ne Win, whose multiple wars have been on a far smaller scale than the conflict in Vietnam, has given greater attention to the "nationalization" of his country's economy than to its modernization or development, as illustrated by his successful policy of driving out large numbers of ethnic Indian and Chinese entrepreneurs.

Long-Term Objectives. Vietnam and Burma are not the only countries where other priorities have competed with modernization for the attention of the leadership and the resources to translate such attention into accomplishment. Indonesia's onetime nationalist hero Sukarno sought international political leadership for his country—or himself (whom he often confused with his country)—while Marcos and previous Philippine Presidents, though to a lesser degree, seemed ordinarily to be more concerned with their personal predominance than anything else. But, even in these four politically preoccupied lands, development was one of the main proclaimed goals of government.

In the long run, economic modernization for almost all the lands of Southeast Asia has meant freedom from forced dependence on the developed lands for the purchase of largely unprocessed agricultural and extractive exports—food products, rubber, timber, minerals, and oil. Before the "energy crisis" of the mid-1970's, at least, most of Southeast Asian leaders perceived the "raw material countries" like themselves as perpetually and uncontrollably at the mercy of the industrial consuming nations. This meant that economic independence—even relatively speaking—could be achieved only as a result of some amount of industrialization (including steel mills and automobile factories), greater diversification of national economic activity and trading partners, and less reliance on foreign sources of consumer goods, raw materials, services such as shipping and insurance, and energy.

Short-Term Objectives. While almost all the Southeast Asian countries have welcomed economic and technical aid from other governments, and particularly international agencies, and some have also wooed private foreign capital, most of their leaders have been aware of the desirability of paying much of modernization's costs themselves. And this has meant an expansion and modernization of the agricultural sectors of their national economies, as well as industrialization, to earn dollars and other vitally needed international currencies.

Both agricultural and industrial development, however, require infrastructures to permit their growth to begin—and to continue. Roads, ports, and power stations, accordingly, have received high priority in development plans. The creation of an entirely new kind of labor force is also under way, which has meant not only expansion of literacy but, beyond that, development of technical schools and institutions of higher learning and training.

POLICIES

The policies for achieving both long- and short-term goals have varied considerably from country to country. In general, countries

like Singapore and Malaysia have placed "economics above politics," but even their economic policies often have also had non-
economic objectives, such as giving potentially pro-Communist
Singaporean Chinese a stake in their small but successful nation
or permitting the Malay majority in Malaysia to play a greater
role in their country's economic life through Malay political leadership–controlled state economic agencies. Governments in North
Vietnam and Burma have sought the attainment of their economic
objectives almost wholly through state means, while "free enterprise" has been responsible for much of the economic growth of
the Philippines and Thailand and might have accomplished more
in South Vietnam but for the past and continuing war in that
country.

Singapore, Malaysia, North Vietnam, Thailand, Indonesia,
Burma, and Cambodia under formerly ruling Prince Norodom
Sihanouk have all pursued four- or five-year "economic plans."
The Philippines and South Vietnam have also sought to plan their
development but in far less systematic government-directed fashion, while economic planning as such has never really been attempted in Laos. Plans in Indonesia, Burma, and Cambodia, however, were often very unrealistic and were abandoned or altered
beyond recognition.

Singapore, Malaysia, Thailand, and the Philippines—the four
most successfully modernizing countries in the region—have actively welcomed foreign private capital through the years, but Indonesia, Burma, and Cambodia were formerly highly suspicious
of such investment, as the Burmese still are. North Vietnam, because it is a Communist country and because of its recent war
with the Americans, has received only foreign government assistance, most of it from other Communist countries.

In general, the governments of Southeast Asia since independence have greatly expanded local processing of various raw materials and foodstuffs, such as the Philippine fruit-canning industry,
and have established a few heavy industries, like Indonesian steel
production. Internal transportation and communications have
been improved, but much still remains to be done in most of
the countries. The governments have encouraged the growing of
new crops and the export of various of these for the first time.

They have emphasized labor-intensive and often rural small manufacturing and reformed and rationalized fiscal and banking institutions and operations.

RESULTS

The results have been uneven, not just because of country-by-country differences in policies pursued or in the intensity with which they were pursued, but also because of other factors: size and complexity of the country, ideological and work attitudes, willingness of foreigners to help, and, not least of all, the incidence or nonincidence of internal political or even foreign wars. Singapore, the fastest-growing national economy in the area, had a nearly 15 per cent expansion in gross national product in 1973 and has been the most impressive of the Southeast Asian countries in terms of general as well as economic modernization. But, then, Singapore is a small country with no vast hinterland to develop, is an almost wholly urban state, and has a largely Chinese population that is extremely industrious. Furthermore, it inherited an established infrastructure and level of development from the colonial British. One-third of Singapore's GNP is derived today from manufacturing, but, though wholly self-supporting in services and capital through its exports of goods, Singapore has also never been more dependent on various other parts of the world, both for its raw material and the purchase of its exports and for the oil or other forms of energy to operate its increasingly industrialized economy.

Malaysia, which will complete its second five-year plan in 1975, has also experienced a booming economy with an annual growth rate of approximately 8 per cent in the first years of the 1970's. But Malaysia's exports remain for the most part primary ones, the traditional tin and rubber plus timber, of which the Malaysians became the world's leading exporter in the early 1970's. Malaysia, however, is second only to Singapore in Southeast Asia in the establishment of new industries, for which it has imported increasing amounts of machinery and related equipment.

Other countries have been less successful in their modernization efforts. Thailand in the late 1960's and early 1970's, partly as a result of economic benefits it derived from the nearby Vietnam war, seemed to be booming, but some of its heralded development turned out to be less than solidly based, and its economy was suffering serious difficulties in the mid-1970's. The Philippines, on the other hand, fell far short of expectations economically in the first quarter century of its independence but was coming on strong in the mid-1970's, assisted by unprecedented international demand and high prices for its primarily raw material exports. Indonesia, which made an extraordinary recovery from the economic mismanagement of the Sukarno years in the late 1960's and early 1970's, encountered stiffer going by the mid-1970's; its earlier economic growth of about 7 per cent annually was too concentrated in a few extractive industries like oil and so heavily dependent on foreign capital and expertise. Burma, which stagnated during much of the 1960's under General Ne Win's restrictive "Burmese Way to Socialism," was still losing ground in the 1970's under its first four-year plan. Its population growth slightly outstripped economic growth.

North Vietnam, which gave greater priority to the war with South Vietnam than to economic development in the years 1960–72, was engaged in a "crash program" in 1974 to re-establish and expand its onetime promising industrial base in order to support its agricultural sector. The economy of South Vietnam, however, had become so dependent upon the United States during the war that it was having extraordinary difficulty in the mid-1970's adjusting to a steadily diminishing American interest in the country, particularly since it still had to carry one of the proportionately heaviest military budgets in all Asia. The Cambodian and Laotian economies were in utter disarray as a consequence of the conflicts that had confronted them in recent years, and which continued in 1974 in Cambodia.

PROBLEMS

The economic problems of the mid-1970's, for the most part, were different, at least in form, from those experienced in the previous twenty-five years. The world inflationary spiral, for example, for the first time very seriously threatened to undermine the genuine growth accomplishments of the highly successful Singapore and Malaysian governments. Primary producers like the Philippines, Malaysia, and Indonesia were finding international demand for many of their exports to be the highest ever and with prices also at unprecedented levels; but the same inflationary demand also dramatically increased the costs of goods and services they needed to buy abroad, which were essential to their modernization efforts. Countries like Singapore, Malaysia, the Philippines, and Thailand had made great strides in modernizing their economies and other aspects of their national life, but they were still very vulnerable economically in the mid-1970's, particularly to the pressures of the oil-producing Arab states as well as the West, Japan, and the two Communist giants.

The historically surplus agricultural economies of the mainland countries experienced a quite different but no less serious type of trouble in the early 1970's. Bad weather and their own growing populations forced formerly ranking rice exporters Burma and Thailand to ban temporarily rice shipments abroad. This action also hurt the importing countries of Indonesia and the Philippines, which experienced short harvest and so could not meet domestic demands for the grain. Once rice-rich South Vietnam and Cambodia, meanwhile, appeared to have become nearly chronic importers of the grain as a result of the devastation and dislocation resulting from the wars with the Communists.

Despite such problems, however, much development did take place in Southeast Asia as a whole in the quarter-century 1949–74, and more of it occurred in the rural areas, especially in Malaysia, the Philippines, Burma, and Thailand, than has been generally appreciated. Modernization has "spread out," so to speak, no longer taking place only in the capital cities but extending to parts of the countryside where it was hardly felt a decade ago. In addition, hopes were high in the mid-1970's for early breakthroughs in petroleum exploration and exploitation in several countries, particularly in Malaysia, Thailand, Burma, the Philippines, and South Vietnam. But growing populations, higher domestic consumption levels, international inflation, and continuing or renewed internal political wars could pose still more problems in the years ahead.

POLITICAL IMPLICATIONS

The political implications of what has taken place in terms of economic, educational, health, and general modernization in Southeast Asia to date, and what may yet happen, are far-reaching. New kinds of societies are being shaped, albeit slowly, and this means new problems, such as those associated with urbanization, industrial labor, pollution, and energy supplies. It also promises creation of new interests and new political actors working on behalf of more and new kinds of interest groups. The progress to date, moreover, in lands like Singapore, Malaysia, and Thailand has stimulated popular economic expectations to new levels, and there will be growing political demands for their satisfaction.

Southeast Asia, in addition, is not a series of unconnected lands where developments in one country do not influence neighboring nations. There was once the fear in Washington and many Southeast Asian capitals that Communism would threaten the whole of the region if it triumphed militarily in one of the countries of the area. It is very possible, however, that this "domino theory" may work more decisively in other (and largely nonmilitary) ways; that is, development progress in one country may strongly stimulate modernization efforts or possibly dissatisfaction with the lack of such efforts in nearby lands. As an illustration, the Malaysian "modernization example" has not been lost on many persons today in both Indonesia and Thailand, while at least some Burmese question why their land lags far behind the neighboring Thai in terms of development.

The precise political results of what has been accomplished economically in Southeast Asia in the last quarter-century cannot be predicted. But, if politics is in any way economically influenced, then the largely politically induced economic changes of the past twenty-five years will have a feedback effect in the quarter-century to come. The new economies will surely aid the emergence of new political processes, just as the new politics and independence have already dramatically altered national economies.

12

Foreign Policy

Two aims dominated the foreign policies of the Southeast Asian states through the mid-1970's: the preservation of national independence in a world of military and other dangers and the acquisition of some of the surplus resources of the richer countries to facilitate modernization of their economies. Burma alone of the ten nation-states of Southeast Asia did not participate in, or otherwise support, a war in (or against) another country in the years after World War II. The Burmese, however, did receive foreign aid through these years from a variety of sources, as did all the other countries of the area. Malaysia and Singapore received much less assistance than the other lands of the region, but their political leaders were among the most successful in attracting foreign private capital—for the same purposes as most of the other lands accepted direct aid from the United States, the Soviet Union, and China, among others: to assist them to become more economically modern, diversified, and self-supporting states.

Other problems also presented themselves in the twenty-five-year period 1949–74 that required foreign-policy responses from the Southeast Asian governments, but none of these was anywhere nearly as important as the quest for security and development resources.

THE SEARCH FOR SECURITY

Almost from the start of resumed independence, two very different approaches guided the Southeast Asian governments in their respective searches for security. Some of the states, particu-

larly Thailand and the Philippines, sought their security in partnership with a larger and more powerful nation, the United
States. Both the Bangkok and Manila governments very much
feared the new People's Republic of China, proclaimed by Mao
Tse-tung in 1949, but neither land possessed the means to deter a
potentially aggressive China. Their strategy, accordingly, was to
mobilize some of the resources of the United States, front-ranking
among the world's military powers in the early postwar years, to
protect themselves against a possible Peking challenge. Other
governments, however, such as that of Burma under both U Nu
and Ne Win, sought to remain aloof from great-power rivalries by
not associating themselves closely with any of the major nations
of the world. The Burmese aim was to avoid becoming the enemy
of one of the great powers as a result of its relations with a rival
of such a power.

Nonalignment. The first "neutralist" government in Southeast
Asia probably was Thailand, although its attempted nonalignment occurred during the first forty years of the century and was
very successful. Burma, however, was the first of the former colonies to pursue a nonaligned foreign policy after independence.
Premier U Nu, however, initially sought some kind of military
guarantee from the British and the Americans following the Communist victory over the Nationalists in China and adopted a foreign policy of neutralism only after London and Washington both
declined to give his Rangoon government any such commitment.
By the mid-1970's the most truly nonaligned of all the Southeast
Asian governments was still Burma, which has never been the
ally of either of the Communist countries, despite its present
Communist-type economy and political system, or of the United
States. The Burmese, indeed, have so far refused to join the five-
nation Association of Southeast Asian Nations (ASEAN) because
that would represent an abandonment of their strictly honored
policy of noninvolvement (which is even more neutral than "nonaligned").

Indonesia also pursued a foreign policy of nonalignment from
the start of independence, for essentially the same reason as
George Washington urged such an approach on his countrymen
in the formative years of the United States—the avoidance of en-

tanglement in the dangerous power politics of the older and less idealistic states of the world. While avoiding any semblance of an alliance with a great power in their initial years of resumed independence, the Indonesians nonetheless played an increasingly active diplomatic role in their part of the world and among the nonaligned lands of the "third world" in general; they described their foreign policy as one of "active independence." In the early 1950's, indeed, the Jakarta government consulted increasingly regularly with four other nominally nonaligned countries—India, Pakistan, Burma, and Ceylon (now Sri Lanka)—who were known as the "Colombo Powers." And the first international conference of independent Asian and African states in history was convened in 1955 in Bandung, Indonesia. Recipient of military aid from the United States, Indonesia's pro-American government was by no means neutral in sentiment or behavior by the mid-1970's, however, although Jakarta still attended nonaligned nations' conferences.

Cambodian Prince Norodom Sihanouk, who made his country's foreign policy almost by himself from 1954 to 1970, was widely known as a "neutralist" leader, but, like Burma's U Nu, he initially sought a security partnership with one of the great powers. The Prince, who feared Communist Vietnamese conquest of his militarily weak country, proposed Cambodian membership in SEATO to the United States in 1954. He became an outspoken "neutralist" and frequent critic of the Americans only after President Dwight D. Eisenhower responded that the Phnom Penh government's participation in the Southeast Asian security alliance would be too obvious a violation of the 1954 Geneva Accords.

Nonalignment was supposed to be the foreign policy of both Cambodia and Laos following the Geneva Accords. It was hoped that this would insulate these two weak lands from exploitation by the major contestants in the great confrontation between the Communists and the anti-Communists on the international scene and in Southeast Asia. The Laotian leader Prince Souvanna Phouma made a genuine effort to pursue a neutralist foreign policy, but his attempt was undercut almost from the start by the anti-Communist and antineutralist Americans, to the great cost and later regret of Washington and to the much greater cost of Laos.

Although Prince Souvanna Phouma would now like to resume a policy of genuine neutrality, and his military patron of the years 1964–74, the United States, would like to see him do so, Laotian rightist military elements are not universally sympathetic to such a strategy.

The most important newcomer to the ranks of the avowedly nonaligned nations of Southeast Asia in the 1970's was Malaysia. Neither Malaysia nor Singapore followed nonaligned foreign policies in the first years of independence, but neither were they allies of the major powers of the cold war.

Although the Malaysians remained partial to the Americans and the Saigon government in the Vietnam war through the January, 1973, "settlement," they were also the first of the non-Communist countries of the area to exchange diplomatic representatives with Hanoi after the American combat disengagement from the otherwise continuing Vietnamese conflict. Despite their past partiality to the Saigon side, the Malaysians' official reaction to Vietnam has been strongly negative. Premier Tun Abdul Razak and his chief supporters believe that South Vietnam suffered more than it benefited from American participation in the war with Hanoi. The crux of the Malaysian position—which can be described as a "better red than dead" posture—is that the U.S. performance in defense of South Vietnam was excessively destructive and was probably not worth it. As Kuala Lumpur sees it, other Southeast Asian governments would be wise to avoid ever being placed in a situation requiring such destructive foreign help.

The Malaysians, who have become active participants in the meetings of the world's nonaligned nations, have proposed a method for avoiding "more Vietnams": neutralization of Southeast Asia as a whole, as contrasted with the neutralization of only a few countries of the area, such as Laos and Cambodia. In 1972, the other ASEAN countries endorsed the principle of such a "zone of peace and neutrality" in Southeast Asia, but they all expressed the fear privately that China might exploit the area's neutralization. What the Malaysians have urged is that the ASEAN lands—and the other countries of the area—abstain from alliance or other preferential relations with any of the great powers. According to the Kuala Lumpur government, this would result in none of the great powers having a reason to move against any Southeast Asian country, because no country would be allied with any of its rivals. In the case of Vietnam, as the Malaysians see it, the United States fought on Saigon's side—and destroyed much of the country in the process—because of Hanoi's relationship with Peking and Moscow. The real point of "neutralization," however, would appear to be the elimination of any possible justification for China to take action against one or more Southeast Asian states, because none of the states of the area would be an American, or Soviet, ally.

Partnership. The Philippines, a former American colony, and Thailand were the first Southeast Asian countries to enter into security partnerships with the United States. The Vietnamese Communists, however, were a party to such a relationship with the Soviet Union and China very early in the post–World War II period and were recognized by Moscow and Peking as the government of all Vietnam in 1950. For all three Southeast Asian parties—Manila, Bangkok, and Hanoi—the object was the same: to harness the surplus resources of a friendly major power to fulfill the goals of a smaller state. The point was to make the smaller country's "enemy" the "enemy" of the great power, so that the major government would henceforth treat the lesser state's aims almost as its own.

The United States retained bases in the Philippines when it ended its rule over the islands in 1946, but the 1951 mutual-defense treaty between Manila and Washington was more of Filipino than American urging. U.S. military aid to Thailand began as early as 1950, when the Thai were already working for a SEATO-like regional alliance, which came into being in 1954 (including as its members, besides Bangkok and Washington, the Philippines, Australia, New Zealand, Pakistan, Britain, and France). Thailand and the Philippines had both wanted such a military grouping for several years, which makes it difficult to accept the old criticism that the Americans manipulated various of their friends in the area into the alliance.

Cambodia under Sihanouk desired SEATO membership but was denied participation, as Burma had earlier been refused British and American security guarantees before it adopted its foreign policy of "neutralism." Malaysia and Singapore had—and still have—defense ties with Britain, which is not the same as being members of SEATO or formal allies of the United States but is also quite different from being nonaligned. Of necessity, South Vietnam, Laos, and Cambodia became very close allies of the Americans in the years leading up to the mid-1970's. Similarly, the Indochina war forced North Vietnam into even greater dependency upon the Chinese and the Soviets as the price of gaining access to their resources for use in its war against Saigon and the Americans.

The increasing attention accorded Malaysia's proposal for neutralization of Southeast Asia notwithstanding, there were probably more *de facto* (as contrasted with formal) allies of the United States in the area in 1974 than there had been twenty years earlier. The Philippines, Thailand, South Vietnam, Laos, and Cambodia were still military partners of Washington, and Indonesia, the region's biggest country, and Singapore, its smallest, were strongly urging the United States not to pull back too far. Jakarta and Singapore—no less than Manila. Bangkok, Saigon, Vientiane, and Phnom Penh—wanted to use surplus U.S. power for the furtherance of their own foreign-policy security objectives.

ECONOMIC AND TECHNICAL AID

Nonalignment or partnership as strategies of survival in a dangerous world were largely short-term policies, accommodations to the threats, real or imagined, of the 1950's through the mid-1970's. Even alliance-inclined governments like Manila and Bangkok included some persons by the mid-1970's who argued a marked decrease in the need for a military partnership with the Americans, while the once pro-Communist Indonesian Government wanted the United States to remain in the region at least until 1980, by which time Jakarta hoped to be able to play a larger military role in the region's defense. Security policies clearly were undergoing alteration in the mid-1970's in response to Sino-American *"détente,"* the disengagement-motivated "Nixon Doctrine" that placed greater reliance on the Southeast Asian states for their own defense, and the new multipolar relationship in East Asia among the Chinese, Japanese, Soviets, and Americans. Since the friends, or even enemies, of the Southeast Asian governments increasingly appeared to be far from permanent ones, the policies creating or accepting existing relationships could hardly be regarded as stable.

The quest for resources for development purposes, however, was a greater long-range necessity. Policies in pursuit of such foreign help also changed in the 1970's, but their objective remained constant: to obtain economic and technical help from abroad to support modernization processes that might well fail—and bring down ruling elites—if additional resources were not found. Only North Vietnam received no American Government aid in the years 1950–74; Malaysia and Singapore received only modest amounts of such U.S. public assistance but did benefit immensely from American private investment and related technical and managerial assistance. The U.S.S.R. provided aid to North Vietnam, Indonesia, Laos, Cambodia, Burma, Thailand, and Malaysia at different times in the same quarter-century. Hanoi, Jakarta, Vientiane, Phnom Penh, and Rangoon also received Chinese help. Even anti-Communist Bangkok and Manila were aided by China in the early 1970's, with much-appreciated "sales" of oil and rice.

The policies of individual Southeast Asian governments with respect to foreign aid were an extension of their internal ideologies, institutions, and development policies. In the early 1950's, already quasi-socialist Burma was a recipient of U.S. foreign assistance, but Premier U Nu terminated such aid because of American CIA involvement in the internal affairs of his country. Under General Ne Win from 1962 on, Burma became increasingly socialist economically and politically; it accepted aid from Moscow and Peking but not from Washington and sent most of its overseas students to Communist countries and none to the United States. But the Burmese did enter into contracts with American petroleum firms for offshore oil exploration and exploitation to take advantage of U.S. technical expertise and marketing connections as well as to boost its sorely depleted foreign-exchange reserves and its sadly lagging development plan.

Indonesia under Suharto welcomed both U.S. foreign aid and private investment, as have the Philippines, Thailand, Malaysia,

Singapore, and South Vietnam. Japanese aid, investment, and trade have been sought by nearly all the Southeast Asian states, but Japanese tactics and behavior, which have led to rioting, continuing student protests, and angry editorials, alienated the countries of the area even more than an earlier generation of "ugly Americans." Soviet trade with the area also increased dramatically in the 1960's, and China seemed to be expanding its commercial relations with most of the Southeast Asian lands in the 1970's.

OTHER PROBLEMS

The quests for security and development assistance have preoccupied nearly all the Southeast Asian governments for the past quarter-century. But there have been other problems they have had to deal with in their foreign relations, although none of these have been of the same commanding importance.

A case can be made—and a very good one!—that, over-all, the states of Southeast Asia have used other nations, like the United States, more than they have themselves been used by such countries. South Vietnam, Thailand, and the Philippines probably took greater advantage of the United States through the years than the United States took of them. Nonetheless, the Americans did also use the Thai and the Filipinos for ends that were more narrowly American than Thai or Filipino. The U.S. "containment" policy of the years after 1949 did not reflect real American concern for the nations of Southeast Asia but rather fear of the People's Republic of China and determination to mobilize all the lands of Southeast Asia against it. In the mid-1970's, a strikingly similar attempt to "contain" China was being made by the U.S.S.R. and its ally, India, both of whom had reasons, not unlike those of the Americans earlier, for checking China. The Malaysian proposal for a neutralized Southeast Asia was designed in part to avoid just such "use" of Southeast Asia. Throughout the quarter-century since 1950, Southeast Asians have had to be on their guard against being used in this manner, and there is no reason to believe that they will not have to keep up such a guard for the rest of the century.

The Southeast Asian countries have also had to be careful not to be dominated, economically and culturally no less than politically, militarily, or ideologically. Indonesia in the 1970's sought a continued American economic presence in the area, partly to offset feared Japanese economic domination, and sought expanded Australian technical assistance to acquire some of the skills that the more economically powerful Japanese were not willing to share. Similarly, North Vietnam sought to play off China and the Soviet Union to avoid being dominated by either.

Relations among the nations of the area have predictably increased in the quarter-century since independence as "new states" got to know one another, developed more active foreign policies, and discovered common interests. The Association of Southeast Asian Nations (ASEAN), formed in 1967, had become by 1974 a major forum and foreign policy–harmonizing instrument of Indonesia, Thailand, Malaysia, Singapore, and the Philippines. Ostensibly economic and cultural in character at the time of its inauguration, ASEAN endorsed in principle Malaysia's neutralization proposal, sought to coordinate the China policies of its five-member states, and played a mediating role among its members when they fell out, as Malaysia and the Philippines did over the latter's still unsatisfied claim to the easternmost Malaysian state of Sabah.

ASEAN also sought to coordinate various international commodity marketing activities of its members, to increase trade among these countries and with such outsiders as the European Economic Community, and to further regional economic specialization. The individual member countries and other lands, however, also sought to expand their commercial relations with new trading partners, like the Soviet Union and the People's Republic of China, by other means.

TRENDS

Several trends were apparent in the foreign policies of the Southeast Asian states in the mid-1970's. Expanded cooperation among the states of the area was one of the most important of these, within and outside ASEAN. Malaysia agreed to diplomatic relations with China in 1974, and there were talks between the

Chinese and the Thai, Filipinos, and Indonesians that could lead to early improved ties between Peking and these other ASEAN governments. Indeed, both the Soviet Union and China seemed destined to play larger roles in the region's affairs in the years ahead, as trade partners no less than as intervening great powers (although the U.S.S.R., in particular, increased its political influence in the area in the late 1960's and early 1970's, when both China and the United States were concentrating so much of their attention on Indochina). And Japan also will probably exercise more influence in the future, but it may be less of a friend and benefactor and more that of threat—and possibly not just economically.

With the exception of landlocked Laos, all the Southeast Asian nations may possess petroleum deposits of varying significance off their shores, and this could make them even more important to outside nations in the 1980's and after. Indonesia was experiencing an oil boom in the mid-1970's, and operations were under way in both Burma and Malaysia that could prove highly profitable to these two countries. Oil, however, could be as much a bother as a blessing. Large new petroleum finds could tempt outsiders to try once again to dominate the region.

The international relations of Southeast Asia will probably be lively—if not bloody—for many years to come. And foreign policy will continue as a major preoccupation of its different political elites.

13

Rights and Freedoms

The balance between liberty and restraint has been constantly shifting in Southeast Asia over the past quarter-century. There was probably greater freedom, particularly of speech, in a few of the lands of the area in the mid-1970's than there had been earlier in the postcolonial period. But during the past decade there has also been much erosion of civil liberties in the region as a whole, and the state of human rights and freedoms is not a generally favorable one today.

All the states of Southeast Asia have been at war—internal or foreign—at one time or another during the last twenty-five years, and some countries have been involved in both types of military conflict simultaneously. Domestic and external opponents of existing governments have sought to subvert governments that are unusually vulnerable because of their shallow roots and limited experience and to induce the general population to alter their political, ideological, and even national loyalties. Extensive subversive operations have also been conducted by all of the major powers—the United States as much as, if not more than, China or the Soviet Union. And nationalist, religious, and other zealots have tried to make the new era of accomplished independence also an age of the restoration of old orthodoxies or the establishment of new doctrines.

The general climate, in short, has not been conducive to the kind of tolerance and mutually respected liberties that are the essence of true human freedom—political or otherwise.

"POSITIVE" FREEDOMS

Freedom of speech and association underlay the democratic governmental systems with which nearly all the new states of Southeast Asia began their resumed independence. Two other freedoms—of movement and religion or belief—were also part of the early postcolonial ideological setting. These four freedoms, however, which never became firmly established institutionally in most of the Southeast Asian societies, have been the objects of almost constant attack. In many lands they have perished almost altogether, while in other countries they are partly alive but seriously endangered. In no nation of the area are they fully applicable and meaningful today.

Speech. In only one country, Thailand, formerly one of the less liberal of the lands of Southeast Asia, was there anything really resembling freedom of speech in 1974. The freest press in all Southeast Asia was to be found in Thailand after the antimilitary uprising of October, 1973, and, even under the former and fairly benevolent Thanom soldier dictatorship, the Thai press had not been severely restricted. But people were saying things in Thailand in the mid-1970's that they would not have dared to say at the decade's start, although it is not certain that they would have been jailed or otherwise punished if they had done so. Part of the old restraints in Thailand, which may have had their roots in the far from distant age of unrestricted monarchical rule, were of the mind and tradition and persisted without the need of governmental sanctions.

Four countries—the Philippines, Burma, Singapore, and Malaysia—suffered serious losses of once very free speech in the 1960's and early 1970's. Filipino politicians and journalists formerly constituted almost a caricature of unrestrained political license. Even the best Filipino publications, such as the subsequently repressed daily *Manila Times* and weekly *Philippine Free Press*, carried much material that would never have been printed because of its questionable accuracy in the older democracies (and the *Times* and *Free Press* were models of responsibility compared with some of their competitors!). Politicians in the Philippines also engaged

in endless mud-slinging with opponents that knew no limitations
on the kinds of baseless charges leveled in pursuit of political objectives. Yet, although the Philippine political system was a free
one as far as what members of the ruling elite could say about one
another is concerned, it was also a system very much manipulated
by a comparatively small number of men who owned empires of
newspapers, magazines, and radio and TV stations that monopolized the "public media" as in no other democracy.

Even this kind of freedom of speech died in the Philippines in
September, 1972, when President Marcos proclaimed martial law
and closed down all the newspapers and magazines as well as the
country's radio and TV stations. Those that were subsequently allowed to resume operations, or that replaced the former giants of
Filipino communications, have not been permitted to criticize
Marcos's so-called New Society. Similarly, General Ne Win, when
he seized power in 1962, shut down a once free Burmese press
that was far more responsible in its heyday than its Philippine
counterpart. Singapore's Lee Kuan Yew has also selectively closed
down newspapers, while great pressure has been brought on such
publications in Malaysia not to print what the government does
not want to see in print. In the three lands—Malaysia, Singapore, and Burma—broadcasting has been government-operated,
after the formal model of Britain's BBC, but misused to an increasing extent through the years.

The press is more free today in Suharto's Indonesia than it used
to be under Sukarno, but it is still not free to say everything it
wants to say. In the two Vietnams, Cambodia, and Laos, there has
never been real freedom of speech since independence, partly,
but not exclusively, because of the wars that have been waged in
these lands.

Association. Freedom of association—or of organization and assembly—is an essential element of a free political society, but it
has probably never been as restricted in Southeast Asia as it is today. In Burma, the 1974 constitution effectively prevents the
country's citizens from forming political parties of their choice;
that is, it makes all parties illegal, except the government-created
Burma Socialist Program Party. Thailand also banned political
parties before the 1973 overthrow of the Thanom military dic-

tatorship, and free association in political parties is not possible today in either North or South Vietnam. Communist parties, too, are banned everywhere in Southeast Asia—except in North Vietnam—whether they are in revolt against the government or not; the restrictions are against Communists *per se* rather than against acts that Communists might commit. Other parties are specifically prohibited in some countries, such as the anti-Communist Muslim *Masjumi* party in Indonesia, some of whose members participated in a revolt against former President Sukarno. And opposition parties have been required to combine in new government-sponsored umbrella organizations or are otherwise harassed, as in Indonesia and Singapore.

Other political—or potentially political—organizations like labor unions have been similarly restricted, harassed, or controlled, as under the dictatorships of Burma, South Vietnam, and Thailand. Prohibitions have also been issued against political meetings above a government-determined size or for particular purposes in Malaysia, Singapore, South Vietnam, Cambodia, Burma, and the Philippines. And, in Malaysia, the subjects of race, religion, language, or "Malay privileges" cannot be publicly discussed.

The purpose of such restrictions on free association is the same throughout the region: to control or even eliminate organizations that are perceived to threaten the ruling elite.

Movement. Men and women are not free to leave most of the Southeast Asian countries—when they want to do so—at the present time. There are even criminally and politically innocent persons who are held as hostages because relatives deemed unfriendly to the government are abroad speaking critically of the government. A case in point is the Philippines, where the wife and family of opposition leader and former Senator Raul S. Manglapus had to flee the country clandestinely by boat because the Marcos government would not allow them to leave as an act of retaliation against Manglapus' criticism of Filipino dictatorship before audiences in the United States. The reasons for restraint on travel by Filipinos are not economic, as the government has argued. Even Filipinos whose travel would be financed by friends, companies, or educational institutions out of funds outside the Philippines have been prohibited under martial law from leaving their once free country. For many Filipinos, their lovely island-country became, after 1972, a veritable political jail.

In Burma, among other Southeast Asian countries, nationals do not even retain possession of their passports when they return from abroad; these are surrendered to immigration authorities at the port of arrival. The result is that the government must be petitioned for permission for any departure from the country, whatever the purpose, destination, or financing. A consequence of such restrictions is to keep persons deemed opponents of the regime virtual prisoners of their country. Not irrelevantly, it keeps such men and women from telling others in freer lands of the extent to which human liberties have been restricted in their nation and from forming embarrassing, or even threatening, expatriate political movements.

Religion. Most of Southeast Asia's constitutions proclaim the freedom of their citizens to practice the religion of their choice, and there has probably been a modest increase in real religious freedom since independence. Many, though not all, of Southeast Asia's leaders are themselves secularists, and they have vigorously opposed recurrent efforts—in Indonesia, for example—to give the followers of the majority religion a privileged status in the society or to provide new or greater state support to such a religion. Non-Buddhist Burmese, especially among the hill people, regarded former Premier U Nu's decision to make Buddhism the state religion as a potential threat to their freedom of belief, despite U Nu's passionate public espousal of the simultaneous right of freedom of religion. The non-Buddhists argued that, if nothing really would be changed, as U Nu asserted, there was no point (but much danger) in giving Buddhism such official status. (U Nu's reason for taking the action, incidentally, was probably to earn religious "merit" for himself, indicating the overlapping spheres of the personal and the public, the religious and the political, in Burma under his leadership.)

Roman Catholicism clearly possessed a privileged position in South Vietnam under President Ngo Dinh Diem, but this was no longer the case in the mid-1970's, although Catholics remained politically important in the Buddhist-majority country out of proportion to their numbers. The Islamic faith has not been the object of political discrimination in the Philippines, but Muslims have been treated as second-class citizens because of their limited number and low educational and economic status. But the majority Thai and Malay populations of Thailand and Malaysia have equated national identity with Buddhism and Islam, respectively, to the political and general disadvantage of their minorities and "nonbelievers."

"NEGATIVE" FREEDOMS

There are two freedoms that can be best expressed in terms of freedom *from* something. They are freedom from arbitrary arrest or other restraint and freedom from want. The first of these freedoms is largely nonexistent in Southeast Asia today, while "freedom from want" does not really exist in those lands in which degrading work conditions exist and the victims of such conditions can do little to alter their cirmumstances.

Freedom from Arbitrary Action. One of the most able and dedicated public servants in recent Philippine political history—Senator Benigno S. Acquino, Jr.—remained unjustifiably under detention by the self-imposed government of his country in 1974 wholly because of the fear he caused on the part of President Marcos. Treason and other charges were belatedly brought against Acquino, who remained in the custody of the Marcos government, which believed that the young and very popular legislator could successfully lead a national revolt against it. Senator José W. Diokno, freed in September 1974 after two years' detention, was one of the outstanding defenders of civil liberties in all Philippine history and, more than any other Filipino, might have successfully resisted various of the Marcos government's limitations on political freedoms. In Burma, U Nu was also jailed from 1962 to 1966 to allow Ne Win to consolidate his political position. Hundreds of other Burmese and Filipinos have also been held without charges in the wake of the overthrow of elected governments in their once democratic countries. South Vietnam, however, has probably been the most notorious of the Southeast Asian lands for jailing its political prisoners for years on end without trial, but Singapore and Indonesia have jailed opponents, too, often for largely political reasons.

Those who have been detained in this manner in Southeast Asia have ranged the political spectrum from Communist to extremely conservative, with many very dedicated democrats among their ranks. Their "crimes," on the whole, have been their availability and credibility as alternative leaders to those in power. The conclusion to be drawn from the first twenty-five years of independence in many Southeast Asian countries is that it has become increasingly dangerous to be viewed by the country's leadership as a rival for control of government.

Freedom from Want. Freedom from want means economic security—at least to the extent of having enough of the right kinds of foods to eat, a decent place to sleep, and sufficient clothing. But there is no freedom from want in much of the area today. Nor is there—and this is equally important from the perspective of human liberties in the region—the freedom to seek to change prevailing patterns of inequity, exploitation, deprivation, and near-slavery.

The Philippines is a particular case in point. Conditions on sugar plantations in some parts of the country are among the most oppressive in the world, but efforts by the agricultural proletariat or its sympathizers, like socially conscious Catholic priests and laymen, to protest or alter such conditions have been met by various types of oppression, including physical brutality and even murder. Burmese peasants are by no means as oppressed—indeed, they may not even be oppressed at all—but they are required to sell their produce to the government on the government's terms, and they are denied any real means of protest except self-punishing reduction of agricultural output or dangerous resort to black-marketing. *Most* Indonesians are less well-off today than they were in Dutch colonial times, although *some* Indonesians are *very* well-off. Many Vietnamese, Laotian, and Cambodian peasants enjoy neither economic freedom nor freedom from a war that drastically restricts their ability to feed themselves and others.

The Free—and Not So Free—States

Comparative evaluation of the civil freedoms of the states of Southeast Asia is not easy for a number of reasons. There often are great variations in the degree of freedom in different areas of

human activity within a single country, and there have been no
less great fluctuations in the support of civil liberties within individual nations over time during the past quarter-century. Civil
liberties were probably more genuinely respected in more ways
in the Philippines before the 1972 declaration of martial law than
anywhere else in the area—but, even in the Philippines before
1972, both police and politicians were often unbelievably brutal
in their treatment of less privileged Filipinos, and so for such
Filipinos there was little real freedom. Under President Marcos's
"New Society," ordinary citizens have been treated with far
greater respect than previously, and they are no longer bullied by
their leaders or other public officials. But there is no freedom of
speech or assembly in the country today.

There is no state in Southeast Asia where there is strong across-
the-board institutional support for human rights and freedoms as
there is in America, Britain, or the continental European countries. Probably the greatest freedom of person—and of the right to
legal defense and protection—is to be found in Malaysia and transitional Thailand. There are limits, however, on free speech and
association in Malaysia, while Thailand's new-found freedoms
have been so recently obtained that it is not really possible to do
more than point them out and hope that they will last. Political
freedoms are more restricted in Indonesia, Singapore, and the
Philippines than in the first two countries, but the legal rights of
those who do not politically oppose the government do not seem
to have been curtailed. Burma and Laos have even fewer freedoms than the latter three countries, while human rights are probably even less respected in the two war-ravaged Vietnams and
Cambodia.

THE REASONS WHY

Civil liberties lack roots in the political and social soil of Southeast Asia. Men had no rights under the arbitrary governing institutions that existed before the European colonial era, and their
subsequent foreign rulers variously limited freedom of speech,
association, movement, and even religion. The nationalist Sukarno
and other anti-Dutch Indonesians were detained for long periods

in disease-ridden New Guinea, a veritable tropical Siberia, by the Netherlands. There was no freedom of speech at all, in written or spoken form, in old French Indochina or the former Dutch East Indies. And Spain literally forced Filipinos to become Christians when it took over their islands.

During World War II, Japanese rule over all Southeast Asia was much more restrictive of human freedoms than colonial government under the Americans and the British—or even the French and Dutch—had ever been. After the war, Indonesians and Vietnamese fought to free themselves from foreign rulers who wanted to re-establish their previous dominance. The eight-year anticolonial war in Vietnam, moreover, was followed by a second and even longer conflict. And externally aided civil wars have raged in adjacent Laos and Cambodia as well as Burma, Malaysia, the Philippines, Indonesia, and Thailand.

Against such a background, and in such an environment, it would be surprising if civil liberties had not suffered a steady decline and erosion. Many of the rulers of Southeast Asia, moreover, have been, and still are, despotic men, who seized power by force. A political climate of respect and support for human rights and liberties would be the kind of setting in which the rule of such men could be more easily challenged. For this reason, progress toward greater human freedom in Southeast Asia can be expected to be very slow in the years ahead.

14

Criticism and Competition

The concept of a loyal opposition is foreign to the political experience of most of the Southeast Asian states. There is no shortage of opposition to governments in this part of the world, but much of it is armed and some of it is even loyal to "distant aunts," as the Burmese colorfully put it. Largely because of the conspiratorial character of opposition to continued colonial rule before independence, many political leaders have genuine difficulty in comprehending the concept of opposition that is loyal and constructive instead of subversive and destructive. And those who have opposed existing governments have often been so completely hostile to such rulers that any means seemed to them to be justified to topple such regimes—even terror, rebellion, and murder.

So small were many of the new political elites of Southeast Asia at independence that they rarely included enough men and women to form both a government and a loyal opposition. In Burma and Indonesia, there almost literally were not enough experienced political actors to go around—even though Indonesia seemed superficially to have an excess of politicians. It was expected that time would change this situation, but it has not really done so. And there have been two reasons in particular why it has not done so: "Postdemocratic" dictatorial politics have dramatically limited political participation in a new way; and military and civilian dictators alike have reacted very negatively to opposition to their rule and placed many more persons in jail for political reasons than had been imprisoned in the first years of independence. The human cost of playing the role of opposition has increased dramatically in Southeast Asia in the last quarter-century.

LIMITS OF CRITICISM

Criticism took place in the mid-1970's in nearly all the Southeast Asian political systems, though least of all in North Vietnam and Cambodia, two countries that were otherwise very dissimilar. But this was everywhere "restricted criticism," and it was a criticism that everywhere fell short of honest opposition to an incumbent government, except in an occasionally veiled sense. Opposition there was, of course, but almost all genuine opposition was illegal, either because it had been so declared or, no less important, because it sought to overthrow the system rather than to change its policies and political leaders peacefully.

Programs, Not Policies. Programs may be publicly criticized in Burma and the Philippines—but not ex-General Ne Win's "Burmese Way to Socialism" or Filipino President Marcos's "New Society." The policies of Burmese socialism and a new Philippine society must be accepted by all participants in the legitimate political process; those who criticize the fundamental assumptions or policies of the ruling elites in these two countries are very likely to become political detainees. Indonesia and most of the other lands of the area similarly limit the extent to which basic policies—as contrasted with implementing programs and the manner in which they are implemented—can be criticized publicly. It is not politically permissible anywhere in the area to ask any more, "Where should we go?" But it is still possible to inquire, "How can we get there?"

Secondary, Not Primary, Problems. Malaysia's primary problems involve race, religion, and language; those of South Vietnam and Cambodia concern the Communist alternative to the present ruling groups in these two countries and how to deal with the Communists. Nothing is more important to Burma than the applicability and acceptability of its new political arrangements to the country's minorities; to the Philippines, what is becoming increasingly important is the grievances of its Muslim minority and how this minority is being handled. But none of these primary problems could be publicly discussed in the formal political systems of the four countries in question at the mid-point of the 1970's. Secondary issues could be raised—but the questions on which the very survival of states may depend are more often than not politically out of bounds as far as public criticism is concerned.

Domestic but Not Foreign Policies. Public discussion of domestic issues is, as indicated, very much restricted, but there is greater freedom to disagree openly with the government position on internal than foreign-policy questions. In the mid-1970's, it was not politically permissible in Indonesia to offer public criticism of the Suharto government's opposition to resumed active diplomatic relations with China, although often outspoken Foreign Minister Adam Malik periodically came close to indicating the extent of his personal disagreement with President Suharto's fear that renewal of such links between Jakarta and Peking would be followed by Chinese-sponsored subversive activity.

Only the government could criticize government policy toward China (or any other country) in Burma. Continuing ties with the United States used to be a favorite target of congressional, press, and demonstrating critics of the Marcos regime in the Philippines, but opposition to close "Fil-Am" relations or other aspects of Filipino foreign policy was not possible in the "New Society." Public criticism of foreign policy was everywhere a very dangerous activity to undertake.

"Hirelings" but Not "Bosses." Singapore's Lee Kuan Yew, Cambodia's Lon Nol, Indonesia's Suharto, South Vietnam's Thieu, Burma's Ne Win, the Philippines's Marcos, and even Malaysia's Razak are literally above criticism in their nations' political processes. Southeast Asian politicians, like those of Malaysia and Singapore, found *Washington Post, New York Times,* and other American press opposition to President Nixon almost incomprehensible. "We would never let our newspapers talk that way about our leaders," one Malaysian minister very accurately asserted in the early 1970's. Middle- and lower-level public servants, however, are a different matter. They can be criticized; it "helps" them to do a better job, according to a Singapore official. They can even be made examples of—to improve the performance of other public servants.

Privately, but Not Publicly. Even in North Vietnam apparently, criticism of policies is possible within the circle of the small number of men who run the country. Vigorous opposition to favored personal positions of Indonesian strongman President Suharto is known to have been expressed by various of the former soldier's advisers. And the Malaysian Government has often been of more than a single mind—internally—on various important questions.

In some countries, however, even such private criticism has its limits, particularly if it is given to such stubborn personalities as Burma's Ne Win, Singapore's Lee Kuan Yew, or Cambodia's Lon Nol.

LIMITS OF COMPETITION

There are two key kinds of political competition: for position and for policy. Competition for primary political position was almost completely restricted in Southeast Asia in the mid-1970's. Juniors might jockey for second or third place behind soldiers Suharto and Ne Win, but they could never seem to rival the leader, as former Burmese Brigadier Aung Gyi, stripped of his previously influential position, found out in the early 1960's. Competition for policy influence, however, was still politically permissible in the mid-1970's in both Vietnams no less than in the Philippines and Burma.

Within the Party. The political history of North Vietnam since 1954 has been a seemingly constant struggle within the ruling *Lao Dong* Party among such key Communist political figures as civilians Le Duan and Truong Chinh and military leader Vo Nguyen Giap. Le Duan, for example, opposed the 1972 Communist Vietnamese "Easter offensive" that had been urged by Giap. When the offensive failed to accomplish its objectives, Le Duan led the fight within the Hanoi politburo for the kind of "settlement" that was reached with the Americans in January, 1973, as well as for a higher priority for economic reconstruction subsequently.

Similar political competition also took place within the "ruling" Burma Socialist Program Party in the early 1970's, although, in general, that party was very much under the political thumb of

Ne Win and his chief military lieutenants. But there was real competition to serve as delegates to the first and second BSPP party congresses and to stand for election to the first "People's Assembly" under the new constitution in 1974.

Competition need not take place only among strongly opposed ideological opponents; indeed, such competition, often a political fight to the finish, can be very destructive to both government and opposition, as well as to the country as a whole. Competition within a narrow ruling elite or a single official party, on the other hand, while unquestionably more competitive than no opposition at all, should still be recognized for what it is: "regulated" or "controlled" competition.

Within Participatory Institutions. The parliaments of such controlled political systems as those of Indonesia and Singapore, where the winners of elections can confidently be predicted beforehand, are by no means altogether lacking in competition. In Indonesia, where the government's *Sekbar Golkar* party has a commanding two-thirds majority, there is still competition among factions of that majority as well as among rival ambitious politicians within the *Golkar* organization. Singapore's parliamentary majority has ordinarily been even more commanding—100 per cent, in fact—but there has been competition for both policies and position within the legislature, albeit among members of the ruling People's Action Party.

Such participatory institutions—like Burma's People's Assembly or the two houses of South Vietnam's legislature—are not the loci of political power in any Southeast Asian country, as is, for example, Parliament in Britain or Canada. But these bodies are "proving-grounds," for ideas and personnel, where new men and proposals can be tested in nearly complete safety as far as the continuation of the regime and its policies is concerned.

Competition for Favor. Many of the Southeast Asian political systems in the 1970's resembled kings' courts of a bygone era, with "ministers" and "advisers" jockeying with one another for favor with the ruler. The Philippine Government in 1974—lacking a legislature, political parties, or open opposition—was very much a modern-day equivalent of the medieval monarch's favor-dispensing entourage. Sometimes, however, the favorites fall by the political wayside, as happened to Brigadier Aung Gyi and, later, Brigadier Tin Pe in Ne Win's nondemocratic Burma in the 1960's. Such competition for favor or position is almost the antithesis of modern competitive and pluralistic democracy, involving, as it does, the pursuit of preference by the few rather than the representation of the interests of the many.

No Real Opposition

In the mid-1970's, in civilian- and soldier-ruled countries alike, there was no real criticism, competition, or opposition within the legally defined political systems of Southeast Asia. Controlled criticism and limited personal competition existed, but there was no opposition at all to the ruling elites and their policies. The men who governed Southeast Asia in the 1970's believed criticism, competition, and opposition to be dangerous not only to themselves but also to their countries. Philippine President Marcos was probably the least sincere of these leaders in such self-serving evaluations of the dangers of dissent. But Singapore's Lee Kuan Yew, Indonesia's Suharto, and Burma's Ne Win unquestionably believed themselves to be men of destiny, opposition to whom was tantamount to treason.

Consequences

Criticism and competition—from loyal politicians, journalists, and others—could be what Southeast Asia most urgently needed as the decade of the 1970's passed the halfway mark. The ruling autocrats, however, argued that criticism and competition had a disunifying effect. They seemingly failed to perceive that the political orders over which they presided were brittle and inflexible and might tumble overnight, as that of Thailand's Thanom Kittikachorn did in 1973. The policies pursued by such regimes, moreover, were not flawless. The "Burmese Way to Socialism," enunciated in 1962, was one of the most ill-conceived and poorly implemented economic strategies in all the "third world," but even in 1974, it could not be criticized, having been placed above debate in the new constitution adopted on the twenty-sixth anniversary of the country's independence. No nation in all Southeast Asia, however, needed criticism—and competition—more than Burma at the mid-point of the 1970's.

Unchallenged political institutions have a tendency to wither, weaken, and finally collapse, even under slight pressure. The Diem, Sihanouk, Sukarno, and Thanom regimes were all pushed from power, however gently in the Indonesian case, but they were already petrifying for lack of meaningful criticism and competition. What passed for policies—or were proclaimed as such— had long lost whatever pertinence and vitality they once possessed, and this partially explains why the regimes that proposed and pursued them collapsed so completely.

This is not to say that politics should—or can—be played in Rangoon, Manila, or Kuala Lumpur as it is in Westminster and Washington. But it should be recognized by Southeast Asian leaders that the policies of their governments *must* be subjected to some criticism and some competition, and, not least of all, some opposition, if they are to be purged of inadequacies that could prove costly to national development hopes and even the country's survival. Southeast Asia's nations cannot afford many major mistakes; criticism and competition are two means of trying to correct them.

15

Different Paths

All the Southeast Asian governments except Thailand's have become less democratic through the years. Not all these lands, however, were dictatorships in the mid-1970's, although most of them were. The two Vietnams, Burma, and Cambodia were probably the most authoritarian of the Southeast Asian regimes at the midpoint of the 1970's, even though Lon Nol's Phnom Penh administration was notoriously inefficient and in danger of being overthrown. The Philippines was becoming increasingly autocratic under President Marcos's "constitutional authoritarianism," while Indonesia and Singapore retained many of the formal trappings of competitive systems—such as contested elections—even though there was no doubt who would win such voting and continue to control the country. For most of the time since 1954, surprisingly perhaps, Laos had an elected government and a legislature that shared power with the executive, despite the ongoing war with the Communists. Transitional Thailand possibly excepted, the most democratic government in all the area in 1974 was Malaysia, where an independence-winning, "Alliance" party—led "national front" governed as the electoral choice of the people.

The trend toward autocratic government notwithstanding, there were different paths of political development that the various Southeast Asian ruling elites seemed to be following through the mid-1970's. An analysis of these different paths might well yield some insights into the possible political future of this much-troubled corner of the world.

SINGLE-PARTY SYSTEMS

Only two Southeast Asian countries had or were developing single-party political systems in the mid-1970's. These were Communist-ruled North Vietnam, where the *Lao Dong* Party monopolized political power, and Burma, which adopted a new constitution in 1974 that legitimatized the *de facto* exclusive political role of the still very much soldier-controlled Burma Socialist Program Party. Single parties dominated the politics of both Indonesia and Singapore, too, and had earlier done so in Cambodia in Prince Sihanouk's time, but the leaders of these countries were not willing in the mid-1970's to make their countries party dictatorships.

It would seem highly unlikely, from the vantage-point of the mid-1970's, that either North Vietnam or Burma would soon change its one-party political system. No Communist government in the world's history has yet been overthrown, and no Communist party has ever relinquished or reduced its exclusive control over a national government. North Vietnam is highly unlikely to become the first to do so, even in the 1980's, although the possibility that a coalition regime to unify the country will change this political outlook cannot be discounted altogether. Burma is probably the more likely of these two lands to change, particularly if there is a fall-out among former and continuing soldiers, field and political soldiers, or junior and senior soldiers. Ne Win, who resigned his general's rank in 1973 and became "U" (or Mr.) Ne Win, is the human cement that holds the country together politically. There may be soldiers, young and unknown, who are more democratically inclined than their leader, although this is not particularly likely. In any event, a struggle for power within the military is possible, and a more liberalized political system could follow in its wake.

SOLDIER-RUN STATES

Besides being a one-party system, Burma is also still very much a soldier-run state. The military controls the government, but, no less important from the viewpoint of possible political change, it also controls the single party permitted by the constitution, the

BSPP. Brigadier San Yu, Ne Win's heir-apparent, is secretary-general of the BSPP, in which the military is represented wholly out of proportion to the civilian population. Army and party are, for all practical purposes, one and the same at this time, but there were indications in the mid-1970's of a growing gap between the soldiers who continued in the role of soldiers and those soldiers who had effectively departed military careers and had become the leadership and senior bureaucracy of the BSPP.

South Vietnam, Indonesia, and Cambodia were also soldier-run states in the mid-1970's but in more political danger probably than the ruling Burmese military. South Vietnamese President Nguyen Van Thieu in 1974 was in an early stage of constructing a soldier-controlled, one-party system of the sort that already exists in Burma; he had a fair likelihood of success if the Hanoi Communists meant what they were publicly saying about according higher priority to economic reconstruction of the north than enlargement of the military struggle in the south. Like Burma, Indonesia's soldier-politicians also were endeavoring to "civilianize" their regime, and, while three definable parties remained on the political scene, the possibility of *Sekber Golkar,* the government party, becoming the only permitted party in the future was a real one.

The essence of the Burmese, Indonesian, South Vietnamese, and Cambodian political systems, however, was that the soldiers were in charge and were, indeed, the ranking politicians in these systems. The army was thrown out of office in Thailand in 1973, but there is a very strong likelihood that it will be back in power before the end of the decade. No less likely is the prospect of a military takeover in the Philippines, where the army is the chief support of civilian dictator Marcos. In short, there are likely to be more military regimes before there are fewer of them in Southeast Asia.

CONTROL WITHOUT DICTATORSHIP

Malaysia and Singapore are examples of political systems in which established elites—and particular personalities—predominate without recourse to heavy-handed dictatorial rule. Premier Lee Kuan Yew is no less the unchallenged leader in Singapore than Ne Win in Burma, but elections are regularly held in Singapore, opposition elements have contested such voting, and the ruling People's Action Party probably is the overwhelming political choice of most Singaporeans.

Lee and his PAP lieutenants, however, are among the most astute politicians in Southeast Asia, and they have been able to control their country without recourse to conventional dictatorial means—through tight party discipline, frequent house-cleaning of corrupt and undesirable elements, leadership of labor unions and other such organizations, recruitment and promotion of promising young persons and related replacement of those who no longer serve their purposes, and skillful strategies concerning the calling of elections and other political maneuvering.

Malaysia is a less-controlled political system; its control is the consequence of cooption, skillful allocation of rewards, and exploitation of the widespread fear that the government might just become even less democratic if it really became necessary. Malaysia, however, is *not* a dictatorship; indeed, it is the least dictatorial of all the Southeast Asian political systems. The ruling "Alliance" party's domination of the political system has been challenged—and was genuinely threatened in 1969—but the "national front" it formed easily triumphed in the 1974 elections. Nonetheless, Malaysian political control is no less control for being benevolent and willing to permit popular participation in politics; this style of rule is possible as long as participation does not seriously threaten the Malay political elite's direction of the system.

NONPARTY LEADERSHIP

The Philippine Government of Ferdinand Marcos is the most conspicuous example of nonparty leadership in Southeast Asia today. Marcos, of course, may still launch a "single party" to institutionalize and support his largely one-man direction of Philippine politics, but this has not happened to date. Moreover, it never really did happen in Thailand under any of the military autocrats who led the land between 1947 and 1973: Phibun Songkhram, Sarit Thannarat, or Thanom Kittikachorn. Each of these soldier-politicians created a party at one point or another to buttress his sagging political position—or to contest an inconveniently necessary election. But leadership under the "big three" of Thai soldier-dominated government over the past quarter-century has largely been "nonparty" leadership, thus indicating that partyless politics is possible and can survive for a fairly substantial period of time.

It probably could also be said that the various governments in non-Communist-ruled Laos through the years really were not party governments—nor was the Lon Nol regime in Cambodia in the early 1970's a party one. Previous Cambodian ruler Prince Norodom Sihanouk, however, did preside over a single-party-type of government, although the party had none of the relative separate institutional identity even of Lee Kuan Yew's People Action Party in Singapore or ex-soldier Ne Win's Burma Socialist Program Party.

DEMOCRATIC DEVELOPMENT

The four most common paths of political development in Southeast Asia over the past quarter-century have been one-party systems, soldier-run states, exercise of control without dictatorship, and nonparty leadership. Democratic political development has not been one of the chosen means of governing man and improving his welfare. Indeed, there has been an almost steady retreat from democratic politics through these years. The Philippines, Burma, Singapore, and Indonesia have all departed the ranks of democratic political systems. Countries like South Vietnam, Laos, and Cambodia that were never democracies have shown no recent inclination to liberalize their political processes. Malaysia, however, has remained more of a democracy than a nondemocracy, and Thailand was flirting with democracy again in the mid-1970's, although the flirtation may turn out to be very brief.

At the same time, many of the countries may be closer to popularly controlled governing systems today than ever before. Thailand, indeed, may well be showing the way to the other lands, as it did earlier by having the first "neutralist" foreign policy in the area and being ruled by the first "soldier-politicians" in the region. Never a colony, Thailand has experienced many of the political developments that subsequently influenced the rest of the area before any of the other countries of Southeast Asia. Military autocracy appeared to fall in Thailand in 1973, at least partly because it was out of step with the modern level of development of the society in general. Economic, educational, and social change had made Thailand quite a different country by 1973 from what it had been in the late 1930's, when Phibun Songkhram and his fellow officers seized political power.

The political story of Thailand, in a very real sense, may be in the process of being acted out in other parts of Southeast Asia today. Even where the trend seems most recently to have been strongest against democratic rule—that is, in the Philippines—the argument can be made that Marcos-style politics is already out of step with the general trend of a country that is in many respects even more modern than Thailand. Indonesia and South Vietnam have undergone changes over the past ten to fifteen years— changes that were accelerating in the 1970's—that may make it likely they will have more liberal, if not yet outright democratic, regimes some time in the years immediately ahead. Malaysia, one of the most rapidly modernizing states in all Asia, may never lose its democratic character as a consequence of the pace of its development.

This is not to say that democracy is just around the corner in any of the nondemocratic lands of Southeast Asia. For it probably is not. But the first postcolonial governments in most of the Southeast Asian lands were extreme artificialities; they had no roots at all in the countries in question. It was probably necessary for a political step backward to be taken—or many such steps in some instances—before a firm footing could be obtained. Such a footing may well exist today, and it could be that tomorrow's Southeast Asian governments will move progressively, if slowly, toward more popular rule. Societies, as contrasted with political systems, are being modernized in the area. And, while political systems may well lag quite a distance behind them, change will probably occur in them, too, in time. This may well be the most important message of the overthrow of Thai military autocracy in 1973—a message with a meaning for the other lands of Southeast Asia as well as the Thai themselves.

Selected Bibliography

This bibliography is designed to identify some of the most valuable book-length studies of the area and countries that make up Southeast Asia. Much valuable information is to be found as well in the rapidly growing periodical literature on the region both in general publications and, particularly, in the specialized periodicals listed in the final portion of the bibliography. Especially recommended for identifying past articles, books, and monographs is the annual bibliographical issue of the *Journal of Asian Studies*. Another outstanding bibliography, with accompanying critical essays, is Paul Bixler's *Southeast Asia: Bibliographical Directions in a Complex Area* (published by *Choice*, Middletown, Conn.).

Books

GENERAL

ALEXANDER, GARTH. *The Invisible China: The Overseas Chinese and the Politics of Southeast Asia*. New York: Macmillan, 1974.

BASTIN, JOHN, and HARRY J. BENDA. *A History of Modern Southeast Asia*. Englewood Cliffs, N.J.: Prentice-Hall, 1968. A very readable general history.

CHAWLA, SUDERSHAN, MELVIN GURTOV, and ALAIN-GERARD MARSOT, eds. *Southeast Asia Under the New Balance of Power*. New York: Praeger, in press.

CLOUGH, RALPH N. *East Asia and U.S. Security*. Washington, D.C.: Brookings Institution, 1974.

EVERS, HANS-DIETER, ed. *Modernization in South-East Asia*. New York: Oxford University Press, 1973.

FIFIELD, RUSSELL. *Americans in Southeast Asia: The Roots of Commitment*. New York: Crowell, 1973.

FISHER, CHARLES A. *Southeast Asia: A Social, Economic and Political Geography*. 2d ed. New York: Dutton, 1966. The best geographical work on the area.

FITZGERALD, C. P. *China and Southeast Asia Since 1945*. New York: Longman, 1974.

FITZGERALD, STEPHEN. *China and the Overseas Chinese: A Study of Peking's Changing Policy, 1949–1970.* New York: Cambridge University Press, 1972.

GURTOV, MELVIN. *China and Southeast Asia: The Politics of Survival.* Lexington, Mass.: Heath, 1971.

HLA MYINT. *Southeast Asia's Economy: Development Policies in the 1970's.* New York: Praeger, 1972. One of the best economic works on the area.

LAU TEIK SOON and LEE SOO ANN, eds. *New Directions in the International Relations of Southeast Asia.* 2 vols. Singapore: Singapore University Press, 1973. Vol. I deals with economic relations; Vol. II deals with the great powers. Papers are from a 1972 conference.

LEIFER, MICHAEL. *Dilemmas of Statehood in Southeast Asia.* Vancouver: University of British Columbia Press, 1972.

MCALISTER, JOHN T., JR., ed. *Southeast Asia: The Politics of National Integration.* New York: Random House, 1973. The best anthology of politically related writings on the area, superbly organized around a very important theme.

MEHDEN, FRED R. VON DER. *South-East Asia, 1930–1970: The Legacy of Colonialism and Nationalism.* New York: Norton, 1974. An outstanding treatment of a complex subject.

POOLE, PETER A. *The United States and Indochina: From FDR to Nixon.* Hinsdale, Ill.: Dryden Press, 1973.

PYE, LUCIAN W. *Southeast Asia's Political Systems.* 2d ed. Englewood Cliffs, N.J.: Prentice-Hall, 1974.

SHAPLEN, ROBERT. *Time Out of Hand: Revolution and Reaction in Southeast Asia.* New York: Harper and Row, 1969.

SMITH, ROGER M., ed. *Southeast Asia: Documents of Political Development and Change.* Ithaca, N.Y.: Cornell University Press, 1974. An outstanding collection of documents.

STEINBERG, DAVID JOEL, et al. *In Search of Southeast Asia: A Modern History.* New York: Praeger, 1971. A work of great depth and perception.

TILMAN, ROBERT O., ed. *Man, State, and Society in Contemporary Southeast Asia.* New York: Praeger, 1969.

WADDELL, J. R. E. *An Introduction to Southeast Asian Politics.* Sydney: Wiley, 1972.

ZASLOFF, JOSEPH J., and ALLAN E. GOODMAN. *Indochina in Conflict: A Political Assessment.* Lexington, Mass.: Heath, 1972.

BURMA

BA MAW. *Breakthrough in Burma: Memoirs of a Revolution, 1939–46.* New Haven, Conn.: Yale University Press, 1968. By an important Burmese nationalist leader of the 1930's and wartime head of state.

BADGLEY, JOHN. *Politics Among Burmans: A Study of Intermediary*

Leaders. Athens: Ohio University Center for International Studies, 1973.

BUTWELL, RICHARD. *U Nu of Burma*. 2d ed. Stanford, Calif.: Stanford University Press, 1969. An updated and revised version of a 1963 study.

CADY, JOHN F. *A History of Modern Burma*. Ithaca, N.Y.: Cornell University Press, 1958.

DONNISON, F. S. V. *Burma*. London: Benn, 1970. Best single-volume work on the country.

JOHNSTONE, WILLIAM C. *Burma's Foreign Policy: A Study in Neutralism*. Cambridge, Mass.: Harvard University Press, 1963. No longer current but a very illuminating study of the setting of Burmese foreign policy.

MAUNG MAUNG. *Burma and General Ne Win*. Bombay: Asia Publishing House, 1969.

PYE, LUCIAN W. *Politics, Personality, and Nation-Building: Burma's Search for Identity*. New Haven, Conn.: Yale University Press, 1962. Highly insightful study by a ranking political scientist.

SILVERSTEIN, JOSEF, ed. *The Political Legacy of Aung San*. Ithaca, N.Y.: Southeast Asia Program, Cornell University, 1972.

SMITH, DONALD E. *Religion and Politics in Burma*. Princeton, N.J.: Princeton University Press, 1965.

TRAGER, FRANK N. *Burma: From Kingdom to Republic—A Historical and Political Analysis*. New York: Praeger, 1966.

CAMBODIA

CHANDLER, DAVID P. *The Land and People of Cambodia*. Philadelphia: Lippincott, 1972. A good introductory book.

LEIFFER, MICHAEL. *Cambodia: The Search for Security*. New York: Praeger, 1967. A well-written, perceptive study of Cambodian foreign policy during Sihanouk's rule.

NORODOM SIHANOUK. *My War with the CIA*. Hammondsworth, England: Penguin, 1973. His memoirs, as related to Wilfred Burchett.

POOLE, PETER A. *Expansion of the Vietnam War into Cambodia: Action and Response by the Governments of North Vietnam, South Vietnam, Cambodia, and the United States*. Athens: Ohio University Center for International Studies, 1970.

SIMON, SHELDON W. *War and Politics in Cambodia*. Durham, N.C.: Duke University Press, 1974. The best study of the country since Sihanouk's overthrow.

SMITH, ROGER M. *Cambodia's Foreign Policy*. Ithaca, N.Y.: Cornell University Press, 1965. Dated but still perceptive study of Cambodia's former foreign policy.

INDONESIA

BRACKMAN, ARNOLD C. *The Communist Collapse in Indonesia*. New York: Norton, 1969.

FEITH, HERBERT. *The Decline of Constitutional Democracy in Indonesia.* Ithaca, N.Y.: Cornell University Press, 1962. An excellent examination of early postindependence Indonesian political development.

FEITH, HERBERT, and L. CASTLES, eds. *Indonesian Political Thinking.* Ithaca, N.Y.: Cornell University Press, 1970.

HUGHES, JOHN. *Indonesian Upheaval.* New York: McKay, 1967. The best account of the events preceding and following the September 30, 1965, affair.

JONES, HOWARD P. *Indonesia: The Possible Dream.* New York: Harcourt Brace Jovanovich, 1971. The very valuable account and analysis of the late (and longtime) U.S. Ambassador to Jakarta.

KROEF, JUSTUS M. VAN DER. *The Communist Party of Indonesia.* Vancouver: Publications Centre, University of British Columbia, 1965.

LEGGE, J. D. *Sukarno: A Political Biography.* New York: Praeger, 1972. The best study of the late Indonesian nationalist dictator.

MORTIMER, REX. *Indonesian Communism Under Sukarno: Ideology and Politics.* Ithaca, N.Y.: Cornell University Press, 1974. An excellent study.

————, ed. *Showcase State: The Illusion of Indonesia's "Accelerated Modernisation."* Cremorne Junction, Australia: Angus and Robertson, 1973.

NEILL, WILFRED T. *Twentieth Century Indonesia.* New York: Columbia University Press, 1973.

ROEDER, O. G. *The Smiling General.* Jakarta: Gunung Agung, 1969. A biography of Indonesian President Suharto.

SIMON, SHELDON W. *The Broken Triangle: Peking, Djakarta and the P.K.I.* Baltimore: Johns Hopkins University Press, 1969. An outstanding study of both international and internal politics.

LAOS

Committee of Concerned Asian Scholars. *Laos: War and Revolution.* New York: Harper and Row, 1971. Edited by Nina S. Adams and Alfred W. McCoy.

DOMMEN, ARTHUR J. *Conflict in Laos: The Politics of Neutralization.* Rev. ed. New York: Praeger, 1971. A good contemporary account of earlier efforts to "neutralize" Laos.

FALL, BERNARD B. *Anatomy of a Crisis: The Laotian Crisis of 1960–1961.* Garden City, N.Y.: Doubleday, 1969. Edited and completed by Roger M. Smith.

LANGER, PAUL F., and JOSEPH ZASLOFF, JR. *North Vietnam and the Pathet Lao: Partners in the Struggle for Laos.* Cambridge, Mass.: Harvard University Press, 1970. A Rand Corporation study.

TOYE, HUGH. *Laos: Buffer State or Battleground.* New York: Oxford University Press, 1968. A somewhat dated but valuable overview.

ZASLOFF, JOSEPH J. *The Pathet Lao: Leadership and Organization.* Lexington, Mass.: Lexington Books, 1973.

MALAYSIA

BOYCE, PETER, ed. *Malaysia and Singapore in International Diplomacy.* Sydney: Sydney University Press, 1968. A very comprehensive collection of documents.

ESMAN, MILTON J. *Administration and Development of Malaysia: Institution Building and Reform in a Plural Society.* Ithaca, N.Y.: Cornell University Press, 1972.

GAGLIANO, FELIX V. *Communal Violence in Malaysia 1969: The Political Aftermath.* Athens: Ohio University Center for International Studies, 1971.

GOH CHENG TEIK. *The May Thirteenth Incident and Democracy in Malaysia.* New York: Oxford University Press, 1971.

MEANS, GORDON. *Malaysian Politics.* New York: New York University Press, 1970. An excellent study.

RABUSHKA, ALVIN. *Race and Politics in Urban Malaysia.* Stanford, Calif.: Hoover Institution Press, 1973. A very perceptive study.

RAHMAN, TUNKU ABDUL. *May 13 Before and After.* Kuala Lumpur: Utusan Melayu Press, 1969. The account by the then Malaysian Prime Minister of the rioting of May 13, 1969, and subsequent events.

RATMAN, K. J. *Communalism and the Political Process in Malaysia.* Kuala Lumpur: University of Malaya Press, 1965. A first-rate book.

ROFF, WILLIAM R. *The Origins of Malay Nationalism.* New Haven, Conn.: Yale University Press, 1967.

SCOTT, JAMES C. *Political Ideology in Malaysia: Reality and the Beliefs of an Elite.* New Haven, Conn.: Yale University Press, 1968. A most insightful study.

VASIL, R. K. *The Malaysian General Election of 1969.* Kuala Lumpur: Oxford University Press, 1972.

PHILIPPINES

ABUEVA, JOSE VELOSO. *Ramon Magsaysay: A Political Biography.* Manila: Solidaridad Publishing House, 1971. First-rate study of the Philippines's most respected postcolonial leader.

ABUEVA, JOSE VELOSO, and RAUL P. DE GUZMAN, eds. *Foundations and Dynamics of Filipino Government and Politics.* Manila: Bookmark, 1969. The best anthology of serious political writings on the Philippines.

AGPALO, REMIGO E. *The Political Elite and the People: A Study of Politics in Occidental Mindoro.* Manila: College of Public Administration, University of the Philippines, 1972. One of the best studies on Philippine politics.

AVERCH, HARVEY A., *et al. The Matrix of Policy in the Philippines.* Princeton, N.J.: Princeton University Press, 1971. Very revealing —and myth-shattering—empirical study of selected aspects of Philippine politics.

FRIEND, THEODORE. *Between Two Empires: The Ordeal of the Philippines, 1929–1946.* New Haven, Conn.: Yale University Press, 1965. A prize-winning history.

GROSSHOLTZ, JEAN. *Politics in the Philippines.* Boston: Little, Brown, 1964. A first-rate effort to explain the basis of Philippine politics.

GUTHRIE, GEORGE M., ed. *Six Perspectives on the Philippines.* Manila: Bookmark, 1968. A collection of outstanding essays.

LARKIN, JOHN A. *The Pampangans: Colonial Society in a Philippine Province.* Berkeley: University of California Press, 1972. An unusually well-done historical study.

LIGHTFOOT, KEITH. *The Philippines.* New York: Praeger, 1973. The best full-length book through the Marcos "takeover" of September, 1972.

MACAPAGAL, DIOSDADO. *A Stone for the Edifice: Memoirs of a President.* Quezon City, Philippines: Mac Publishing House, 1968. Autobiography of the Philippines's fifth President.

MAJUL, CESAR ADIB. *Muslims in the Philippines.* Quezon City, Philippines: University of the Philippines Press, 1973. Excellent study by a ranking Filipino political scientist, himself a Muslim.

MARCOS, FERDINAND E. *The Democratic Revolution in the Philippines.* Englewood Cliffs, N.J.: Prentice-Hall International, 1974.

SPENCE, HARTZELL. *Marcos of the Philippines.* New York: McGraw-Hill, 1969. A revised and enlarged edition of a campaign biography of the Philippines's sixth President.

STANLEY, PETER W. *A Nation in the Making: The Philippines and the United States, 1899–1921.* Cambridge, Mass.: Harvard University Press, 1973.

SINGAPORE

BELLOWS, T. J. *The People's Action Party of Singapore.* New Haven, Conn.: Yale University Press, 1970.

BUCHANAN, IAIN. *Singapore in Southeast Asia: An Economic and Political Appraisal.* London: G. Bell, 1972.

CHAN HENG CHEE. *Singapore: The Politics of Survival, 1945–1967.* Singapore: Oxford University Press, 1971.

GEORGE, T. J. S. *Lee Kuan Yew's Singapore.* London: Andre Deutsch, 1973. A journalist's critical biography.

JOSEY, ALEX. *Lee Kuan Yew.* Singapore: Donald Moore Press, 1968. A sympathetic treatment.

OOI JIN-BEE and CHIANG HAI DING, eds. *Modern Singapore.* Singapore: University of Singapore, 1969.

PANG CHENG LIAN. *Singapore's People's Action Party: Its History,*

Organization and Leadership. New York: Oxford University Press, 1971.

THAILAND

BASCHE, JAMES. *Thailand: Land of the Free.* New York: Taplinger, 1971.
DARLING, FRANK C., and ANN DARLING. *Thailand: The Modern Kingdom.* Singapore: Donald Moore for Asia Pacific Press, 1971. A good introduction to the country.
INGRAM, JAMES C. *Economic Change in Thailand, 1850–1970.* Rev. ed. Stanford, Calif.: Stanford University Press, 1971.
RIGGS, FRED W. *Thailand: The Modernization of a Bureaucratic Polity.* Honolulu: East-West Press, 1966. An exceptionally good work by a well-known political scientist.
SIFFIN, WILLIAM J. *The Thai Bureaucracy: Institutional Change and Development.* Honolulu: East-West Press, 1966. A perceptive study by one of the most qualified observers of Thai politics and administration.
WILSON, DAVID A. *Politics in Thailand.* Ithaca, N.Y.: Cornell University Press, 1962. The onetime standard political study—now dated but still very valuable.
———. *The United States and the Future of Thailand.* New York: Praeger, 1970. An excellent recent foreign-policy study.

VIETNAM

BUTTINGER, JOSEPH. *A Dragon Defiant: A Short History of Vietnam.* New York: Praeger, 1972. The best single-volume introduction.
ELLSBERG, DANIEL. *Papers on the War.* New York: Simon and Schuster, 1972.
GOODMAN, ALLAN E. *Politics in War: The Bases of Political Community in South Vietnam.* Cambridge, Mass.: Harvard University Press, 1973. The best study of the war-influenced politics of South Vietnam.
FITZGERALD, FRANCES. *Fire in the Lake: The Vietnamese and the Americans in Vietnam.* Boston: Atlantic-Little, 1972.
HALBERSTRAM, DAVID. *The Best and the Brightest.* New York: Random House, 1972. About the men who made America's Vietnam policies.
HO CHI MINH. *Ho Chi Minh on Revolution: Selected Writings, 1920–66.* New York: Praeger, 1967. Edited by Bernard Fall.
HUYEN, N. KHAC. *Vision Accomplished? The Enigma of Ho Chi Minh.* New York: Macmillan, 1971.
JOINER, CHARLES A. *The Politics of Massacre: Political Processes in South Vietnam.* Philadelphia: Temple University Press, 1974.
LACOUTURE, JEAN. *Ho Chi Minh: A Political Biography.* New York: Random House, 1968.

LE DUAN. *The Vietnamese Revolution: Fundamental Problems and Tasks.* New York: International Publishers, 1971. An illuminating study of North Vietnam.

MCALISTER, JOHN T., JR., and PAUL MUS. *The Vietnamese and Their Revolution.* New York: Harper and Row, 1970. A penetrating study of South Vietnam.

PIKE, DOUGLAS. *War, Peace, and the Viet Cong.* Cambridge, Mass.: MIT Press, 1969.

RACE, JEFFREY. *War Comes to Long An: Revolutionary Conflict in a Vietnamese Province.* Berkeley: University of California Press, 1972.

SHAPLEN, ROBERT. *The Road from War: Vietnam 1965–1971.* Rev ed. New York: Harper and Row, 1971.

VAN DYKE, JON M. *North Vietnam's Strategy for Survival.* Palo Alto, Calif.: Pacific Books, 1972.

Periodicals

American Universities Field Staff Reports (Southeast Asia Series). Hanover, N.H. Periodic, from-the-field reports on current topics.

Asia. Quarterly journal published by the Asia Society, New York. Some issues are devoted to country or topical themes.

Asia Research Bulletin. Singapore-published digest of recent political and economic information. Highly reliable and very comprehensive monthly publication.

Asian Affairs. Published for the American-Asian Educational Exchange by Crane, Russak, New York.

Asian Survey. Highly reliable short-article monthly published by the Institute of International Studies, University of California, Berkeley. January–February issues are country surveys of previous years.

Bulletin of Concerned Asian Scholars. Published by Bay Area Institute, San Francisco.

Far Eastern Economic Review. Hong Kong–published news and commentary weekly. A veritable "bible" for students of the current Asian scene.

Index

Acquino, Benigno S., Jr., 170, 212
adat (Indonesian common law), 55
administrators, colonial, 122–26
Afro-Asian conference (Bandung),
  58, 66, 115, 199
agitators, political, 123–26
"Alliance" (Malaysia), 65–67, 100,
  141–46, 151, 158, 223, 226
Angkor Wat, 35
antidemocracy, 111–12
Anti-Fascist People's Freedom
  League (AFPFL), 47, 49, 137,
  139–42, 144–45, 151–52, 168–69
anti-"powerism," 116
Arab Muslim nations, 77, 87, 162,
  182, 195
Association of Southeast Asia (ASA),
  77
Association oí Southeast Asian Nations (ASEAN), 54, 62, 68, 70–
  71, 77, 114–15, 117, 198, 200,
  205–6
astrology, 117
Aung Gyi, 199, 221
Aung San, 140
Australia, 53, 62, 65–67, 201, 205

Ba Maw, 124
Bandung conference, *see* Afro-Asian
  conference
Bao Dai, Emperor, 24, 156
baranguy (Philippines), 11, 92
Barisan Socialis, 71, 149
Bhumibul Adulyadej. 44
Bornean states, *see* Sabah; Sarawak
Boun Oum, Prince, 32

British colonialism, 8, 40–42, 47–48,
  53, 62–65, 76, 82, 87–91, 102,
  128, 137, 139, 198, 201–2, 215
Buddhism, *see specific countries*
Budi Utomo, 136
Burma, 4–6, 14–15, 22, 40, 42, 51,
  73, 81, 91, 93, 94, 104, 114, 116,
  185, 203, 206; Britain and, 40–42,
  47–48, 91, 119, 198, 201; Buddhism in, 93, 96, 106, 133, 134,
  164, 179; Chinese role in, 7, 8,
  46–50, 53, 95, 104, 105, 172,
  190; colonial experience of, 84,
  85, 86; communalism in, 103;
  Communists in, 47–49, 107, 130,
  139–41, 148, 149, 164, 183, 187;
  economy of, 86, 100, 177, 190,
  192, 194; elites in, 25, 91, 92, 101,
  105, 106, 113–14, 119, 120, 122,
  124–30, 133, 134; 135, 167–69,
  171, 172, 187, 217; ethnic minorities in, 12, 29, 46–51, 88, 89, 90,
  95, 96, 100, 103, 104, 105, 121,
  139, 148, 149, 163, 171, 177, 178,
  179, 184, 185, 190; foreign interferences in, 10, 25, 40–41, 46–48,
  91, 128, 137, 139, 215; foreign
  policy of, 46, 47, 115, 197, 199;
  liberties in, 208–14; modernization in, 190, 195; nationalism in,
  90, 97, 105, 178, 183, 185, 186,
  188; political representation and
  institutions in, 13, 16, 21, 49–52,
  82, 86, 110–12, 136–45, 147–52,
  155–60, 163–64, 166–69, 177, 184,
  187, 216–19, 221–24, 227; separatism in, 104–5; socialism in,

Thailand *(cont.)*:

7–8, 44–45, 95, 180, 205–6; Communists in, 45, 149; economy of, 106–7, 109, 186, 192–95; elites in, 14–15, 21, 42, 88, 100–101, 113, 120, 126, 128–30, 133–34, 167; foreign interferences in, 10, 40–42, 44, 82, 90; foreign policy of, 41–42, 45, 53–54, 68, 72, 77, 81, 86, 88, 116, 198, 201, 205; Islam in, 93, 96, 105, 149, 163, 179–80; liberties in, 113, 208–10, 212, 214; minorities in, 12–13, 29, 45, 51, 88, 90, 178, 185–86, 188; modernization of, 41–43, 190, 192, 195–96; nationalism in, 44, 51–52, 178, 185, 188; North Vietnam and, 44–45; political representation and institutions in, 13, 41–45, 51–52, 81, 83, 112, 143, 145, 149–52, 155, 158–61, 167, 169, 173, 223, 225–28; U.S. and, 42–45, 47, 71, 131, 172, 198, 201–4

Thanom Kittikachorn, 15, 43–45, 126, 129, 131, 157, 161, 173, 182, 208–9, 221–22, 226

Thieu, Nguyen Van, 15, 26–27, 35, 104, 110–11, 127, 148, 155, 170, 172, 218, 225

United Malays National Organization (UMNO), 65, 67, 143, 158
United States, *see specific countries*
"Unity Development" group, 61, 146

U Nu, 4, 14–15, 46, 48–50, 93, 101, 104, 106, 110–12, 125–26, 130, 134, 144–45, 147, 156, 160, 163–64, 168–69, 172, 183, 185–87, 198–99, 203, 211–12

Viet Minh, 23–25, 30–31, 36, 139–40, 148, 163

Vietnam, 21, 30, 46, 48, 53–54, 92–93, 181, 215; Buddhism in, 16, 26; Chinese role in, 6–7, 23, 95, 101; colonial experience of, 30, 36, 84, 85, 119; Communists in, 4, 22–28, 47, 83, 94, 125, 201; elites in, 23–28, 92, 119–20, 135, 167; nationalism in, 23–26, 51, 86, 92, 97, 125, 178–79; political representation and institutions in, 13, 83, 111, 138–41, 163, 179; U.S. and, 11, 23–24, 26, 28, 45, 159, 164, 206

Vietnam war, 3, 22–28, 72, 194, 200–202, 215; internationalization of, 24; U.S.-Communist agreement in, 33; U.S. military role in, 3, 11, 22–28, 164–65; *see also* North Vietnam; South Vietnam

Visayan (Philippines), 181
Volksraad, 56–57

West Irian (western New Guinea), 89
Workers' Party, *see Lao Dong* Party
World War II, 23, 81–84, 90–91, 124, 138–40